KEEPING
YOUNG
&
LIVING
LONGER

KEEPING YOUNG & LIVING LONGER

By JOSEF P. HRACHOVEC, M.D.,D.Sc.

SHERBOURNE PRESS

How to stay Active & Healthy past 100

LOS ANGELES

Published by Sherbourne Press, Inc., 1640 So. La Cienega Blvd.
Los Angeles, CA 90035

Library of Congress Catalog Card Number 72-85486
ISBN 0-8202-0150-2
Composed by Datagraphics, Phoenix, Arizona.
Printed and bound by The Maple Press Company, York, Pennsylvania

DEDICATION

To my old medical school teacher for his enthusiasm, which he knew how to communicate to others, to Dean L. S. Goerke for his support at the University of California School of Public Health at Los Angeles, to Jean S. Felton, Professor and Head, Division of Environmental Health, UCLA School of Public Health, to Vice-Chancelor Foster H. Sherwood and the Academic Personnel Office at UCLA for action which provided the impetus and much-needed time to write this book, to Bernard C. Abbott, Professor and Chairman at USC, and to James E. Birren, Director of the Gerontology Center at the University of Southern California, for their support, to colleagues at this Center, and particularly to Bernard L. Strehler, Professor at USC, for his encouragement; to my wife for her patience and understanding, to them all and to many others not mentioned by name, I extend my deep appreciation.

CONTENTS

PREFACE

ALL MY LIFE HAS BEEN SPENT STUDYING THE MAJOR MEDICAL and biochemical ways that man can use to live beyond the limits of the average human life expectancy. My interests in the efforts to live longer were awakened during my medical studies some 25 years ago by one dedicated teacher who aroused my interest in these rather neglected matters. Then, after graduation from medical school and during my medical practice, I very soon became keenly aware of a great number of questions concerning efforts in helping people to live longer. I realized that some answers can come ultimately only through scientific research on aging, which brought me back to the university in order to do such research.

Several years later, after having received my Doctor of Sciences degree, I did research on aging at the Faculty of Medicine in Paris, France, then at the College of Physicians and Surgeons of Columbia University in New York, and for five years at the New York University School of Medicine. For the past seven years I have been doing research at the University of California, School of Public Health, Los Angeles, and have recently joined the Gerontology Research Center at the University of Southern California. My studies at this center deal mainly with the molecular biology of aging, particularly with the age decline in tissue protein synthesis and its relationship to age decline in resistance to stress and chronic diseases of old age. During these studies I have had firsthand, ample opportunity to evaluate most of the major scientific attempts to help people live beyond the limits of the average life expectancy. This book, then, is the result of my lifelong studies.

Countless efforts have been made along numerous lines toward the elusive aim to stay young and live longer. What are the realistic possibilities and limitations in research efforts to achieve prolongation of human life within our lifetime? A major portion of the first part of this book answers that question. However, many of the possibilities lie in the future, are not available at the present time. This finally leads to the question: What can a lay person do *now,* at the present time, in order to maximize his chances to live beyond the limits of an average human life expectancy? The answer, above all, lies in the avoidance of countless errors of everyday life which make us grow old faster than necessary. Anybody who knows what these errors are and how to avoid them can live past 100 years of healthy, vigorous, active life.

The whole point of this book is to enable you to face reality: to show what can be done about keeping young and living longer —and what cannot be done, no matter how ardently we may desire it or what various rejuvenationists would like people to believe.

In recent years the bookstores have been flooded with all kinds of diet and health books written by people who claim to be disciples or gurus of various oriental, mystic ways of life. Often these men have no real understanding of the religious and philosophic concepts they teach and even less understanding of the nutritional and other needs of the human body. These books may be easy and enjoyable to read, but many of them are filled with misleading and dangerous advice about how to eat, exercise, and live in order to keep healthy. A diet limited to one food or a limited number of foods cannot provide the building blocks the body requires to manufacture and replace the cell components. There have been recorded instances of persons who became sick and even died following a rigid adherence to diets prescribed by some of these books.

Nutrition and dieting have always been the happy hunting ground of food faddists, science fiction writers, and self-styled prophets. Some of the claims made over the last two decades have been truly extraordinary. This food will purify the soul, that food will cure cancer, a third will give unlimited sexual potency. Unfortunately, the men who write these books seem to have the ad man's skill in catching the reader's interest and encouraging his belief. Even more unfortunately, medical authorities and scientists are more skilled in their research and their medical activities than in writing. Too often their books turn out to be overly long, difficult to follow, and too dry for the taste of the average lay person.

Nevertheless, these are the books that are worthwhile to read because the advice in them has already been tested and retested on animals and humans before it comes to you. These books will also help you exercise your own judgment. They provide descriptions of the experiments on which their advice is based and the names and professional competence of the men who made the observations and conducted the experiments. As you become more familiar with the solid foundation of research behind the advice, you will be able to apply it more efficiently to your own life and come to prefer it to promises made on the basis of wishful thinking and verbal legerdemain.

This book is intended to be the kind of book that physicians recommend to their patients because it answers most of the usual questions about keeping young, living longer, dieting, and exercise, which patients like to ask their physicians. Because these more general questions are answered in this book, the patient and the physician will have more office time for handling and discussion of the specific questions about the patient's present health.

I hope this book will inspire you to take an honest look at yourself and your everyday life. With its help, you may uncover various errors which make *you* grow old faster than necessary. Once you know what these errors are, it will then be relatively easy to avoid them in order to live a long, vigorous, healthy, and active life.

—Josef P. Hrachovec, M.D., D. SC.
Los Angeles, Calif.
June 1972

PART I:
Keeping Young

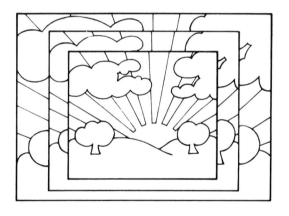

1 | The Challenge of Life-Shortening Errors

WHEN YOU ARE YOUNG, YOU DO NOT MERELY FEEL ALL RIGHT; you feel like walking on the ceiling—or at least like climbing trees, fences, and mountains. Such a surplus of energy means that the young can not only endure the ills to which the flesh is heir but also can fight off and be free of the ailments that plague us in our thirties and forties.

While we are still young and feel strong, actually our functional capacities are already beginning to decline. This gradual decline sets in long before we are willing to admit it. Careful tests reveal that our strength and swiftness begin to lessen in the middle twenties. An athlete reaches his peak performance around the age of 25 or 30 years. From that point onward, his performance begins to decline no matter how much effort and will power he forces himself to exert. Our automobile steering coordination, for example, peaks at 25 and then declines rapidly.

Concurrently, this decline in strength and performance is accompanied by a decline in recuperative powers. At age 20 we can stay out until 3 A.M., and still be at the office at 9 A.M. without the boss knowing the difference, but double this age and, if we are out after midnight, it may take a day or two to regain normal efficiency. And this is only an outward expression of inner changes. For example, the skin wound that heals on a 20-year-old in one week, needs two weeks to heal on a 40-year-old.

Many facets of this early decline in functional capacities and recuperative powers are so subtle that we do not notice them or, if we do, do not let ourselves think about them; we prefer the self-deception that we are different, that this universal process will not affect us. We know that there always have been athletes who did prove somewhat exceptional. This decline of physical powers with age did not seem to apply to them; and we like to believe that similarly it will not apply to us. We refuse to face the fact that the athletes have bought their extension of vigor with discipline and careful planning.

The guiding concept of this book is that the human body is designed to function efficiently to an age numbering in three figures. But most people are robbed of achieving this potential by the accumulated effects of a variety of stresses. Permitting these stresses to act upon us day after day, month after month, year after year comprises the disease-inducing, life-shortening errors which sap our strength and shorten our lives. On the other hand, preventive health maintenance is a program designed to put an end to or reduce these stresses before they have had a chance to do us permanent harm. Preventive maintenance functions to allow us to achieve the potential life span past 100 years that is our birthright.

As the stresses are many, so are the errors we commit that encourage or tolerate them. For convenience sake, these errors can be ordered into three categories: bad nutrition, lack of exercise, and overstrain or lack of relaxation. It is literally true that we are what we eat. If our eating habits are poor, we are not going to be as healthy and strong as we can be. Bad eating habits include not eating enough of the foods that make for strong bones and muscles and eating too much of the foods that make us fat and susceptible to disease. The second part of this book is devoted to both aspects of nutrition. The astronauts dramatically illustrated that our bodies begin to deteriorate without use. Lack of exercise is becoming an increasing health hazard in urban America. The third part of this book describes the types of exercise most conducive to health and vigor, and suggestions for those who are short of both time and facilities. The fourth section of the book deals with man-made stresses, overstrain or lack of relaxation, including techniques for detecting various errors of everyday life that, left unchecked, could develop into major health hazards, and with suggestions for controlling them. The first part of the book I am mentioning last because it is perhaps the most exciting. It deals with the research, now under way in countless laboratories in the United States and around the world, to extend human life and vigor beyond the hundred year mark.

You are holding a key to long life in your hand. No matter who you are, where you live, what your profession is or how much your income, you are not immune to committing the various health-endangering, disease-inducing, and life-shortening errors of every-day life which make you grow old faster than necessary. Most of these errors look innocent and are inoffensive, if committed only occasionally. However, if committed daily for years or even decades, their effects pile up and may seriousl*y* endanger your vigor, well-being, health, and even your life. These errors are relatively easy to avoid, if you know what to avoid and are determined to apply a certain amount of self-discipline in order to avoid them.

It is amazing how much time is wasted and how much frustra-tion generated by millions of uninformed or gullible persons; they are willing to apply various remedies for old age, offered by all kinds of rejuvenationists who are usually very expensive but bring no results worth mentioning. Whereas the really helpful remedies cost nothing except the avoidance of various errors of everyday life described in this book and some self-discipline. Don't allow your-self to be trapped. After the damage has been done and com-pounded, it may become much more difficult to do something about it.

Most recent scientific observations indicate that, contrary to general belief, each person has an inborn potential to live past 100 years, and that each person, even if he has short-lived parents, can live up to his potential of 100 years of healthy, vigorous, active life. This can be achieved very simply by relatively small efforts to avoid various errors of everyday life that make us grow old faster than necessary.

This book can tell you what to do to achieve a long, vigorous, healthy and active life, but it cannot do it for you. You will not be asked to follow any difficult programs or procedures, but you will have to develop a certain amount of consistency and self-discipline in following the advice presented. Lack of consistency may cost you decades of your individual life expectancy.

Since it is impossible in a book written for a large audience to cover every single human contingency, the author can only give you an idea of what these various errors are—these life traps—what they do to your body, and how they make you grow old faster, how scientists have uncovered them and how you can avoid them with the least effort. Then you will be on your own and, if your motivation and persistence are strong, you will enjoy a vigorous, healthy, and active life past 100 years of age.

Whatever the future outcome of research efforts toward life prolongation, try to remember that you are fighting for very high stakes—the prize is several decades of vigorous, healthy life for you.

If your body is still lean and hard muscled, quick and hardy, this book will show you the easiest, most reliable and realistic means of keeping it so.

If your body is already beginning to show the wear and tear of middle age, you have even more reason to follow the advice in this book. You have nothing to lose but your bad habits, your overweight flabby muscles, and possibly also high blood pressure, heart disease, arteriosclerosis, diabetes, and other ailments.

Give yourself a realistic amount of time to achieve a change; once the change begins to show, keep going.

2 | Is It Possible to Prolong Life?

THERE ARE GOOD REASONS TO BELIEVE THAT A DRAMATIC prolongation of human life will soon be more than mere exuberant imagination. The fields of biology and medicine have advanced to the point where scientists can realistically aim at prolonging human life and controlling aging within our lifetime, depending on the amount of research efforts and financial support given toward this aim.

Forecasting studies by the Rand Corporation (Santa Monica, California) predict that an increase of 50 percent in human life span will be achieved by the year 2020. Robert W. Prehoda in his book *Extended Youth, Promise of Gerontology,* predicts that the next 20 years should give man the necessary knowhow for complete control of the aging process. Recent studies by Smith, Kline and French Laboratories, a large pharmaceutical company, predict that a 50 percent increase in human life span will be achieved in the early 1990s.

Before discussing how prolonging life and controlling aging can be or will be achieved, let's see first how the human body grows old. The components of the human body are in a dynamic state, being continually rebuilt, renewed, and replaced through the biosynthetic processes inside the tissue cells. These dynamic processes of renewal, or turnover, lead to an almost complete replacement of all the components of each cell in all the tissues of the entire body. In this continuous process, some components are being replaced more slowly than others. It has been observed that, while some parts of the body are entirely replaced within a few weeks, the replacement of other parts takes several months, and still other parts several years. But one of the most amazing aspects is the fact that through these processes of replacement, nearly all of the components and all the molecules of the human body are entirely replaced within a few years by new components and new molecules from outside the body.

The form of the human body remains the same, or almost the same, but the materials that fill the form have been replaced. The new molecules and components are almost identical with those that have been replaced—almost, but not entirely identical. And this is how the human body grows old: in the dynamic process of continual replacement, some components have been slightly changed and become slightly different from the components they are replacing, others are not entirely replaced, and some simply disappear.

In this way about 100,000 brain cells disappear every day from the brain of every living individual and are lost irretrievably. Nevertheless, none of us notice these losses on a daily basis, because the human brain contains about 10 billion cells from which a daily loss of even 100,000 is a very small portion. Similar cell loss takes place in all other organs and tissues of the body.

Probably the most important feature of these processes is that their pace can be modified by various influences from outside the body. There is even more to it! The possibility exists of slowing down the pace of the aging process, and of reversing it, if we know the nature and effects of the influences which can modify the pace of the dynamic processes of renewal within the human body.

Some of these influences are relatively easy to achieve and fall within the field of nutrition and physical exercise and are discussed in the second and third parts of this book. Other influences are more complicated and are subjects of research on aging, research which ultimately will lead to the control of aging and life prolongation.

It is almost certain that life prolongation and control of aging will be achieved in steps rather than in a single leap, because there are many causes of aging. As each cause is analyzed and removed or alleviated, it will provide its own contribution to prolongation of human life. The first step in life prolongation most probably will be achieved through the application of chemicals called antioxidants.

ANTIOXIDANTS: A KEY TO LONGER "SHELF LIFE"

Antioxidants are substances which have been used for a long time in the food industry to slow down or to prevent excessive oxidation of polyunsaturated fats. The addition of antioxidants to fat-containing food products effectively slows down their deterioration and thus prolongs their "shelf life."

It was Dr. Denham Harman from the University of Nebraska School of Medicine who advanced the idea that deterioration through excessive oxidation of polyunsaturated fats might be among the contributing factors or causes of aging in living organisms. Experiments have been done in which various antioxidants were fed to laboratory animals, resulting in their living 40 to 50 percent longer than their normal life span. So we know that these antioxidants have life-extending properties, but not enough experimental work has been done to permit their application to humans.

As fantastic as it seems, there may exist already a possibility of extending indefinitely the life of people now living. However, to obtain these startling results a massive financial support for research on all the factors and causes of aging at once would be necessary, comparable to financial support for atomic research, space exploration, or cancer research.

Life prolongation through the use of selected antioxidants or related substances could buy us the time to work out other steps in prolonging human life. An exciting new approach to the problem is Dr. Björksten's theory that cross-linked molecules (formed between protein molecules with the passage of time) could be eliminated from the cells, freeing the space they had occupied and permitting the cells to function more effectively—if they can first be broken down. The problem is locating a specialized enzyme that can accomplish the delicate and selective task of breaking down the cross-linked molecules while leaving the rest of the cell intact. Funded by the Upjohn Company, Dr. Björksten is engaged in a major research program to find and isolate such enzymes.

Dr. Björksten believes that some strains of soil bacteria contain suitable enzymes. He proposes to obtain the proper soil bacteria by starting with cross-linked protein material from old animals, breaking it down with known enzymes which would digest and wash out all soluble material. He then would make the remaining cross-linked substances the only nitrogen source in a mixed culture of soil bacteria, where nitrogen is essential for survival.

Out of many thousands of soil bacteria strains, only the strains capable of breaking down the cross-linked protein could then survive. These selected strains of bacteria would be grown in quantity and the enzymes could be extracted, purified, and finally a rejuvenating elixir prepared. This elixir, however, would have to be injected into the body rather than swallowed because most enzymes do not survive passage through the digestive tract.

THE "ACCUMULATION" THEORY

Another interesting theory is that the accumulation of toxic substances in the blood, or inside the cells, is in part responsible for the body's gradual deterioration with age. If this approach is productive, it should be possible to achieve life prolongation by the elimination or slowing down of the accumulation of these substances. But by what means could this be achieved?

It is well known from tissue culture studies that inhibitory (or toxic) substances are released from the cells of a tissue fragment explanted into the medium *in vitro* (that is, outside of the body) and that this results in a sort of rejuvenation of the cells. Further, a colony of cells cultured outside of the body can be rejuvenated to some extent by removing the old medium (containing the released inhibitory substances) and replacing it by a fresh medium.

This is basically what experiments applying the blood washing, or the so-called plasmapheresis, try to achieve with the whole animal. In these experiments, done by Dr. Orentreich at the New York University, larger amounts of blood are periodically withdrawn from the animal and the blood cells are washed clean of plasma with its inhibitory substances. Washed blood cells are then mixed with a synthetic plasma and returned to the animal's blood stream from which they were taken. Dr. Orentreich's results with rats and dogs are encouraging and it appears that plasmapheresis may eventually become available for people as another step in life prolongation.

Other steps may involve the immunologic causes of aging. It is known that the human body, as it grows older, produces antibodies against the proteins of its own organs. In addition to the organ damage these antibodies cause, they also precipitate organ-specific proteins into the intercellular spaces (that is, in the spaces between the cells) of our organs.

These spaces between the cells have a very necesssary function in the dynamic processes of renewal of the body. Through them, oxygen and food diffuse from the blood capillaries to the cells, and various waste products stream from the cells to the blood. If these intercellular spaces gradually become clogged as we grow older, less and less oxygen and food manage to get to the cells, and less and less waste products manage to get out of the cells. This contributes heavily to a general slowdown of all the metabolic processes of the body.

Research on this problem can be approached from several directions: finding the means of preventing the formation of these antibodies against organ-specific proteins, finding the means to prevent the formation of the precipitates of such antibodies with organ-specific proteins, or finding the means of getting rid of such precipitates once they are formed in the intercellular spaces. Any of these approaches may lead to another step in life prolongation.

As encouraging as the possible steps in life prolongation may be, they nevertheless deal with only a small portion of the contributory factors of aging and none of the basic causes of aging. An enormous amount of research still remains to be done. If man wants to achieve unlimited life prolongation or physical immortality, which is not impossible, he will have to find how to treat or eliminate *all* the existing factors or causes of aging; because if he found treatment against all but one, this last one would ultimately do him in.

The quest of the elusive fountain of youth is a fascinating story of searching and researching, with countless failures and dead-end streets on roads in the unknown, because originally none of the explorers had the slightest idea where exactly to look for the fountain, or what it is going to be like, once it is found. It is becoming increasingly clear that the only road to the discovery of the fountain of youth leads through modern, scientific research laboratories. The elusive "fountain" will be another hard-fought-for and hard-won scientific discovery.

BASIC "FOUNTAIN-OF-YOUTH" RESEARCH

Research on the biology of aging basically has followed the same path as research in other areas of biochemical sciences, except at a much slower pace. This development can be divided into three stages, widely overlapping in time—early experimental, descriptive, and molecular gerontology.

In the early experimental stage, some research on aging was based on too much wishful thinking and intuition. It was marked by unjustified and exaggerated claims, and accompanied by unfulfilled public expectations. This invariably was followed by disillusionment, ridicule, and a skeptical attitude toward all research on aging, with the result that now many scientists avoid such research because of concern for their professional reputation. It is mainly these early experimental efforts, however, which have received the greatest publicity and continue to be discussed in various contemporary lay articles about achievements in research on aging.

Descriptive gerontology, the second stage, includes practically all the research into the changes in chemical composition, enzymatic activities, physiological functions, and others, which have been investigated during the past decades in animals and humans. The results indicate that everything changes during aging, and that there probably does not exist one single biological entity or parameter that would not change with the age of the animal. Some entities increase during aging, others decrease, and still others increase up to a certain age and then decrease again. Descriptive gerontology mainly described how individual entities change during aging, whereas the important question, which usually remained unanswered, was how these various changes of different entities are related to one another.

The extent of research efforts in descriptive gerontology is well illustrated by *A Classified Bibliography of Gerontology and Geriatrics,* prepared by N. W. Shock in 1951, which lists over 18,000 references of articles on aging, published in English and other languages. Its supplement, published in 1957, lists another 16,000 references covering the years 1949–55.

In most recent years gerontologists have been turning to methods of molecular biology. This marks the beginning of the third stage, molecular gerontology. Our knowledge of the processes of aging can be compared to a composite picture; countless scientific observations from various areas of biomedical sciences are being put together like pieces of a mosiac puzzle; new pieces are continually inserted or continue to be investigated in various laboratories of this country and abroad, but a great many pieces are still missing.

The results of research on aging confirm that there are several *basic* factors or causes of aging and a number of *contributory* causes of aging, and it is evident that no researcher can possibly investigate all of them simultaneously. My own investigations of basic factors in aging, which my staff and I first pursued in my laboratory at the University of California at Los Angeles, School of Public Health, and now continue at the University of Southern California (USC)

Gerontology Research Center, have centered around the theory that the age-related decrease in resistance to disease, and aging itself, might be due to an accumulation of some toxic substances in tissue cells.

Experimental evidence from a number of our studies indicates that toxic substances do accumulate in the endoplasmic reticulum of cells. The endoplasmic reticulum is a lacelike network of inter-connecting tubules and vesicles that permeates the cell. The endoplasmic reticulum itself contains units (ribosomes) on its outer surface that manufacture or synthesize protein molecules from amino acids that come into the cell. These protein molecules are then secreted into the cavities of the endoplasmic reticulum where they accumulate with age and gradually inhibit the process of protein synthesis.

When the cells are homogenized, the endoplasmic reticulum is broken into fragments (called microsomes) which look like small bags surrounded by membranes. Recently we discovered that the ability of these live fragments to manufacture or synthesize protein molecules decreases with the age of the animal. Investigating further, we found that the liver cell sap contains substances which inhibit the manufacture of protein molecules by liver microsomes and that the liver cell sap taken from old animals inhibits protein synthesis more than the liver cell sap taken from young animals. Inhibition of protein synthesis in turn inhibits cell divisions.

These observations have led us to speculate that aging takes place in a "falling domino" fashion. When one structure inside a cell "falls" or becomes inhibited, the other structures inside the cell tend to become inhibited. With each "fall"—that is, each structure within the cell that becomes inhibited—the cell's ability to function normally is weakened that much more.

According to the "falling domino" theory, then, as the animal ages the inhibitory substances in the intercellular space and inside the cells increase in amount (or grow stronger in their effect) which results in a slowdown of protein synthesis. Inhibition of protein synthesis during aging is followed by a gradual slowdown of all the metabolic and biosynthetic (body-manufacturing) processes and ultimately leads to the individual's growing failure to resist stress and the chronic diseases of old age.

In addition to the "falling domino" theory of aging there are some 20 to 25 known theories of aging, each centering around some other causes of aging, now being investigated in various laboratories around the world. Not just one but many important breakthroughs in preventing the harmful effects of aging are just around the corner. All that is needed to achieve them is time, increased research efforts, and research funds. In the meantime let us keep ourselves in as sound physical shape as is currently possible in order to live long enough to realize the benefits personally.

3 | Why Are There No Life-Extending Procedures Available Now?

W HY IS IT TAKING SO LONG TO DEVELOP LIFE-EXTENDING PRO-cedures? Is it so terribly difficult to work out some of these procedures to the point where they could be applied safely by people? Why hasn't anything been done yet?

The ultimate answer is simply: for the past several decades, literally research on aging and life prolongation has been a "disaster area" in the biomedical sciences.

There is probably no other field in biomedical research which has been so utterly neglected. And yet the desire to live longer than one's forefathers is an ancient one. Aristotle was interested in this possibility, so were the Chinese, especially the Taoists. Eager, if crude, experimentation flourished in the Middle Ages; the results are now only of historical interest. The more disciplined experimental efforts to conquer the rundown feeling that comes with age only began toward the end of the nineteenth and the beginning of the twentieth century.

One of the earliest experimental efforts was by Charles Eduard Brown-Séquard. On June 1, 1889, he told the forum of the Societé de Biologie in Paris about his experiment. It is now hardly more than an historic milestone, but on that day in 1889 it was sensational. Brown-Séquard reported that he removed one of the testicles of a vigorous two-year-old dog, cut the organ into little pieces, put the pieces into a mortar adding a little water, and mashed them to obtain as much juice as possible. He filtered the juice and collected about four cubic centimeters of a "rather transparent" pink liquid, which he injected into the muscles of his own leg. According to his report, the following day and even more so afterward, he recovered all the strength he had possessed many years ago. He resumed his old habit of running up and down stairs, and tests with a dynamometer showed that his strength increased considerably.

Subsequent investigators who repeated Brown-Séquard experiments, however, seemed unable to obtain his results and considered them to be a psychological or placebo effect brought on by autosuggestion. Many ridiculed his efforts and experiments as senile aberrations. Nevertheless, whatever the shortcomings of his experiments, Brown-Séquard deserves credit for giving an imaginative start to endocrinology, the science of glandular or inner secretions which has continued to flourish ever since.

THE "MONKEY-GLAND" PRACTITIONERS

In his quest for rejuvenation, or revitalization (a term more acceptable in medical circles than rejuvenation), by sexual gland therapy, Brown-Séquard was followed by many others. Probably the most famous of his followers was Serge Voronoff, son of a rich Russian manufacturer. Voronoff emigrated to France in 1884 and later occupied the chair of experimental surgery at the Collège de France in Paris. He introduced and practiced transplantation of testicles from chimpanzees, gibbons, and orang-utans to his patients, and at the height of his career lectured all over the world about his newly discovered "Fountain of Youth." It is estimated that Voronoff did some two thousand transplants, for which he charged about $5,000 each.

Another of Brown-Séquard followers was Eugen Steinach (1861–1944), a Viennese physiologist-endocrinologist, who invented the so-called vasoligature. Vasoligature, or tying off the canal through which sperm flows, was supposed to produce a rejuvenating or reactivating effect by stimulating the production of testosterone, the male sex hormone.

In the mid-1930s the analysis and synthesis of testosterone by Adolph Butenandt, a German biochemist, replaced Voronoff's transplantations and Steinach's vasoligatures with simple, inexpensive injections of pure synthetic testosterone and with subcutaneous implantations of testosterone tablets. Today, in women going through the menopause, a similar procedure is estrogen replacement therapy (ERT). Estrogens are female sex hormones produced by the ovaries. Hormone therapy for old age has always been a controversial subject, and even now there are clinical professors of endocrinology and endocrinologists who believe that sex hormone therapy is a great help to their aging patients. Nevertheless, the effects of sexual hormone therapy do not last long and are not able to slow down the processes of growing old.

CELL THERAPY

Cell therapy, intramuscular injections of cut-up animal tissues, is another early experimental effort to fight the effects of old age. It was originated by Paul Niehans, a Swiss physician. Niehans and his followers use tissues of sheep fetuses approximately one month before their scheduled birth. However, for injections of adrenal, parathyroid, pituitary, testes, and ovary tissues, they use organs of adult animals.

After cell injections, patients are required to stay in bed for several days. In addition, they are asked to avoid all alcohol, tobacco, or vaccines for several months following the cell treatment. Beside this "fresh-cell-therapy," in which cut-up tissues of freshly killed animals are injected, preparations of cells preserved by lyophilization are also used. This is a technique which removes water by vacuum-drying frozen material and which does not denature the protein, as normal drying does. Niehans developed the technique of lyophilization of animal cells in 1949, and since 1954 his Siccagell factory in Heidelberg has marketed some 60 varieties of organ preparations.

In western Europe there are now hundreds of physicians who specialize in cell therapy on a full-time basis, and thousands of physicians who use it occasionally. Niehans' cell therapy is very similar to the so-called impulse therapy which was known in Europe long before cell therapy appeared. Impulse therapy has been recommended for treatment of leg ulcers and other chronic ailments, and consisted of injections into leg muscles of several milliliters of milk sterilized by boiling, or of several milliliters of the patient's own blood. The reabsorption of the injected material was supposed to give an impulse to the body's defense mechanisms and an impulse to the reabsorptive and healing processes, which in turn gave an impulse to healing processes around the ulcer.

Niehans has made a fortune treating personalities of international repute; his treatment of Pope Pius XII in 1954 earned him vast publicity. The list of celebrities treated by Niehans since 1957 includes Konrad Adenauer, Bernard Baruch, Charlie Chaplin, Christian Dior, Wilhelm Furtwangler, Lillian Gish, Sacha Guitry, Hedda Hopper, Somerset Maugham, King Ibn Saud, Gloria Swanson, and others. Chancellor Konrad Adenauer is said to have taken cell therapy every year since about 1958 from a clinic in Bühler-Höhe.

According to an interview with Somerset Maugham's secretary, the famous writer had three series of cell therapy injections. The first series gave Maugham some trouble. Possibly because he was a heavy smoker, enjoyed alcohol, and had some difficulties with Niehans' directions. However, following the second series of cell injections, Maugham carefully abided by Niehans' admonition to abstain from tobacco, alcohol, etc. After the initial trouble Maugham's sleeplessness disappeared and his creativity reawakened abruptly. He felt inspired, he began to write again, and his imagination worked overtime, but he didn't have the physical strength to keep up with it.

His secretary, Mr. Searle, took cell therapy at the same time to please Maugham. To Searle's surprise his memory rapidly improved, his nervous condition vanished, and the skin disease, psoriasis, from which Searle had suffered ever since puberty and which covered his entire body except his face, disappeared. Two years after the first treatment Maugham decided to have another go with cell injections. Once again the results were good and there were no unpleasant aftereffects. Maugham plunged again into creativity, which appeared to be restored by the treatment.

The third series of cell injections which Maugham took, however, did not bring about any improvement at all. Years later his secretary revealed that Maugham continued to have 80 cigarettes a day, double Scotches on the rocks, cocktails, and after dinner brandy.

It is difficult to ascertain how much of Maugham's improvement after the first two series of cell therapy injections was due to complete avoidance of cigarette smoking and alcohol drinking, how much to nonspecific impulse therapy effect, how much to the placebo effect—and how much, or how little, to the specific revitalizing effect of cell therapy. It would come as no surprise if the specific revitalizing effect of cell therapy were found to be nonexistent. In fact, even physicians who have been applying cell injections to their patients for years do not believe that cell therapy can extend the life span, although they like to insist that it can help man to age more comfortably. It is of interest to speculate how much confidence Niehans actually had in his own therapy, because he never applied cell therapy to himself. He died in Montreux, Switzerland, in the summer of 1971, at the age of 88.

GERIVITOL H3

Among contemporary efforts to fight the effects of old age possibly the most widely known is the treatment by procaine hydrochloride (Novocain,® a form) or its long-action form, Gerovital H3, orginally initiated by the Rumanian doctor, Anna Aslan. Dr. Aslan's attention was attracted to the particular effects of procaine years ago, in 1951, after she tried a new treatment for rheumatic arthritis on a 20-year-old patient whose leg was locked stiff at the knee, who was totally immobile, and who suffered great pain. Immediately after she injected procaine solution into his (femoral) artery, the pain vanished and he could bend his knee. After further injections he left the hospital within a few days.

When Dr. Aslan applied prolonged treatment with procaine injections to older arthritic patients, she found not only that the pain disappeared but also that various complaints of old age, unrelated to arthritis, began to improve—she observed increased mental and physical activity, improved memory, disappearance of depression and she began to apply procaine injections on a large scale to her older patients. When she read in a foreign medical journal that an alkaline procaine solution deteriorates faster and could cause complications she began to use acid solutions of procaine, buffered between pH 3.4 and 4, which later she developed into a more complex preparation and marketed under the name of Gerovital H3.

In subsequent years Gerovital H3 has become the subject of more than 300 medical and scientific publications, many of which are highly appreciative of its effects. The main claims are that Gerovital H3 used in older persons (1) relieves depression, lack of physical energy, decreased mental activity, loss of memory and induces a feeling of well-being, optimism, orientation, and attention, (2) relieves pain of patients suffering from degenerative arthritis of the aged, (3) lowers and normalizes the blood pressure in persons suffering from high blood pressure and improves arteriosclerotic and senile brain disorders, (4) is beneficial in various skin

WHY ARE THERE NO LIFE-EXTENDING PROCEDURES AVAILABLE NOW?   19 disorders and induces changes in the aging skin, which result in a more youthful appearance.

These various beneficial effects of Gerovital H3, which may often appear unrelated, can possibly be explained by our recent findings that Gerovital H3 is a powerful inhibitor of a special enzyme called monoamine oxidase. Drugs belonging to the group of monoamine oxidase inhibitors are known to be effective against depression, high blood pressure, and related disorders.

Monoamine oxidase inhibitors were discovered accidentally in 1951 when a drug called iproniazid, used in the treatment of tuberculosis, was found to have some unexpected effects. These were characterized by a return to vitality with a sudden burst of optimism, so that even patients who were on their death beds "miraculously" recovered and were able to leave the hospital. Later it was found, however, that most of these drugs had severe side effects and many have been withdrawn from the market.

It has been claimed that Gerovital H3 injections have much better effects against complaints of old age than do regular procaine injections. There have been claims, and some research studies tend to bear it out, that Gerovital H3 injections, in addition to the overall improvement, also increase life expectancy by up to 30 percent. However, only carefully prepared research work over long periods of time will give a clear-cut answer to this question in the future.

It is interesting to note that in addition to the Gerovital H3 injections, Dr. Aslan gives her patients regular physical exercises, a well-balanced diet, intellectual activity, and entertainment. Some physicians therefore, believe that perhaps the *care* alone, even without Gerovital, may be responsible for the good results she has with her patients. However, statistical evidence seems to indicate that Gerovital H3 was indeed responsible for the beneficial results.

There are now over 100 imitations of Gerovital being sold in Europe and in England. Oral versions of Gerovital, often called the youth pill, eliminate the need for painful injections and frequent expensive visits to a doctor or a certified nurse.

At the present time, Gerovital H3 cannot be obtained legally in the United States. Before it can be approved for marketing, it must pass the Federal Food and Drug Administration regulations, which stipulate that the drug has to be safe and effective for the claims made. However, research work aimed toward this approval is currently in progress in the United States.

In the United States, only a few years ago the thought of experimenting with a youth pill was almost unthinkable; today, scientists talk more freely about finding a chemical compound capable of influencing the processes of aging. Adding strength to this concept is the beginning revolt of the 40 million Americans over 55 who do not want to be pushed aside or to have a nursing home as their final destination. They want to be active, enjoy life longer, and have more opportunities to live their lives fully to the last days of their allotted time.

Other antidotes for old age, like Bogomoletz's antireticular cytotoxic serum, were more in vogue years ago than they are now. These and many more recent serums are characterized by randomness in experimental approach, intuitiveness in application, and wishful thinking in describing their effects. They seem to be aimed mainly at commercial exploitation.

As we have seen, all the contemporary therapies or remedies of old age are inadequate and inefficient for the aims they are intended to achieve. Most rejuvenators or "youth doctors," applying one or the other of these therapies to their aging clients, are frank enough to admit their doubts about the life-span-extending effects of their particular brand of therapy. They are satisfied that their therapy will help their patients (in exchange for a lucrative fee) by making their later years more productive and more enjoyable. Those rejuvenators, who claim that their therapy also has a life-span-extending effect, have difficulties in presenting proof in the form of experimental or statistical data to support their claims.

WHY CONTEMPORARY REMEDIES FALL SHORT

Possibly the most important reason for the shortcomings of all the contemporary remedies for old age is the fact that they ignore practically everything which has been learned since the turn of the century about the functioning of living matter and about the processes of aging. In fact, all the contemporary therapies for old age apply nothing better than the out-dated approaches and methods of the nineteenth century. The amount of knowledge on which any of these contemporary therapies of old age is based is so small that it does not scratch the surface of what we already know, which in turn is still very little compared to what we have yet to know. Using these out-dated approaches is like fighting the enemy with stone-age weapons. We can approach the problem of aging with the most modern scientific research and develop weapons against old age comparable in efficiency to atomic weapons.

It is increasingly evident that the speed with which scientists can move toward the goals of prolonging life and the eliminating chronic diseases depends largely on the amount of financial support for research toward this goal. Too often in the past, funds for innovative research have been insufficient and slow in coming.

A similar fate of "too little too late" hampered the work of Dr. Robert H. Goddard, the pioneer in space exploration. It has been recognized that the inadequate financial support Dr. Goddard received from governmental agencies and private foundations resulted in a slowdown and retardation of space exploration by some 20 to 30 years.

A comparable slowdown now exists in research on aging and life prolongation because of inadequate financial support. This problem is (or should be) everybody's business. If low financial support for research on aging postpones the achievement of life prolongation by some 20 to 30 years, as actually happened with space exploration, most of the adults and practically all of the middle-aged persons now living will be deprived of the possibility of living longer.

If you feel concerned about this possibility, express your concern in letters to your senators and congressmen, urging them to support (or to initiate) legislation in favor of intensified research on aging and life prolongation, and to vote for appropriations of funds for such research. Congressmen and senators are guided in their decision-making by the desire for the well-being of our society and by the wish to satisfy the voters and taxpayers.

It appears that increased financial support for research on aging will be made available only if and when the voters and taxpayers become aware of the importance to themselves of this research and urge their congressmen and senators to vote for appropriations of funds for such research. Surprisingly, there is a close relationship between the indifference of voters and taxpayers toward the problems of growing old and the existing lack of financial support for research on aging. Research on aging and life prolongation has never been an issue in political campaigns as, for instance, Medicare and Medicaid have been.

Another way to become part of the research team working on life prolongation is to send tax-deductible contributions to nonprofit organizations supporting research on aging and life prolongation, such as the American Aging Association (University of Nebraska, Department of Medicine, 42nd and Dewey Ave., Omaha, Nebraska), or its affiliate member, the California Aging Association (3959 Laurel Canyon Blvd., Suite C, Studio City, California 91604).

It has been estimated that if it were possible to channel into research on aging and life prolongation at least one-tenth, and no more, of the money which each year is being spent in the United States on various remedies against old age, life prolongation would become a fact within a few years.

4 | The Benefits and Drawbacks of Prolonging Life

THE MOST COMMON CONCERN EXPRESSED ABOUT LIFE PRO-longation is the fear that it might lead to the extension of that last period of life which is so often accompanied by general weakness and dependency, senile decline, and chronic ailments. Fortunately, this need not be the case. From what scientists already know about the process of aging, there is no doubt that the elimination or alleviation of any of the numerous causes of aging will automatically be accompanied by an increased vitality and by an increased resistance to senility and chronic diseases.

In unpublished experiments by the author, life prolongation was achieved through long-term addition of chemicals called antioxidants to the food of laboratory animals. The most striking observation—beside life prolongation itself—was the increased vitality, vigor, and youthful appearance of those animals which received the antioxidants such as alpha d-tocopherol, BHT, and BHA.

At the time when senile decline sets in, and when the animals that did not receive antioxidants had lost over 30 to 40 percent of their adult body weight and were losing hair and showing all the usual signs of age, their litter mates which had been receiving antioxidants looked quite different. They showed the vitality, vigor, and appearance of early middle age; they showed no loss of body weight and no loss of hair. They finally lived about 40 percent longer than their litter mates and proved that life prolongation (by antioxidants) is accompanied by an increased vitality and vigor, and by an increased resistance to senile decline.

It is anticipated that life prolongation will extend the prime years of life, the working years of people in all professions. An increase in productive life span will substantially increase the net return that the individual makes to his society. If about 30 years are required to rear and educate a human being into full professional usefulness in a technoscientific society, then the ratio of productive to consuming years is only about 1 to 1 with present life expectancy. But if the productive life span were expanded to 90, the ratio would become 2 to 1.

WHY EXTEND THE LIFE SPAN?

Extending the human life span will become an economic advantage and even a necessity if human knowledge and the time required for education keep increasing at the same rate that they have in the past decades. The time will come when man will have to spend most of his life getting educated and will not have enough time left to work productively before retiring or dying of old age—unless his life span is extended. With some professions we already may be closer to this point than we like to admit. Some Canadian medical schools often reject applicants who are 30 years old or more because "they cannot practice medicine long enough to make a full contribution to society," according to William Davis, Ontario's minister of education.

The second major concern about these current approaches to life extension is the doubt that they will fit into the budget of the average person when they do come. Life extension measures, which only the rich can afford, would be cruelly tantalizing to the rest of us. However, the hope and goal of the researchers is to find means of prolonging life and vigor that will cost as little as possible. Unquestionably, some methods will be expensive, especially when first available, before the pharmaceutical companies and the medical profession have worked out less costly methods of applying them. Even so, some of these methods will be generally affordable from the very beginning.

The antioxidant step in life prolongation will be very inexpensive or the least expensive of all the future life-extending steps. Antioxidant drugs most probably will be taken in the form of pills two or three times a day. Most antioxidants, such as the butylated hydroxytoluene, can be produced inexpensively and in large quantities. The cost may be 20-30 cents a day or less for each person.

Such an inexpensive and simple therapy for old age will be within the reach of the entire population of developed countries and the relatively affluent citizens of less-developed countries.

It is expected that the enzymes which break cross-linkages between molecules inside the body will be more expensive than the antioxidants. In general, enzymes are temperature sensitive and destroyed at room temperature; this requires storage and transportation at low temperature. They would have to be injected into the body with a hypodermic syringe, which adds to the cost of the therapy. It has been estimated that the cost of treatment against old age by such enzymes might amount to $3 or $5 a day, and might run between $1000 and $1500 a year for each treated person. This price is possible for most working people, though it may be beyond the reach of many older persons.

Even more expensive would be the blood washings or plasmapheresis-treatment of old age. An optimum treatment might require two blood washings a week, or about 100 treatments a year. Similar to kidney dialysis for patients with insufficiency of kidneys, blood washing or plasmapheresis is a very delicate and potentially dangerous measure that cannot be done at home. Highly trained medical specialists are required and the cost is comparable to kidney dialysis in a hospital, which at the present time runs between $10,000 and $20,000 a year for each person treated. However, it can be expected that innovations and large-scale operations will reduce foreseeable costs of plasmapheresis to $5,000 a year for each person; even this price makes the blood-washing treatment practically inaccessible to large sectors of the adult population.

There is no doubt that the aged represent (with or without extended life span) both a potential additional resource and a drain on resources, which even an affluent society can find difficult to support. In the past, each of us individually has been responsible for whether we are an additional resource for our loved ones and society or a burden in old age. With Medicare and Medicaid the responsibility is being shifted increasingly from the individual to the state and federal agencies. This problem, which is becoming more important as the numbers of people over 65 in our population increase, will be further accentuated by the extension of human life span. Certainly we should not postpone our efforts to develop, as N. W. Shock once emphasized, a "clear conception of what the role of the aged should be in our society."

To develop such a conception the main problems will probably center around the question of how to avoid the additional burden, on state and federal agencies, and on society in general, of providing financial support for people who are living longer than their natural life span. Should only some and not the others be allowed to benefit from life-span-extending measures? And if so, which criteria apply for their selection? It appears that in a democratic society the future criteria for deciding who benefits from such measures will be based in one way or other on a sort of "natural selection"—that is, on the usual criteria of supply and demand, the amount of "salable" services an individual can provide compared to the amount of services which he would "need to buy."

DRAWBACKS OF LIFE EXTENSION

The extension of human life span will create problems as soon as the innovation reaches large segments of the population. Just imagine what would happen if large numbers of retired persons who are drawing retirement benefits began to live on the average of 10, 20, or 30 years longer. The need to pay retirement benefits (to people who would have died long before if they had not been using some life-span-extending measures) would represent a heavy drain on retirement funds. Eventually the administrators of retirement funds would have to reduce and even stop the monthly payments of retirement benefits, increase monthly contributions by the working segments of the population (as they pay for their future retirement benefits), or have the retirement funds simply go broke. It may appear that the logical solution would be to increase the retirement age, or the monthly contributions, or both. But suppose some people would not want to live longer than their natural life span. Should they then pay the same higher monthly contributions as those who plan to apply life-span-extending measures and therefore live longer?

One thing is certain: the solution to any of the social problems dealing with an increased life span will not be found until such an increase has become a reality. As each of us has had ample opportunity to observe, society usually deals with problems as they become urgent, not in anticipation of future need.

Technological possibilities are irresistible to man; if man can achieve life prolongation he *will*—and we now know that he *can*.

Life, our own and the lives of those we love, can be enjoyable. And a healthy vigorous active life is the most enjoyable of all. The value of increasing the time allotted to each individual is great enough to make the problems related to it worth solving.

5 | Fear of Growing Old and of Death

THERE IS AN UNDERSTANDABLE LACK OF UNANIMITY REGARDing *when* middle age begins. It is believed to appear somewhat earlier in women than in men. This statement reminds me of what an unknown high school student said about the author of the *Iliad:* "We do not know whether Homer lived, but we do know that he was blind." Anyhow, most people probably will agree that middle age begins somewhere around the time when we become aware that our bodies and minds are less responsive to the joys and demands of life.

The awareness of physical limitations seems to come to the middle-aged person with a shock—as if these changes had occurred overnight. One day, the middle-aged person looks into the mirror and finds that his waistline is no more what it used to be and that the amount of visible flesh on his face seems to have increased twofold overnight. The time of this awareness, however, varies from one person to another, depending on the kind of physical appearance or mental responsiveness that he values most and also because middle age is still capable of impressive mental growth.

Recent intelligence-type tests on middle-agers, who had previously been examined at the age of 19–21, have found not a decline, but a significant increase in total score, with more than one-third of the 45–49 age group scoring as well or better than the average of the 19–21-year-olds. Middle-agers make particularly high scores on general information and vocabulary tests; they do not slip much on arithmetical problems, even though they score less well on analytical thinking. Actually, there are no mental slippages that would indicate a significant handicap for middle age.

Nevertheless, the physical signs of middle age are easy to read, but those who read them differ greatly in their interpretation. Many a person simply denies the signs and insists that he is "still as good as ever" and that he "never felt better." Others note the signs but insist that these are only warning signs, and that all they need to do is to take more rest and, maybe, some vitamin pills. Still others cushion the impact of advancing years by a simulated youthfulness, but neither the denial, nor the continued youthfulness nor any other stratagem give solace from the increasing opaqueness of the senses and the cooling of the passions. They do not shy away the awareness of chronic small aches, nor the necessity for compensating fading vision, slower movements, infirm muscles and missing teeth, nor can they help to rid one of the recurrent fear of growing old.

The middle-aged man is likely to be near his peak of earning power, or he may be trying to land the top job in his profession. Often he is depicted as a dollar-mad, tension-ridden, ulcer-coddling, sex-obsessed, and culture-anemic individual, too busy making a living to enjoy life. Nevertheless, middle age is the time of major roles in the individual's life, such as the realization of one's potential in terms of achievement and life satisfactions. Middle age also is the time when many parental duties are over, and the time of the individual's preparation for the later years of life.

Early middle age may be the time of testing in which the individual compares the level of his youthful aspirations or goals with the level of his actual achievements and satisfactions. Such testing or comparisons are not inherent in this or any phase of life, but rather are a consequence of certain cultural conditions. Such comparisons often take place in cultures where the individual's life goals can be achieved earlier in life, that is in the first half of the life course. Anyhow, the individual may decide on the basis of his comparisons, in which also the relative achievements of his friends and colleagues play an important role, that he is successful, partially successful, or a failure. In Western societies, for example, it is possible for a businessman to become a millionaire or for an academician to become a professor, while he still has half his productive life before him, and the problem of what to do with the rest of life may arise.

Success, however, is not a guarantee against dissatisfaction. Even the individual who considers himself to be successful may become dissatisfied with the fruit of his success. The dissatisfied success, even though he has achieved his original goals, realizes that his dominant desires still have not been satisfied. In such case, various alternatives are possible. If, for example, the individual believes that he made a mistake in choosing his original life goals, he may desire to choose a new life course and often the most important question he will ask himself is, "Will I have enough time?" or "Am I not too old to start all over again?"

The fears of growing old and of death are fears all human beings experience in one way or another. They rarely exist when we are young, but develop gradually as we approach middle age, and then intensify. Countless books have been written on the subject of how to face the fact of death from the religious, philosophical, and other metaphysical points of view. Even though these various views are fascinating in so many different ways, they will only be summarized here, just enough to assist the main objective of this chapter: to help the reader in his realization that he, too, is afraid of growing old, so that he does not feel ashamed, for instance, to discuss this fear with his physician.

The famous composer, Igor Stravinsky, before he died, was so afraid of growing old that he did not hesitate to fly to Switzerland to consult the Swiss doctor-rejuvenationist, Paul Niehans, author of the so-called cell therapy against aging (this therapy has been discussed in more detail on pages 17-19).

Admitting to oneself the fear of growing old is an excellent way to start a personal program of avoiding the various known errors of everyday life which make one age faster.

Besides the fears that there is not much time left to achieve one's life goals, and even less to change one's life course or to enjoy the fruit of one's efforts, there is the paramount fear of becoming old, decrepit, senile, and dependent. The fear of becoming old and dependent may be even stronger than the fear of death itself. There is something deplorable in senile degeneration that offends the aesthetic sense. When asked about becoming old, people often say that they do not mind growing old as long as they do not become dependent and a burden to others. For many, the idea or the fear of growing old is terrible mainly because it may mean that somebody has to take care of them. Only rarely do they allude to the fear of death itself. Similarly, illness, blindness, and deafness are seen mainly as states involving dependence upon others, and not as threats to bodily integrity.

Dependency is always seen as having two main drawbacks: loss of income and loss of health. But loss of income is usually considered more important. Many express the feeling that they had become old and ill before they had enough time to make or save enough money for the later years of life. Loss of health or loss of wealth, which is the more important?

Whether we want it or not, we are forced by the inevitability of events to take some kind of attitude toward the facts that we are growing old and going to die. Even the attempts to ignore these facts are equivalent to taking an attitude. The possible attitudes in this regard, which are available for man to choose from, fall into three major categories based on:

a) religious beliefs and philosophies
b) nonreligious, pragmatic adjustments
c) revolt and fight against nature and gods.

RELIGIONS, PHILOSOPHIES, AND FEAR OF DEATH

Man has long been obsessed by the fear of death and the desire for immortality. There is only a short step from the desire for immortality to the idea of an indestructible soul, or at least the hope of life after death in the form of resurrection, rebirth, renewal, or reincarnation, each particular name having a special meaning to some persons or groups of persons. To explain death, some religions teach that man must have done something wrong, otherwise there wouldn't be death; consequently, they proclaim that eternal life can be secured, if death not avoided, by proper conduct, demonstrations of love and fear of God, self-denial, and sacrifice. In a similar category falls the conviction that the death of the body assures the everlasting life of the soul.

Gradually, people have acquired a more sophisticated attitude toward life and death and the hereafter. Many individuals feel increasingly deeply and, by the time their forties roll around, very strongly that no philosophy of life, however profound and esoteric, can bring solace from or can avail against the increasing opaqueness of the senses, the cooling of the passions and the signs of growing old. In fact, the most imaginative religions and philosophies of life encounter the problem of death and annihilation simply by refusing to believe it, or by other kinds of self-deception, and they all tend to become irrelevant to the simple fact: sooner or later we all must die.

When the protective orthodoxies, myths, and philosophies are stripped away, we finally come to the realization that the void is waiting for everybody and that each of us is going to vanish into it. The doubts concerning one's future after death, the fears of growing old, of death's void, are among the most unbearable of all the doubts and fears man can experience.

It would seem that the nonreligious, pragmatic adjustments to aging would be easier for those who achieved the life goals they originally set. Unfortunately, only a very small proportion of people feel that they have achieved their goals. To many, middle age brings the shattering realization that one is not going to do some of the things that he always thought he would do. Such a realization does not make the adjustment easier. In middle age many persons realize that their earlier fantasies of romantic prowess, great wealth, and overwhelming prestige will never be realized. Others achieve their dreams, and find out that the efforts have not been worthwhile. For men with responsibilities, for those striving for achievement and success, middle age can be rough; now the only road is a plateau or a downhill course. There may no longer be the thrill of hoped-for achievements or rising to new heights. Unfortunately, a large number of middle-aged persons are still tied up with having to succeed, often for no other apparent reason than to satisfy some basic neurotic needs.

Some men, at the peak of their earning power, find that younger men are challenging their position, authority and know-how. They may feel threatened by the vitality of the young, or by the changes they bring; such men of middle age may be additionally handicapped by their own tendency to look backward to see how things ought to be done. The individual who considers himself only partially successful may reason to himself that conditions were much too unfavorable for him to completely achieve his original life goals, or he may realize that his own abilities were or are too limited.

However, some individuals prefer to ignore that the odds were against them, or conditions unfavorable, and they insist that there is still some chance for them to achieve their life aspirations, even though in a modified form. Those who consider that they have failed to achieve their life goals to an appreciable or satisfying degree not infrequently discover the virtue of calm courage, and seek for another course of life that would finally lead to the essential satisfactions, if not to success. In fact, adjusting to middle age is considered to be the only way to prevent the psychological problems of growing old.

In middle age we start coping with two issues—life does not last forever and we cannot control the future. Properly conceived, the adjustive measures of middle age need not be painful or irksome, nor do they have to be surrender to a philosophy of resignation. They can and should be the adjustment of accommodation including proper assessment of goals, assets, and limitations and the recognition of the neurotic drives behind many goals. Middle age shifts the focus intensively to the acceptance of the real self. One gets real satisfaction from a reasonable degree of accomplishment and takes pride in the way in which one has coped with life and not been deluded. A perfect adjustment to the later years of life was reported by a journalist who once asked Maurice Chevalier, the famous French comedian and singer, "Maurice, how does it feel to be as old as you are?" to which Maurice Chevalier replied, "Considering the alternative, I like it."

The middle-aged person must take pride in himself for what he is and not for what he would have liked to be; old age should be viewed as an extension of middle age. A person who has gracefully adjusted to the traumas of middle age and has gained confidence in handling them will manage his old-age problems reasonably well. The main threats to adjustment in middle age appear to be middle-aged discontent, boredom, and fatigue. Some persons develop a stoic outlook, others become embittered or, in despair, try to escape into alcohol and even suicide (which is a sort of extreme escape), or into other less drastic forms of avoidance. No wonder that more and more individuals look around for ways and means to fight old age!

Many still believe that man must have done something wrong, that death is God's punishment for man's sins. We still believe that the great divide between mortal men and immortal gods is man's mortality and that any attempt to extend the human natural life span is tantamount to man's revolt against the immortal gods, and as such bound to fail. Man may no more believe in immortal gods, but he is still afraid and somewhat ashamed of his desire to extend his natural life span ... as if the gods were envious creatures still watching man's actions, while awaiting the right moment for severe, exemplary punishment, if he ever attempts to snatch something which he is not supposed to obtain and which belongs only to them.

Subconscious fear of immortal gods and the shame of one's desire to live longer than the natural life span, are present in many a person's mind and come to the surface only occasionally under various disguises. What is modern man going to do about his fear of growing old and his desire to extend his life span? Will man's subconscious fear of the immortal gods continue to be stronger than his fear of growing old? for how long?

Since even a limited extension of our life span is not possible at the present time, many a person hopes to make a bargain—and settle for at least a little postponement of his life's end. Many middle-aged persons seem to want most to obtain just a little more time to live longer and to have one more chance to achieve something upon which they can look back with satisfaction. Many people think that any chance to extend the life span is better than no chance at all; they would accept such a chance no matter how limited it may be.

6 How Realistic a Goal is a 100-Year Life Span?

MOST RECENT SCIENTIFIC OBSERVATIONS INDICATE THAT ANY person, even if he has short-lived parents or short-lived grandparents, can live 100 years and possibly more. However, living to such an age requires following advice contained in this book carefully for the rest of one's life. Sporadic efforts will not be enough.

The indications supporting the conclusion that people have an inborn potential to live up to 100 or over can be divided into the following categories:

■ Indications from statistical data about the extent to which the avoidance of all chronic diseases can increase each person's life expectancy.

■ Indications from genetic studies that the inborn potential to live past 100 exists in the human body.

■ Indications from research on the biology of aging that the "biological clock," or the pace of aging, is set up very much the same for all human beings.

In order to outline the above arguments in more detail it will be necessary to explain the difference between human life span and the average length of human life or human life expectancy, because they are often used interchangeably. The expression "human life span" usually means the maximum age which man can attain under the most healthful living conditions possible, with the ultimate in medical care and the best of luck, so that death finally comes from old age alone. If we disregard biblical stories that Methuselah lived to be 969 years old, Lamech 777, and Noah 500, the human life span has been estimated to be 100 years plus or minus 5 or 10 years.

Whereas the human life span does not seem to have changed appreciably in the past several thousand years, the average length of human life, or the life expectancy, which takes into account deaths from various diseases and accidents, has shown a continuous increase. It has been estimated, for instance, that the average length of human life at the beginning of the Christian era, nearly two thousand years ago, was only about 22 years. There may have been a modest increase during the Middle Ages, but there was no rapid advance until about a century ago. Records in Maryland and Massachusetts show that between 1850 and 1860 the average length of life was a little over 40 years. It rose at the beginning of the twentieth century in the United States to about 48 years for white males and about 51 years for white females, with a further increase in 1960 to about 67 years for white males and about 74 years for white females.

Spectacular as this threefold increase may appear it is still several decades less than the human life span—that is, below the maximum age which man can attain under the most healthful living conditions possible. Now compare the reasons for the past increase in the average length of human life to the present, most-frequent causes of death, other than old age. In our time, chronic diseases of old age are killing most of us and preventing us from living the full length of our life span.

The increase in life expectancy of the average American, which took place in the course of this century, was largely due to the spectacular success of the medical profession in treating acute and infectious diseases. Evidence of this success can be seen in the steady decline in deaths caused by these diseases, from 41 percent in 1901 to 9.8 percent in 1955. It is particularly important to note that during the same period there was a steady increase in deaths caused by chronic diseases, from 46 percent in 1901 to 81.4 percent or about 4 out of each 5 deaths, in 1955. Obviously chronic diseases have been more difficult for the medical profession to control. The reasons for this difficulty will be examined later.

How large an increase in life expectancy could we achieve if we did succeed in preventing deaths from chronic diseases? Various investigators have estimated on the basis of statistical data that our life expectancy (which is now about 67 years for men and about 74 years for women), would increase by another 10 years, or even 12.5 years, if it were possible to eliminate deaths from heart diseases and cerebrovascular accidents. After heart diseases and cerebrovascular accidents, most older adults succumb to cancer and high blood pressure in that order. Further, the elimination of deaths caused by high blood pressure would increase our life expectancy by a few more years.

Those individuals who become old without being carried off by the above diseases, fall victim to a number of diseases headed by respiratory infections such as flu and pneumonia. Although these diseases are common to people of all ages, they kill the old more readily than the young people. Once again, the elimination of deaths from respiratory diseases would increase our life expectancy by a few years. That does not yet exhaust the list of chronic diseases which cause death; nevertheless, the above estimations strongly support the notion that our life expectancy can increase by as much as several decades and, unbelievable as it may appear, would approach the maximum human life span of 100 years if every individual were able to avoid death from chronic diseases.

Every person has an inborn potential to live out the full length of human life span. Support for this statement comes from studies of long-lived individuals. You have certainly read or heard about persons who lived to be 100 and over. There are now living in the United States over 5,000 people, or 1 out of every 40,000, who are 100 years old or more. You may even have cherished a secret desire to live to be 100, while at the same time you felt your chances were very small. Your chances are much better than you think. Probably, you have wondered how on earth these people reached such an age. What enabled them to live for such a long time?

Most frequently, it has been pointed out that longevity is inborn or hereditary. The joke is often made that, if you desire to live long, you have to choose four long-lived grandparents. This logic, however, is much too simple and highly fallacious. It is no secret that longevity tends to run in families. Some families consistently produce a high proportion of individuals who survive to advanced ages. Consequently, it comes as no surprise that many studies of human longevity have demonstrated a positive relationship between the longevity of parents, or grandparents, and that of the offspring.

However, the most important factors or causes of human longevity have for a long time eluded investigators. Only recently has it been pointed out that longevity studies of this type did not distinguish between true inborn factors and environmental factors as causes of longevity. These environmental causes are very important in their effects on longevity. Possibly they are more important than the inborn factors.

Some investigators began to look closely at the lives of persons who lived to be 100 and noticed that all these persons in their later years ate simple but well-balanced meals in amounts that kept them slim, maintained their own pace of daily activities, kept busy without hurrying themselves or straining their declining capacities, took care of themselves if not well, and rested when they felt tired. These and other studies indicate that the particular circumstances in which a person lives, that is, his "environmental factors," are vitally important to his chances for a long life.

Research on aging throughout the individual's entire life span, observations concerning the effects of environmental factors on human longevity and observations on inborn factors in chronic diseases taken together, all indicate that longevity is not a kind of inborn privilege which only a few receive from mother nature. All persons, including you, have received the same inborn capacity to live the full length of the human life span. Increasing evidence indicates that mother nature, instead of giving some individuals a longer life span than others, gives some individuals a greater resistance to stress and disease than others. However, the capacity to live the full length of human life span remains the same for disease-susceptible individuals as for disease-resistant individuals.

If some persons die appreciably sooner than others, it is not because they have an inborn shorter life span, but because they have an inborn susceptibility to disease *coupled with their own disease-inducing, life-shortening errors.* These errors may have little or no effect on a disease-resistant individual, but induce chronic disease and shorten the life of disease-susceptible persons. However, even disease-suceptible persons can live as healthy and as long a life as disease-resistant persons if they avoid making these errors in their daily living. If they die prematurely, they have only themselves and their indulgences to blame. Nature has given them the same potential for long life that she gave the disease-resistant persons.

Good strategies of body maintenance, and persistence in following them, will do more than heredity to increase the years of your life.

PART II:
Nutrition

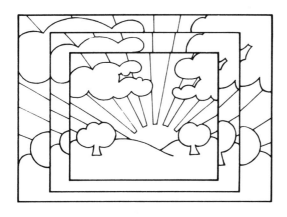

7 | The Dynamics of Nutrition

THE HUMAN BODY IS BEING CONTINUALLY REBUILT; NEW PARTS are being manufactured by the body to replace the old, worn-out parts. In this continuous dynamic process, an essential role is played by the food we eat. A well-balanced diet provides the body with the raw materials it needs for the manufacture of new replacement parts. When the proper foods are missing, the process of manufacture cannot go on efficiently. The phrase "we are what we eat" is all too true.

Digestion breaks down food into building blocks that the body is able to use for renewing itself. For instance, digestion turns the meats we eat and other protein-containing foods into amino acids which the body uses to build molecules of protein for its own cells. During digestion, these amino acid building blocks are split off, or unhooked, by special enzymes present in the digestive tract.

After digestion has taken place, these building blocks are picked up by the blood, which carries and distributes them to countless complicated assembly lines. These assembly lines consist of various enzymes that work in harmonious cooperation to build and rebuild all the components of the body. It is tremendously important that the digested food comes to the assembly lines in the right proportions.

Nutrition is the sum of what we eat each day. Our nutrition is good when we eat the kinds and amounts of food that provide building blocks in the right proportions for the countless assembly lines in our bodies. When a person eats the proper proportions of food nutritionists say he has a balanced diet.

When our nutrition is bad, our diet is unbalanced, and we are sending building blocks in the wrong proportions to the assembly lines of our bodies. If these assembly lines keep receiving too many of the wrong building blocks and too few of the ones they need, trouble begins. The assembly lines try to reject the wrong building blocks or they try to adjust to them. This process tends to overburden the manufacturing process. Sometimes the assembly lines pick up the wrong building blocks and insert them between the components that are being replaced. This may have even more undesirable consequences.

In order to function at all, the body requires fuel. If we starve ourselves, our bodies literally begin to canabalize themselves in order to obtain the fuel necessary for their functioning. First of all, they use their stores of fat; then if outside fuel is still not forthcoming, they begin to break down muscle and other tissue into the needed fuel. The process is somewhat similar to tearing down part of your house to get the wood you need to build a fire to keep from freezing to death.

The most important fuel for the body is the sugar called glucose. It is supplied by carbohydrate-containing foods such as bread, potatoes, rice, corn, and other cereals. These foods used to be called starches. By the process of digestion they are converted from the more complex carbohydrate molecules to the simpler sugar glucose molecules that the body can easily "burn." Triglycerides and fatty acids are another body fuel, found in the fats of meat and the oils of fishes, nuts, and other plant products such as avocados and olives. Although not a carbohydrate or a triglyceride or a fatty acid, alcohol also acts as a fuel. It can be assimilated directly without being digested. Because alcohol is a fuel, a successful weight-reducing program strictly limits alcohol in any form (beer, wine, or distilled liquor). This need to limit alcohol intake may appear unfortunate, but it is based on an unequivocal biochemical fact.

Glucose cannot be readily stored in the body in appreciable amounts. On the other hand, fat or triglycerides can be stored in large amounts. When a person eats too much of the carbohydrate-containing foods that are broken down into glucose, the body turns the excess glucose into fat (triglycerides) and then stores the fat in fat tissues. Sugar glucose, triglycerides, fatty acids, and alcohol are sometimes called caloric or empty nutrients, as opposed to essential nutrients like amino acids, which are the building blocks of the body.

All in all, the role of nutrition and diet is to keep the metabolic processes of the body functioning smoothly by providing blocks in the right proportions and by providing enough, but not too much, fuel for these processes. It is the same old story: too much or too little are equally bad.

There is no excuse for malnutrition in a country as wealthy and as technically advanced as the United States. Nevertheless, we are discovering to our surprise and chagrin that an alarming degree of malnutrition exists among the poor and also among those who are not poor. Many factors in our life today work against the development of good eating habits: the frantic pace of urban life, the increasing number of persons who live alone, often with inadequate facilities to keep food or prepare proper meals, plus the abundance of food stands and of quick-energy and prepared foods.

Greasy and sweet-heavy snacks such as hot dogs and soft drinks comprise an increasing proportion of our diets. As we will see, snacking as opposed to eating large meals is beneficial, but it can be beneficial only so long as the snacks are nutritious in themselves. The next few chapters discuss thoroughly the most dangerous errors in our eating habits and an easy method for providing ourselves with the proper building blocks in the right amounts.

Many people feel that something is wrong with their daily diet, but they do not know how to correct it. They become easy preys of food faddists who have distorted ideas about nutrition. Often the gap between the food-faddist's advice and sober scientific facts is disconcerting. Even though adults can learn the essentials of good nutrition easily, the dietary patterns of many adults are a sad hodgepodge of gustatory preferences, prejudice, capricious self-indulgence, misinformation, indifference, lack of appetite, and fear of indigestion or constipation.

To a great extent, dietary habits are the result of our past experiences. The individual's memories of eating this or that food at his mother's table often determine years later his preferences regardless of logical considerations. Thus, psychological, social, and economic factors contribute heavily to poor nutrition.

It is true that the foods containing protein cost more than foods high in sweets or fats. It is also true that sweets present less of a storage problem than protein-containing foods. One can tuck a candy bar into a breast pocket, but not a chicken drumstick. However, with determination and good planning, fairly inexpensive but very nutritious foods can be had. The extra effort we spend will be paid back in extra years of living.

Recently, it has been found in experiments with animals that a diet which has been unbalanced in one way or another shortens the life span. Indications are accumulating that an unbalanced diet may shorten the life expectancy of man as well. The food we eat, its type, its ingredients, and the amounts in which we take it, have profound effects on our body, our health, our general fitness and our sense of well-being.

8 | Dynamics of Overeating

THERE IS NO DOUBT THAT THE MOST SERIOUS NUTRITIONAL problem in this country is overeating. Chronic overeating not only makes us fat, it endangers our health. Often it is the villain in the development of obesity, atherosclerosis, diabetes, heart disease, high blood pressure, and more subtle diseases.

These diseases and overeating are interrelated and aggravate each other. Even though you may be slim, you may have heart disease and if you allow yourself to become overweight, the heart disease may grow worse. Similarly, it is possible to develop atherosclerosis without being obese—although obesity does tend to hasten its development—and becoming fat will aggravate the atherosclerosis.

Successful dieting not only makes us look better, it also makes us healthier, more efficient in our bodily functions, more able to enjoy life and to live longer. Understanding what happens in the body makes successful dieting easier to accomplish.

As we have noted, after digestion occurs, the blood takes up the caloric nutrients, the sugar glucose, the triglycerides or fat and alcohol, together with the essential nutrients. This intake raises the level of sugar glucose and triglycerides or fat in the blood stream. The more we eat at a given time, the higher the level of sugar glucose and triglycerides or fat in the blood and the longer it takes for the blood level of sugar glucose and triglycerides to reach the low fasting level found in persons who have not been eating for some time. After an especially heavy meal, it can take six hours or more for the glucose and triglycerides in the blood to reach fasting levels.

The blood transports the caloric and essential nutrients to the assembly lines in the tissue cells throughout the body. Sugar glucose and the triglycerides or fat are used to fuel the manufacturing process as well as the other bodily processes and physical activity. When we speak of "burning calories," we refer to the way in which molecules of sugar glucose and triglycerides power these processes, just as gasoline is burned by the engine to power the car.

An unusually high level of triglycerides and glucose in the blood can cause a traffic jam: more fuel is being dumped into the blood stream than can be unloaded and used in the tissue cells. More will be said about this traffic jam later. A moderate rise in the blood levels of sugar glucose and triglycerides or fat that comes about from eating moderately is usual and is not harmful.

During the period of fasting between meals, molecules of sugar glucose and triglycerides continue to leave the blood stream and enter the tissue cells until excess amounts of these molecules have been burned and the level of sugar glucose and triglycerides in the blood returns to fasting levels.

If the low fasting level is not reached before more food is eaten, the excess sugar glucose in the blood is converted into triglycerides or fat and stored along with the excess triglycerides already in the tissues. There is no way around this unfortunate fact: What the body is unable to burn or use as fuel, it has to store inside its tissues in the form of fat.

Allowing the amounts of sugar glucose and triglycerides to reach low fasting levels in the blood stream is the royal road to slimness. Not only does it prevent fat from being stored in the tissue cells, but also during this period the tissue cells release stored triglycerides or fat to be used as fuel.

Unfortunately, many people have the habit of eating much too much food at one time. Often they are not aware of eating too much because this is the way their family has eaten for generations. Unquestionably, the members of their family have also been getting a middle-aged spread for generations. The two are not inevitable, but the relationship is strong.

To make matters worse, the body's capacity to burn fuel declines with age. This means that, as we get older, more of the caloric nutrients that we eat become converted into fat. Next to habitual overeating, this decline in the body's ability to burn fuel is the most significant cause of the weight gain that seems to afflict so many people in their thirties and over.

This decline in the capacity to burn calories, which occurs with age, has been documented and illustrated by a comparison of the differences between younger and older individuals in the rise of fat content in the blood after ingestion of the same amount of fat. In younger individuals the level of triglycerides or fat in the blood rises only moderately and, after three or four hours, drops again to fasting levels. Thus, the excess molecules of triglycerides that result from eating the fats have been delivered to the tissue cells and have been used up or burned in a three- or four-hour period.

Among the older individuals tested, delivery and burning of the triglycerides takes 9 to 12 hours. The traffic jam of high triglyceride levels lasts longer. By implication, if one of the young persons tested had eaten again five hours after consuming the standard fat meal, no storage of triglycerides would have resulted; whereas if an older person had waited as long as seven or eight hours before eating again, excess molecules of triglycerides from the test meal would still be in the bloodstream and in the tissue cells and would be stored as fat to make room for the next load. As we will detail later, the solution for this unfortunate state of affairs is not to put more hours between eating bouts but to eat less at any given time and to continue to decrease the size of the meal as age increases.

Some persons, because of their constitutional setup, even when young are less capable of burning triglycerides than the average person their own age. Without careful attention to their diet, they will begin to gain weight early in life. And, as the age decline in the body's capacity to burn fuel holds for people in this group as well, to be healthy and attractive, they are going to have to resign themselves to a lifetime of discipline.

There are degrees of being overweight. And the difference between overweight and obesity is a matter of degree; the dividing line is somewhere around 20 percent above a desirable weight (found in height/weight tables on page 88, where also the difference between average weight and desirable weight is explained). If a person weighs no more than about 20 percent above his desirable weight, he is considered to be overweight; if he weighs more, he is considered obese. This 20 percent dividing line is entirely arbitrary, however, and some nutritionists use their own dividing line, which may be somewhat more or less than the 20 percent.

The human body is designed to store a certain amount of fat with little harm, although as the age increases so does the importance of not exceeding one's desirable weight. But as we have suggested, there are special tissues whose function it is to store fat. When, however, there is more fat to be stored than the body's fat tissues can comfortably hold or when there are large amounts of fat to be stored at one time, the body tends to shove these excess molecules of fat into tissues which were not intended for fat storage.

If this sounds ominous, it is. Tissue that has been infiltrated by fat is weakened. Its resistance to stress is lessened. And its capacity to function properly is diminished. In some tissues this process can be especially dangerous. When fat infiltrates the walls of the arteries or the heart muscle, the weakening may lead to a serious breakdown.

Did you ever feel tired after a good, heavy meal? It was due to the slowdown of the blood flow in the capillaries of the body tissues and of the brain.

High levels of glucose and fat in the blood after a heavy meal lead, in susceptible persons, to a slowdown of blood flow or sludging of blood cells in the capillaries of various organs. Such a slowdown may even lead to a heart attack, but there are discernible signs that such sludging is taking place. In order to counteract possible dangerous consequences, one can easily learn to recognize these signs.

In few tissues of the human body is it possible to observe directly the slowdown of the blood flow because of high blood levels of fat after a fatty meal. Most suitable for such observations is the outer surface of the white of the eye, where one can see even with the naked eye small blood vessels and, with the help of a microscopic viewer, one can even observe the flow of the blood and the columns of red blood cells streaming through the capillaries.

In susceptible individuals even between meals the continuous stream of red blood cells may be interrupted here and there by a series of clumsily transported irregular masses or aggregates of red blood cells that may cause an intermittence and marked sluggishness of flow. Such a slowdown is never seen in normal unsusceptible individuals; susceptible individuals often have higher blood levels of fat even between meals.

About four hours after ingestion of a fatty meal, these masses or aggregates of red blood cells may in susceptible individuals totally obstruct large numbers of previously open capillaries and induce an intense, widespread lack of blood and oxygen supply, or ischemia, whereas in normal, unsusceptible individuals no obstruction or slowing down of blood flow are observed. This kind of sluggishness of red blood cells may persist even nine hours after a fatty meal in persons with high blood levels of fat (triglycerides), and it also seems that high blood levels of cholesterol are implicated.

The administration of heparin (a complex organic substance claimed to clear up high blood levels of fat or hyperlipemia) prior to the consumption of a fatty meal does not seem to prevent or diminish the sludging of blood cells, nor does it prevent the resulting lack of oxygen, or ischemia. In practically all instances the severity of the obstruction in the capillaries is related to the level of fat (triglycerides) in the blood after a fatty meal.

The sludging of red blood cells and the slowdown of the blood flow in susceptible individuals takes place in blood capillaries of other tissues and organs of the body where it cannot be observed as well as in the capillaries of the white of the eye. Evidently, it takes place in blood capillaries of the heart, because it has been reported by a number of investigators that ingestion of a heavy, fatty meal is often accompanied by an increased rate of the heartbeat and changes in the electrocardiogram, comparable to changes in the electrocardiogram in ischemic heart disease ("ischemic" means: low oxygen supply).

How can a person test for himself whether or not he is one of the susceptible individuals who may develop a dangerous slowdown of the blood flow after a heavy meal?

First of all, it should be emphasized that it really is dangerous for susceptible persons with a weak heart to eat heavy meals. There have been instances where persons with a weak heart had a heart attack soon after a heavy meal, and some did not even survive the attack. But even if the person with a weak heart does not have a heart attack after a particular heavy meal, each heavy meal presents a heavy strain for his heart and in the long run contributes to the aggravation of his heart disease.

How then can a person with a weak heart test whether this or that particular meal has not been too heavy for him, or whether another meal has been light enough for him? Such testing can be done by taking the rate of the heartbeat, or the pulse rate half-an-hour after the meal and each following half-hour for several hours.

If the meal was too heavy, the heartbeat or the pulse rate rises high above normal values within half-an-hour after the meal and stays high for as long as the effect of the heavy meal lasts, often for several hours. A susceptible person with a weak heart may after a heavy meal also develop skipped heartbeats, another very serious danger sign.

What can a person do if he notices a high pulse rate or even skipped heartbeats after a heavy meal? First of all, he can and should slow down in his daily activities which he may have scheduled for the time after the meal (such as the afternoon activities after a heavy lunch). If possible, he should lie down for at least ten minutes and possibly more. He should take the warning: avoid heavy meals, and start having lighter meals. Of course, he should continue taking his pulse rate even after lighter meals and at various occasions, such as after a cup of coffee, etc.

Taking the rate of the heartbeat is a very helpful and easy test, which any person can perform and which affords a person valuable information. If the rate of the heartbeat is too high, it could be a danger sign and means: Slow down, avoid heavy meals, emotional stress, and watch the blood pressure closely. Slow down and reduce the intensity of the strain, no matter what is its origin or character.

The slowdown of the blood flow after a heavy fatty meal probably also takes place in blood capillaries of the brain. This is indicated, among others, by the feeling of tiredness and sleepiness, experienced by susceptible persons after heavy meals which usually are also rich on fat. Incidentally, the feeling of tiredness after a heavy meal was known already to the ancient Romans who incorporated it into their saying, *"Plenus venter studet non libenter"* (the full stomach does not like to study). Moreover, the same fatty meal, which in a young person does not lead to a slowdown of the blood flow, may later in the same person, as he grows older, result in the slowdown of the blood flow in the capillaries of his organs and tissues, particularly the heart and brain, where it can lead to tragic consequences.

9 | Maturity–Onset Diabetes: The Most Dangerous Consequence of Overeating

THE DYNAMIC PROCESSES OF THE BODY CAN EASILY BE THROWN into disorder, or even break down under stressful conditions. When a break down goes by unnoticed and uncorrected, the consequences pile up and contribute to the development of various chronic diseases. One of the most dangerous of such conditions occurs when the body is no longer able to cope correctly with high levels of sugar glucose in the blood—this disease is called diabetes.

Uncontrolled, diabetes can be a killer. There have been instances where healthy-looking diabetics unexpectedly fell into a coma and died. Diabetes has grave effects on obesity, and also on atherosclerosis and heart disease and the ability of the body to resist infection and other diseases.

Today we are fortunate to have methods of detecting diabetes early in its development, in time to prevent its aggravation and most serious consequences. Simple laboratory procedures, which are part of a routine physical examination, will tell your physician whether or not you are a diabetic, prediabetic, or latent diabetic. Diabetes has several forms, some of which are hereditary. For the person who has had diabetes from early childhood, procedures for controlling it are a crucial part of daily life.

One form of the disease is maturity-onset diabetes; it is exceedingly common and comes about through years of overindulgence in such nutritional errors as skipping meals, eating sugar-sweetened foods, or heavy meals at long-spaced intervals.

Some persons are remarkably resistant to this disease; they can eat heavy meals or mountains of candies and sweets every day without developing diabetes. But for us to assume we are among this number is to play medical roulette. There is no way of determining in which category we belong until we check with the doctor. The odds are not good. About one person in three is susceptible to the disease.

There are over two million known diabetics in the United States (and probably over another two million unknown); and maturity-onset diabetes represents approximately 90 percent of all known patients with diabetes. What is even more important, maturity-onset diabetes is prone to occur in *any* person after 45 years of age, if that person is not careful to avoid daily nutritional errors known to induce diabetes. We have a choice: we can learn to eat in such a way as to prevent the disease from developing or we can gamble with our health.

By definition, diabetes is a disorder in glucose regulation. This implies the possible operation of all the many factors, hormonal, genetic, and others, which are known to influence the level of glucose in the blood, either directly or indirectly by influencing the synthesis, secretion, transport, or action of the hormone insulin in responsive tissues.

INSULIN: THE KEY TO FUEL DISTRIBUTION

It is impossible to discuss diabetes without discussing insulin, which is secreted by the pancreas; the pancreatic islets contain the insulin-producing machinery. Insulin plays a very delicate role in the distribution of sugar glucose to all the assembly lines inside the cells of the body. This delicate role can be compared to the role of a coordinator in a large factory (the body). When we eat a meal, it can be compared to a new delivery of building blocks (such as amino acids) and a new delivery of fuel (such as sugar glucose) for the metabolic processes inside the body.

The process works this way. First, digestion breaks down the carbohydrate-containing foods into sugar glucose; then, the blood begins to transport this new supply of sugar-glucose molecules from the alimentary canal; naturally, the level of sugar glucose in the blood rises. This rise in the level of sugar glucose stimulates the pancreatic islets to release the hormone insulin into the blood. The higher the blood level of sugar glucose, the stronger is the stimulus for the release of insulin from the pancreas and, other factors being equal, the larger the quantity of insulin released.

Insulin acts to lower the blood levels of sugar glucose by opening the doors (figuratively speaking) for the molecules of sugar glucose to leave the blood stream and enter the tissue cells where they can be burned to provide energy for the physical activity and to go toward the manufacture of new cells. Once insulin is in the blood stream, it will continue to open doors in the tissue cells for the molecules of sugar glucose to leave the blood stream until the insulin has been used up.

Unfortunately, the pancreatic islets can be fooled very easily. If a person eats a piece of candy or cake, which digests quickly, the level of sugar glucose in his blood will rise quickly and sharply. This sudden rise fools the pancreatic islets into secreting as much insulin as is needed to cope with a large amount of slow-digesting food (such as bread or potatoes). After the molecules of sugar glucose provided by the candy or cake have been delivered to their destination inside the cells, there is still a much-larger-than-normal amount of insulin in the blood stream. This leftover insulin continues to open doors for more sugar glucose to leave the blood stream and enter the tissue cells.

As a result, the level of sugar glucose in the blood stream falls below the normal fasting level. Among other consequences, this low level of sugar glucose, called hypoglycemia, makes a person so urgently hungry that he rarely is able to resist eating again. In this way one sweet leads to another. After a sweet, the person becomes hyperglycemic; he has higher blood levels of sugar glucose than he needs. A short while later, after the insulin has done its work, he has less sugar glucose in his blood stream than he needs; he is hypoglycemic. These fluctations of too high and too low levels of blood sugar glucose and insulin are stressful to the body. They contribute to the development of obesity, diabetes, heart disease, and hypertension.

It is difficult to believe that such a little thing as eating too many sweets, something so many people do all the time, can have such dangerous potential consequences. And yet, this is not scare talk or exaggeration; it is scientific fact, documented by experimental evidence. Fooling the pancreas by eating foods with substantial amounts of sugar or honey (which has essentially the same carbohydrate composition as sugar) is a serious error that can induce diabetes and age us unnecessarily fast.

Overeating—that is, eating in excess of the body's need for fuel —is slightly different in its effect from eating too many sweets, but it is an error just as grave in its consequences, particularly when, as is usually the case, the two errors are combined.

Just as your car can burn only so much gasoline at any given moment, the body's tissue cells need only so much fuel at a time. The level of sugar glucose may remain high in the blood stream after the tissue cells' need for fuel has been satisfied, but the insulin secreted by the pancreas continues forcing or stuffing more molecules of sugar glucose into the cells. In such case, excess sugar glucose molecules, which the tissue cells cannot burn, are transformed into fat and stored in little fat droplets inside the cells. After weeks and months of overeating, the storage areas inside the tissue cells are filled with fat and can hold no more. At this point, the tissue cells take only as much sugar glucose from the blood stream as they can burn at a given moment, no matter how much insulin the pancreas secretes to try to force them to take more.

This point of refusing to take more sugar glucose than can be burned by the cells is called end-organ resistance to insulin. It has been observed in the skeletal and heart muscles and in the connective tissues of obese and diabetic persons. End-organ resistance to insulin is highest in persons who are both obese and diabetic. As the end-organ resistance to insulin increases, the release of insulin from the pancreatic islets increases, too. As a result even in nondiabetic, obese persons, the release of insulin into the blood for a given amount of glucose is about 2 to 4 times greater than it is in nondiabetic and nonobese persons.

Much research in many laboratories in this country and abroad took place before the overall picture of diabetes became as clear as it is now. At first, the process of end-organ resistance was considered to be one theory explaining how diabetes acts and the process of pancreatic islets' insufficiency or breaking down was another theory. Then Dr. J. Vallance-Owen developed a third theory called the insulin antagonist theory. Dr. Vallance-Owen discovered a substance in the blood of diabetic persons that antagonizes or inhibits the activity of insulin. It is believed that 25 to 30 percent of the population of the United States have this insulin antagonist in their blood.

Today, specialists in diabetes consider that these three theories taken together provide the best explanation for the development of the disease:

■ To begin with, some persons are genetically more susceptible than others to develop diabetes. These persons have received through heredity the insulin antagonist in their blood.

■ A long history of overeating and eating sugar-sweetened foods that produce fluctuations of sugar glucose and insulin in the blood lead to being overweight and obese, which in turn tends to produce end-organ resistance to insulin in the muscles and connective tissue. This develops sooner in the "diabetically constituted" persons.

■ Long years of end-organ resistance to insulin, accompanied by the daily powerful stimulations to release increased amounts of insulin (to clear the blood stream of the excessive amounts of sugar glucose), finally exhaust the pancreatic islets.

This vicious circle is self-perpetuating. The swing from too much to too little sugar in the blood stimulates a nagging hunger that usually results in overeating; the eater gets fat so that his fat-storage spaces inside the cells are filled and his body tissues resist insulin's efforts to stuff more sugar glucose into the cells. The sugar glucose remaining in the blood stimulates the pancreas to secrete more insulin and so it goes.

FIGURE 1: THE VICIOUS CIRCLE THAT PRODUCES OBESITY

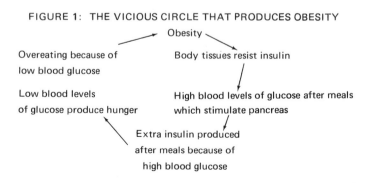

Some persons have a high tolerance for glucose, which means that they can eat heavier meals spaced at longer intervals, that their blood glucose does not rise excessively high after such meals, and that even when the blood glucose rises, it does not stay there for long. Such persons also have a higher capacity to burn calories, and usually it is not very difficult for them to stay lean and to keep desirable body weight.

Other persons have a low tolerance for glucose, which means that, whenever they eat heavier meals or sugar-sweetened foods, their blood glucose rises excessively high and remains at high levels a longer time before it goes down again. Such persons also have a lower capacity to burn calories and usually put on weight very easily; often they are overweight and even obese. In a way, the lower the person's tolerance for glucose, the higher is his tendency toward obesity, diabetes, heart disease, and high blood pressure or hypertension.

A glucose tolerance test has been developed that enables your doctor to determine how your body copes with a given load of sugar glucose. You are instructed to eat no food after midnight and before arriving at the doctor's office in the morning of the test day. Because you have had nothing to eat for at least eight hours, it may be assumed that the sugar glucose in your blood stream is at the fasting level. To make sure, a sample of your blood is taken in the morning and analyzed for the level of sugar glucose it contains. Then you are given 100 gm (grams) of sugar glucose and additional samples of your blood are taken at regular time intervals of two hours (or less) in order to determine how high your blood glucose is rising after the known amount of sugar glucose you have eaten, and how long it takes your body to bring the elevated level of sugar glucose in your blood down to normal fasting levels.

The fasting level of sugar glucose in the blood of normal, healthy, nondiabetic young adults is below 100 mg glucose per 100 ml of blood (for which the usual abbreviation is 100 mg percent, or 100 mg%). This normal level fluctuates around 90-95 mg% but even 85 mg% may be considered almost within normal.

About half an hour or one hour after a meal, or after a glucose-load during a glucose tolerance test, the blood glucose rises above 100 mg% to various levels depending on the age and health of the person and the amount of food eaten. This rise in normal, healthy, nondiabetic, *young* adults does not go much above 100 or 110 mg%. It reaches its peak at 60 minutes and usually returns, after 3 to 4 hours, to normal fasting levels below 100 mg%.

In normal, healthy, nondiabetic, *older* adults this rise in blood glucose level may reach 130 or 140 mg% and possibly even 150 mg%, depending on the age of the person. It peaks around 80 minutes after the glucose load and may take 5 to 6 hours to return back to normal fasting levels below 100 mg%. On the average, the peak glucose levels increase 17 mg% for each decade of life. It is sometimes difficult to decide whether such a rise of blood glucose level in an older adult is within normal limits or whether it indicates the presence of a mild diabetes; the opinion of specialists is not always unanimous about the dividing line between normal and diabetic levels.

In *diabetic* persons the fasting levels of blood glucose may or may not be below 100 mg%. If they are below 100 mg%, it is always a favorable sign, indicating that this particular person's diabetes is probably mild. After a meal, or after a glucose load in a glucose tolerance test, the blood level of glucose in a diabetic may rise way above 150 mg% up to 200 mg% or even above 250 mg%, depending on the age of the person, the severity of his diabetes, and previous conditions such as overeating, irregular eating habits, lack of treatment. In a diabetic, it takes a longer time for the blood glucose to return to normal, (below 100 mg%) which takes a longer time, 6 to 7 or more hours, depending on the age of the person, the severity of diabetes and previous conditions.

When the blood glucose reaches levels between about 130 to 170 mg%, the glucose starts "spilling over" into urine, where it can be easily detected; thus, glucose in urine constitutes an easy test for diabetes. In some persons glucose spills over or penetrates into urine after a relatively small rise in blood glucose levels; in other persons even a relatively high rise in blood glucose levels does not bring glucose into urine. Mild diabetics for days may show no detectable glucose in urine; however, after a feast or a heavy meal, the glucose may reappear.

It has been observed that normal, nondiabetic, young individuals who have been given the glucose tolerance test retain and assimilate in the liver approximately 69 gm of the 100 gm glucose that was eaten. The other 31 gm are transported by the blood stream to the body's other tissues.

On the other hand, in nonobese, normal-weight diabetics, out of the ingested 100 gm glucose, less than 50 gm is retained by the liver and over 50 gm penetrates into the blood stream, to be transported to peripheral tissues.

In obese diabetics only about 25 gm is retained and assimilated by the liver, and about 75 gm penetrates into the blood stream and has to be taken care of by other (peripheral) tissues. Diagnoses are difficult to make, however, because even in normal, nondiabetic, nonobese individuals a deprivation of carbohydrate prior to the tolerance test may produce higher-than-usual and longer-lasting blood levels of glucose. Because of the resemblance to the diabetic pattern, this phenomenon is called "starvation diabetes."

No matter how tolerant of glucose a person's body may have been in youth, it becomes less tolerant with the years as the body's ability to burn glucose lessens. As the person grows older, out of the ingested 100 gm glucose, less and less is retained by the liver, and more and more penetrates into the blood to be transported to peripheral tissues. This results in higher and longer-lasting blood levels of glucose in older persons, as compared to younger ones, and often resembles the maturity-onset diabetes.

The insulin-producing machinery of the pancreas, (the pancreatic islets) requires even more care as we grow older and the body's capacity to burn sugar glucose declines. The higher blood levels of sugar glucose lead to a stronger stimulation of insulin release. However, the amount of insulin released from the pancreas into the blood (in order to cope with a given level of sugar glucose in the blood) also declines with age. Thus, in older persons, insulin only "half-opens the door" for sugar glucose to enter the cells.

Eating a hearty meal is just as hard on the pancreas of a middle-aged or older person as eating a great deal of sugar and honey sweetened food.

Differences among middle-aged persons with and without maturity-onset diabetes are gradual, not of an "all or none" type. Even the beginning of maturity-onset diabetes is gradual; high levels of blood glucose after meals (postprandial hyperglycemia) may exist for 8 to 12 years before the onset of other symptoms. Usually a glucose tolerance test is necessary to establish the diagnosis of diabetes. It is not unusual for a person with a maturity-onset type of diabetes to demonstrate no fasting (that is between meals) hyperglycemia (sugar in blood) or glycosuria (sugar in urine). Various authors call such people prediabetics, potential diabetics, latent diabetics, or persons "constituted as diabetics"; studies of their condition are of intense interest for the understanding of the origin and causes of the disease.

Untreated maturity-onset diabetics respond to the glucose load (during glucose tolerance test) by a delay in the initial release of insulin, followed by excessively high blood levels of insulin, called hyperinsulinemia. Recently, however, it has been reported that the amount of insulin in the blood during a glucose tolerance test rises excessively high in most *obese* maturity-onset diabetics and also in obese nondiabetics, but not in nonobese, maturity-onset diabetics despite very high levels of glucose in their blood. It has been concluded that the excessive release of insulin after a glucose load, often observed in the maturity-onset diabetics, correlates more with the obesity than with the diabetic state.

Persons with high levels of fat (triglycerides) in the blood usually are overweight, and it has been observed that high blood levels of fat are usually associated with acquired (rather than inherited) obesity. Several investigators have also reported the presence of high blood levels of insulin in persons with high blood levels of fat (triglycerides). It appears that the age decline in glucose tolerance, which leads to high blood levels of glucose and of insulin, is also accompanied by high blood levels of fat. Recently, Dr. Harvey C. Knowles, Professor of Medicine at the University of Cincinnati College of Medicine, again confirmed the observations that high blood levels of glucose after a glucose load are commonly accompanied by high blood levels of fat (called hyperlipidemia).

Over 75 percent of persons with maturity-onset diabetes are overweight and obese; therefore, a simple reduction to normal or desirable weight would result in substantial improvement in this large percentage of patients. This all underlines the tremendous importance of reducing to normal or desirable weight, something which some people tend to overlook. Reducing to normal or desirable body weight and keeping this weight is a simple (though not necessarily easy) answer, which may make the difference between developing maturity-onset diabetes or not.

KEEPING DIABETES AT BAY

Recently, convincing evidence has been accumulating to indicate that the processes leading to the development of the maturity-onset type of diabetes are reversible in their earlier stages. They tend to become irreversible only in later stages, and may then result in a complete exhaustion of pancreatic facilities, accompanied by the dependence of the individual on daily injections of insulin. In the case of a chronic disease, the expression "reversible" also means "avoidable" or "preventable," provided the factors or causes that originated or aggravated the diseased state are removed.

People differ greatly in their susceptibility to maturity-onset diabetes; to a great extent, this susceptibility or lack of resistance is inherited. Dr. Victor McCussick, the well-known geneticist, estimates that about 34 percent or one-third of our population is "susceptible" to the development of maturity-onset diabetes. However, nobody is entirely "unsusceptible," or immune to its development. On the other hand, even susceptible persons can avoid the development of the disease, by carefully avoiding nutritional, diabetes-inducing errors. Those middle-aged persons who already have maturity-onset diabetes can keep it from being aggravated and sometimes even alleviate it to the point of almost curing it.

Most important to remember is that even very susceptible persons, who have a very low tolerance for glucose, can avoid putting on of fat, becoming overweight and obese, developing diabetes, heart disease, and hypertension, if they are careful to heed the following basic advice:

- Reduce body weight to a "desirable" weight.
- Do not overeat beyond daily caloric allowance.
- Take your daily caloric allowance in no less than five (and possibly more) smaller meals or snacks, equally spaced during the day.
- Avoid as much as possible all sugar-sweetened foods like pies, cakes, and candy.
- Regular physical exercise is essential (discussed in detail later).

To a great extent, all this is a matter of choice, of preferences and of self-discipline. In a recent interview with the movie star Joan Crawford, she said, "I have trained myself to have disciplined habits. I never touch sweets now, though at one time I adored them. I learned long ago to make myself dislike problem foods. If you think of the fluctuations in weight they cause, you can see why it was easy to teach myself to stay away from them." Here is a way in which we can all profitably try to imitate a movie star.

10 | Why We Gain Weight: Theories and Causes

WHEN WE GAIN TOO MUCH WEIGHT, IT BECOMES IMPORTANT to our health to reduce. The more overweight a person is, the more important it is for him to reduce. However, as many of us know to our sorrow, losing weight is easier to talk about than to accomplish. Various strategies have been devised to help people reduce and stay slim. One of the best is simply to reduce in a natural way, but to do this we must have at least some understanding of the mechanics of the problem.

During war, famine, and economic catastrophe, when food becomes scarce, conditions of overweight, obesity, and related diseases rapidly disappear. On the other hand, within any society that has an abundant food supply, some individuals become overweight, but many do not. Among the overweight group, it is easy for some to lose weight and exceedingly difficult for others. The latter lose weight very slowly even though they limit their daily caloric intake; therefore, there must be factors other than simple calorie overnutrition that create obesity. The many, seemingly contradictory, findings related to obesity have led to a number of theories.

The single-entity theory of obesity views gaining weight as a unitary condition, caused by overeating and nothing else. It holds that people get fat because they eat too much. The chief interest of its advocates center around the mechanisms of overeating, specially the psychological and environmental factors which may encourage overeating.

Some people resort to overeating to alleviate tension, anxiety, worry or frustration; they are fat because life is hard for them. Some depressed persons overeat as a means of showing themselves the outward visible evidence that they are loved and cared for. In more severe cases of eating disorder it is not uncommon to find that the food "addict" has some similarities to the alcoholic and drug addict; food is his liquor.

Years ago, Dr. Walter W. Hamburger, Professor of Psychiatry, Rochester University, listed four categories of overeating that lead to emotional obesity: overeating as a response to nonspecific emotional tensions, overeating as a substitute gratification in intolerable life situations, overeating as a symptom of underlying emotional illness (especially expression of hysteria), and overeating as addiction to food.

Some people who work long hours at night discover that sleep and food are equivalent; they find themselves revived by food in their work without sleep; they overeat to keep awake.

Dr. Stanley Schachter, another researcher into the relation between emotions and the development of obesity, proposed that obesity may sometimes result "from a failure to differentiate between hunger feelings and feelings of anxiety created by emotional states." According to this interpretation, persons who are in a state of anxiety may feel that they are hungry but, in fact, they are only anxious. They overeat in order to relieve their feeling of anxiety. Dr. Schachter points out that treatment of obesity in such persons usually remains unsuccessful unless or until the underlying anxiety has been relieved.

An individual's adult weight can be seen as partly the result of social influences operating in his childhood. Not infrequently, overeating and eating foods heavy in sugar and fat are a familiar feature of everyday life in entire subgroups and national populations. The standards of fashion in regard to fatness and slimness differ in different parts of the world. In the United States, obesity is seven times less frequent in upper-class women than in lower-class women. This tells us what we already know: the idealized American woman is slim. However, in Germany the picture is different. Obesity among the conservative upper middle class is a fleshy badge of professional and social prestige. A recent estimate that one-third of the population in West Germany is overweight has caused the West German government to regard obesity as a national health hazard. The government officially took note that the German custom of eating fatty sausages was heavily implicated in the national problem.

Of the theories that emphasize factors other than overeating, of particular interest are the theories concerned with genetic difference in tendencies to gain weight and concerned with individual differences in body build.

GENETIC OBESITY

The bulk of experimental studies on the genetic and constitutional factors in obesity have been done on animals. The use of laboratory animals permits a strict control of genetic factors. In the laboratory, not only can one use animals sharing the same parents, but those with the same grandparents and with the same genetic line for generations back. For relatively small sums of money the researcher can obtain sizable groups of animals whose genetic histories have been meticulously kept and whose pedigrees are well defined. This type of control simply is not possible with human beings. The closest we can come to controlling heredity in studies of human obesity is by selecting identical twins. On a genetic basis, one would expect that identical twins inherit the same tendency to fat storage more often than fraternal twins do. The difficulties in collecting sufficient numbers of identical twins to make the tests significant have limited the number of studies conducted. Furthermore, no one pretends that the results of these tests are as definitive as the results of the more carefully controlled animal experiments.

Nevertheless, enough evidence has been gathered to leave no doubt that some people eating the same amounts and kinds of food, consumed in the same eating pattern, put on more weight than others. This strongly suggests that some types of obesity are inborn or genetically transmitted. It is just another one of life's injustices.

The accumulated evidence also indicates that the tendency to get fat is not inherited as an all or nothing phenomenon. Rather, as with tallness and shortness, the tendency toward fatness is a continuous variable. Some people seemingly can eat anything without becoming fat. Others have to watch and weigh each mouthful of food. In between in varying positions from each extreme lie the rest of us. Each must take the trouble to discover just where on the continuum he is, how much he can eat on a daily basis without beginning to harm his health.

Some researchers have come to regard obesity and diabetes as related problems. Both may be transmitted as a simple recessive trait with incomplete and variable manifestation or penetrance. Other researchers consider that the hereditary inclination to obesity is due to several genes. Whatever the details of the genetic pattern, both diabetic and nondiabetic obese persons have a reduced capacity to burn sugar glucose. Both show end-organ resistance to insulin and in both excessive amounts of insulin are released after eating sugar-sweetened foods. The greatest dissimilarity is that the diabetic obese person tends to display these abnormal characteristics to a larger degree.

Through research, more and more evidence is piling up that the frequent wail of some overweight persons, "Everything I eat turns to fat," is basically true. In addition to the individual differences in capacity to burn sugar glucose, there are differences in individual body build which correlate with obesity. Some people are lean and long, others shorter and more round, still others are muscular and heavy boned, and some are in between, having a few of the traits of each group.

BASIC BODY TYPES

Sheldon, a well-known physical anthropologist who for the last three decades has tried to describe the various body types, classifies human beings according to their body build as endomorphs, mesomorphs, and ectomorphs. Ectomorphic persons are predominantly the "string-bean" type; they have a relatively small body with long arms and legs, long fingers, long narrow hands and feet (see Figure 2). Mesomorphic persons have a solid, muscular, angular outline, with large bones and joints, heavy leg muscles, thick wrists, and broad hands (see Figure 3). Endomorphic persons have a large body with short arms and legs (see Figure 4). Their abdomen mass overshadows the bulk of that section of the body above it, and all regions of the body are notable for softness and roundness.

Obese persons appear to be more endomorphic, somewhat less mesomorphic, and considerably less ectomorphic than nonobese persons. Endomorphy appears to be an inherited predisposition to the laying on of fat, unless great physical activity, insufficient diet, or voluntary weight control intervene.

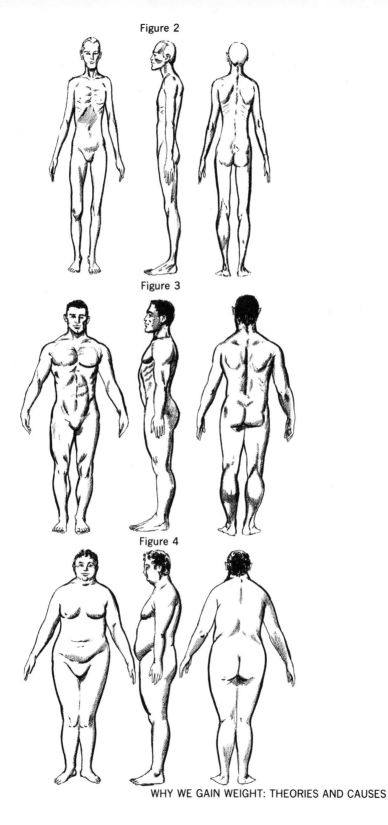

Figure 2

Figure 3

Figure 4

There is such a strong dominance of endomorphy among the obese that Dr. Jean Mayer, Professor of Nutrition at Harvard University, considers obese persons to be inherently endomorphic. In fact, obese adults who were also obese in their adolescent years are all predominantly endomorphs. However, mesomorphy is also relatively strong among obese persons in that the obese often display somewhat greater musculature than nonobese persons, even though the somewhat greater muscle bulk of the obese is, for the most part, associated with relatively poor muscle tone. In addition, predominantly mesomorphic persons, even though they are lean in their adolescent years, often display a tendency to the laying on of fat during adulthood and middle age. On the other hand, ectomorphic people apparently may follow the desires of their appetite without fear of laying on fat, as if nature were intolerant of obesity in ectomorphic types.

At the moment the theories emphasizing plural factors in gaining excess weight are of more value to the researcher than the obese person, whose desire to become and stay slim is hampered by an unlucky inheritance. Perhaps they get a certain cold comfort from having their difficulties publicly acknowledge by medical authorities. However, sympathy is not a substitute for the social, and psychological advantage of being slim. Unfortunately, overweight and obese people must be more resolute, more diligent and, unquestionably, more long suffering in their efforts. The goal, however, is worth the price. They can save their lives.

11 | The Advantages of Nibbling

THE EXECUTIVE'S LUNCHEON—EATING TOO WELL ON AN EX-
pense account—followed by the habit of being late for supper, may
be making him overweight. Actually, executives are not the only
ones who alternately gorge and fast. This nutritional error has many
variations and victims. For decades, dieticians and researchers have
been aware that a wide swath of obese people consume most of their
food within a relatively short period each day.

In addition to the big spenders, there are the midnight raiders
—the executives, students, or housewives who are too rushed to eat
a decent breakfast, too busy to do more than wolf down a sandwich
for lunch, and then famished, stuff themselves in pulsing assaults
on the refrigerator from the moment they reach the kitchen in the
evening until bedtime, often in the small hours of the morning. Dr.
Albert J. Stunkard, a Philadelphia psychiatrist and his coworkers
from the Department of Medicine and Psychiatry of the Cornell
Medical Center in New York, have called this pattern the "night-
eating syndrome."

Dr. Stunkard reported that the night-eating syndrome flares
up during periods of stress when its victims have difficulty in getting to sleep before the small hours of morning. Next day, as might
be expected, they awake without an appetite and often take no
more than a cup of coffee and toast or orange juice for breakfast.
Dr. Stunkard observed that an effective weight-reducing regime is
not possible in the presence of this pattern. Unfortunately obese
persons can spend months dieting only to have their efforts nullified
by a rapid gain in weight following a bout of night eating that was
brought on by emotional distress or vexing problems. Dr. Stunkard

and his coworkers stress that, in order to succeed in a weight-reducing program, one has to stop the midnight raids on the refrigerator, but this can be done only by first taking care of the underlying psychological problems.

The night-eating syndrome is just one example of large food intakes at long-spaced intervals. Another regime that is disastrous to losing weight may be called the commuter's eating pattern. This pattern is easily adopted by persons who have a 9-to-5 work day. Those in this group, which too often includes schoolchildren (but especially commuters and office workers), skip breakfast because they are in danger of being late. Their lunch is often a skimpy affair, dragged out of a brown sack or hurriedly eaten at a short-order restaurant. Only when they return home do these people take the time to enjoy a comfortable meal, which is usually large enough to catch up with the amount of food they missed at breakfast and lunch. This is equivalent to eating larger meals spaced at longer intervals.

In our era of abundance, people of all age groups are beginning to skip meals whenever convenient. The *Wall Street Journal* reported in 1970, "Meal skipping grows as an American phenomenon. From 8 to 14 percent of most age groups forego the midday meal, according to the Market Research Corporation of America. In the 18-to-24 age group, about 22 percent of the men and 18 percent of the women avoid lunch. Another 16 percent in this age group skip breakfast, while 11 percent don't have an evening meal, which brings the total to 49 percent of young people in the 18-to-24 age group who by their own choice live on two meals a day and seem to like it."

The night-eating syndrome, the commuter's eating pattern, and meal skipping all result in large food intakes consumed at long-spaced intervals. We have seen the results of eating large meals on the secretion of insulin and the fluctuations of low and high levels of sugar glucose in the bloodstream. Large meals can trigger other serious problems as well. The fluctuations in blood of sugar glucose due to large meals at long intervals act as a stress on the heart and may, in susceptible individuals, trigger a heart attack. This problem will be discussed in detail later on. If eating one large meal a day with a few auxilliary nibbles is dangerous, spacing the daily food ration or allowance into three square meals is not entirely harmless either.

If one compares the eating patterns in the animal kingdom, one cannot fail to see that many animals eat their daily ration in a number of small portions spaced throughout much of the 24 hour period; they are nibblers. Rats, for instance, by nature nibble their foods throughout the day. Man, on the other hand, tends to eat his food at larger meals taken infrequently, perhaps because of convenience; he is a gorger.

There is no question that in his long evolution, man was at one time by necessity a food-gathering, "nibbling-throughout-the-day" animal, relying for his existence on the constant, day-long plucking of berries, nuts, insect larvae, and the occasional slaying of an animal. He changed from nibbling to meal eating with the advent of agriculture some 10,000 years ago, equivalent perhaps to 300 or 400 generations, which is far too short a period for genetic adaptation to long-spaced meal-eating habits.

Another proof that man by nature is a nibbler is the fact that the human infant for several months is normally a nibbler, whose demands for frequent feedings are usually met by his mother until he becomes old enough to be trained. Then because of convenience, custom, working habits, and sociability, all possible efforts are made to convert him into a meal eater.

TECHNIQUES OF NIBBLING

The pattern of three meals a day is widely followed in western cultures, but in many primitive societies people often remain nibblers throughout their lives. Lean, normal-weight individuals often take small snacks between meals (where the total caloric intake does not exceed the total daily caloric requirements or allowances); this type of "nibbling throughout the day" should not be confused with the "nibbling" by some overweight and obese individuals who, in addition to their generous three meals a day, have many sizable snacks or nibbles between meals, so that their total daily caloric intake far exceeds their total daily caloric requirements or allowances.

Nibbling *in addition* to three hearty meals can be compared to the French farmer's technique for producing the main ingredient in pâté de foie gras: the goose, whose liver is destined to become a delicacy, is inserted in a narrow cage where he can hardly move and force-fed many times a day. The helpless bird can do nothing but swallow the grain that is literally shoveled down its neck. He becomes fatter and fatter; his liver engorges so that it nearly ruptures.

Today too many of us treat our bodies like captive geese, stuffing more food down our throats than we can possibly use or store with economy. Ultimately, as with the goose, something gives. It may be the liver, the pancreas, the arteries, the heart . . . or it may be a general deterioration of our entire bodies, including their outlines.

Nibbling by normal-weight, nonobese persons is understood to be the eating pattern in which the daily caloric requirements or allowances are eaten in more than three (usually five, possibly seven or even more) equal portions during waking hours, as compared to "meal eating" where the same amount of food is taken in only three meals a day. It is opposed to "gorging" where the daily amount of food is taken in less than three meals.

Beneficial effects of nibbling are particularly well illustrated by Dr. Grant Gwinup, professor at the University of California at Irvine, who reports that when man's meal pattern is changed from three meals a day to nibbling, there is a prompt decrease in the levels of fat (triglycerides) and cholesterol in the blood. Nibbling in Dr. Gwinup's experiments was achieved by spreading the same amount of foods that had been used in three meals a day into ten small but identical feedings every two hours, from 8 A.M. one day until 2 A.M., the next day.

Further, Dr. Gwinup reported that, when the meal pattern is changed from three meals a day to gorging, there is a prompt increase in the level of fat and cholesterol in the blood. Again, gorging was achieved by compacting the same amount of foods used in three meals into a single daily meal which was taken between 4 and 5 P.M.; Dr. Gwinup further reported that changes produced by nibbling were rapidly reversed by gorging and vice versa.

Similar observations were made by Dr. Pavel Fábry, a professor in Prague, Czechoslovakia, who observed that an eating pattern of three or fewer meals a day, as compared with a more frequent intake of smaller meals (five or more) led to a tendency toward overweight, and in elderly men also led to high blood levels of cholesterol and to the decrease in glucose tolerance.

The effects of heavy meals spaced far apart, or gorging, as opposed to light meals spaced near together, or nibbling, have also been amply investigated in many detailed experiments with animals. Dr. Clarence Cohn, at the Michael Reese Hospital in Chicago, made experiments in which rats (which by nature nibble throughout the day) were allowed to feed only at one or two mealtimes a day. They reported that in two weeks of meal eating the rats became obese and their body fat content increased to 23.6 percent, as compared to 7.8 percent in control rats which were allowed to nibble at their leisure. At the same time, the body protein content in rats after two weeks of meal eating fell to 17.7 percent, as compared to 22.4 percent in the control rats.

CHANGES IN MEAL PATTERNS

In addition, Dr. C. Cohn reported that the rats allowed to eat only one or two meals a day not only became obese, but also developed high blood levels of glucose, cholesterol, and fat (triglycerides). Similar observations were made by other investigators with dogs, chickens, sheep, and monkeys, indicating that each time when the natural eating pattern of "nibbling throughout the day" is replaced by eating one or two (or three) meals a day, there is an increased tendency toward gaining weight.

It is well known that obese people often have difficulties in following a weight-reducing regimen. Similarly, people who habitually eat heavy meals spaced far apart, experience difficulties in changing this habit. A number of researchers have investigated this problem and found that it is due to an adaptation in the enzymatic machinery inside the body.

Dr. Guy Hollifield and Dr. William Parson at the University of Virginia School of Medicine in Charlottesville, for years have studied changes in the enzymatic machinery and found that shifting rats from their normal pattern of feeding (nibbling) to one or two meals a day (gorging) is followed by pronounced changes of enzymatic activities in the liver and in adipose tissue.

These changes tend toward: (a) an increased synthesis of glucose during *fasting,* in order to improve the decreased availability of glucose and to secure a continued supply of energy in this form for metabolic processes in which glucose is indispensable, and (b) an increased synthesis of fat or "lipogenesis" during gorging, in order to store excess calories.

These studies permit some interesting speculations in regard to human obesity. It is reasonable to assume that the same adaptations in enzyme activities which occur in the liver and adipose tissue of rats forced to take one or two meals a day, would also occur in the liver and adipose tissue of people who eat most of their food within a relatively short period each day, as in the case of the night-eating or of the commuter's eating pattern. Once a person is adapted to such an eating pattern, the enzymatic adaptations in his body tissues tend to perpetuate it. This helps to explain why it is more difficult for obese people to follow a weight-reduction regimen, and why a conscious effort is needed to break the habit of eating heavier meals spaced farther apart.

Another undesirable consequence of eating heavy meals at long-spaced intervals is an increased susceptibility to develop coronary heart disease, attacks of angina pectoris, or a heart attack. This is particularly well illustrated by recent observations made by Dr. Pavel Fábry, in Prague, Czechoslavakia, who presented statistical data from a detailed study of 1,133 men aged 60 to 64, indicating that coronary heart disease was more common among those who took their daily ration in three meals a day or less (30.4 percent) than among those who took the same daily ration in five meals a day or more (19.9 percent), and that among men consuming their daily ration in three or four meals a day the prevalence rate of coronary heart disease was intermediate (24.2 percent).

It has been several years since Dr. Manuel Gardberg, from the Department of Medicine of Tulane University in New Orleans, reported that the ingestion of heavy meals is often followed by changes in the electrocardiogram which prove that heavy meals are stressful to the heart. This observation was later confirmed and enlarged by Dr. Ancel Keys, who found in middle-aged men and women 30-60 minutes after an "ordinary" meal (lunch of 1,260 calories) an increased heart rate and changes in the electrocardiogram, which again proved that the meal was stressful to the heart.

In some persons with heart disease, these changes were even more striking than in normal healthy persons. Comparison of persons having heart disease with normal healthy persons frequently reveals electrocardiographic differences in the response to eating. There is an increase in the incidence of abnormal responses to eating with the increase in heart disease involvement. Persons with heart disease who present normal electrocardiograms while fasting or between meals, often develop marked abnormal changes if the electrocardiogram is taken 30-60 minutes after ingestion of a heavy meal.

The fact that any ordinary meal induces definite changes in the electrocardiogram even suggested the possible use of a meal as a mild and convenient method of testing response to stress in a heart examination. Indeed, some cardiologists have recommended taking electrocardiograms after meals as a diagnostic tool in the detection of a hidden heart disease. There is no doubt that heavy meals spaced at longer intervals present a stress to the heart, especially in susceptible middle-aged persons who are already suffering from heart disease. In such cases, lighter meals spaced at shorter intervals can relieve the stressful burden on the person's heart, and even help to prevent the occurrence of a heart attack at some unexpected moment.

As we have seen, high blood levels of glucose (whether after sugar intake or after a heavy meal) present a strong stimulus for the release of insulin into the blood, followed several hours later, by a decrease in blood glucose to below-normal levels. Below-normal levels of blood glucose, however, are also stressful to the heart, as demonstrated by Dr. Ekrem S. Egeli, Professor at the University of Istanbul, Turkey, who reported that low blood levels of glucose produced by injection of insulin are accompanied by an increase in the heart rate and changes in the electrocardiogram.

Moreover, Dr. H. J. Roberts reported that below-normal levels of blood glucose or hypoglycemia, occurring several hours after a heavy meal, can trigger heart pain and even attacks of angina pectoris in susceptible persons; he considers that high levels of insulin in the blood of the "prediabetic state" are the most important primary cause of ischemic heart disease. These observations indicate that the best advice on how to cope with meal stress is to avoid eating heavy meals spaced at long intervals and instead to divide the daily food allowance into several more frequent, smaller meals or snacks during the day, at bedtime, and even one or more times during the night.

Dr. Roberts also points out that in many "prediabetic" persons the below-normal levels of glucose in the blood (hypoglycemia) are often accompanied by "spontaneous leg cramps" and by "restless legs." Spontaneous leg cramps are sudden, involuntary, and painful contractions of the leg muscles. They usually involve single muscle groups in the calf and foot or in the upper thigh. They occur several hours after the last meal or during the night. Often, they waken the person in the middle of the night and he needs to stretch and walk in an attempt to obtain relief.

Restless legs are characterized by continual involuntary movements of the lower extremities. Often they are accompanied by numbness, crawling or "pins and needles" feelings, pulling or stretching, and weakness. People have described them as "nervous legs, irritable legs, fidgety legs, or leg jitters. Both restless legs and spontaneous leg cramps often occur in prediabetic persons and in maturity-onset diabetics; they are usually intensified several hours after a meal, are related to a below-normal level of blood glucose (hypoglycemia), and are promptly ameliorated by ingesting some food.

Dr. H. J. Roberts noted that in maturity-onset diabetics suffering from angina pectoris, the spontaneous leg cramps precede attacks of angina pectoris during night hours. He found that light snacks taken at 2-hour intervals and avoiding sugar-sweetened foods prevent not only the leg cramps but also spontaneous attacks of angina pectoris at night or in the early morning hours. Dr. Roberts advises frequent small feedings during the day, at bedtime, and during the night one or more times, and a strict avoidance of sugar-sweetened foods (including sugar-sweetened drinks and fruit juices such as orange, pineapple, grape, and prune juice). Some persons may require snacks as often as every 1½ to 2 hours during the afternoon and evening hours because of their accelerated rate of insulin release at these times.

Dr. Roberts also observed that such dietary measures are often sufficient to effect a complete improvement of impaired glucose tolerance within several weeks, even in the absence of weight reduction for obesity. This improvement of impaired tolerance for glucose indicates that a recuperation or "healing" of the exhausted glucose-metabolizing machinery of the body is possible and, in fact, takes place after the stress of heavy meals has been relieved by the relaxing effect of more frequent lighter meals.

There are indications that both sugar intake and heavy meal eating can also contribute to the development of high blood pressure or hypertension, even though it has not been easy to provide experimental and statistical data in this regard. However, high blood pressure and hypertensive cardiovascular disease have been found to be more frequent among certain groups—such as war prisoners who overeat following starvation or prolonged semistarvation.

In the same category fall observations by Dr. Ancel Keys, who reported that acute cardiovascular stress, culminating in heart failure, often takes place in men under conditions of unregulated overeating after experimental starvation studies.

For more detailed information regarding the development of hypertension due to overeating, it was necessary to resort to experiments with animals. Dr. C. W. Wilhelm, at the Creighton University School of Medicine in Omaha, has shown in experiments with dogs that repeated episodes of starvation and refeeding result in the development of persistent high blood pressure or hypertension. Further, they reported that the extent of blood pressure elevation (following repeated starvations and refeedings) was more pronounced and the pulse rate increased only moderately with diets high in protein. They concluded that the fasting–feasting pattern associated with diets high in carbohydrate or protein appeared to have antagonistic actions on the blood pressure of normal dogs. If the same applies for man, it would further underline the need for a diet well balanced in both carbohydrate and protein (that is, not too much carbohydrate nor too little protein in one's diet).

More recently, Dr. B. Connar Johnson, a professor at the University of Illinois, Urbana, in a study funded by the United States Air Force, has investigated the effect of starvation and gorging on the development of chronic hypertension in young adult swine. Swine were selected as subjects for this study because of their willingness to consume various diets in large quantitities following starvation. Repeated episodes of starvation and feeding resulted in the development of high blood pressures which reached and remained in the range of 160-230 mm Hg as compared to blood pressures in the control, normal, nonstarved swine of the same age and weight.

Had these researchers investigated the possible relationship between the increase in the amount of daily sugar intake and the incidence of high blood pressure among individuals around the world, they would have found (1) that the incidence of high blood pressure is very low among people with low sugar intake who live in rural parts of the less-developed countries, India or Africa, and (2) that high blood pressure increases with the increase in daily sugar intake in the more advanced countries.

12 More Sour News About Sweets

WE LIVE IN A SUGAR CULTURE, AND WE SHARE OUR WAY OF LIFE with the rest of the world's more advanced nations. There is a regrettable relationship between a country's degree of industrial advancement and its consumption of sugar.

Some 10 or 15 years ago, Dr. John Yudkin, Professor of Nutrition and Dietetics at the University of London, England, pointed out that the average person's use of sugar had increased tremendously in England. In the 1750s the British were consuming approximately 6 to 8 pounds of sugar a year. A hundred years later the average Englishman's sugar consumption had jumped to around 25 pounds a year. And by the 1950s his heirs were eating about 120 pounds per person a year. That represents a heavy sweet tooth: it has been referred to as "far and away the greatest change in our diets in the last century."

Dr. Yudkin presented data to show that sugar eating increased with the annual income. In the 1950s the wealthy consumed about 50 percent more carbohydrates, about 80 percent more proteins than the poor. But the wealthy consumed at least 400 percent more sugar than did the poor. Worse, the end to this meteoric rise in sugar eating may not yet be in sight. In both England and the United States, sugar consumption has doubled since the turn of the century.

A similar situation exists in much of the world, judging from the statistical data gathered from studies made on sugar consumption. The United States, most of Europe, and Israel are already big sugar users, and sugar consumption is rapidly increasing in Africa and India. Medical knowledge and technology have also increased dramatically with industrialization. However, the havoc caused in the human body by this heavy sugar consumption eludes the skills of modern medicine.

We have seen that sugar eating contributes to the putting on of fat beyond the mere caloric intake. Recent experimental evidence suggests that eating low-molecular carbohydrates such as honey and sugar also leads to an increase in the blood levels of fat (triglycerides) and of cholesterol. In one such study, Dr. Y. Stein, Professor of Medicine at the Hadassah Medical School in Jerusalem, and his associates, observed that the increase in blood levels of cholesterol during a high sugar (sucrose) diet followed the same pattern as the increase in blood levels of fat (triglycerides). In some individuals the fall of blood cholesterol during the subsequent starch diet of high-molecular carbohydrates lagged behind the fall in blood triglyceride level. He also observed that the increase in blood cholesterol and blood fat (triglycerides) levels during sugar (sucrose) eating was much more pronounced than during glucose eating. In another study, Dr. N. A. Olson, Professor at the State University of Iowa, reported that not just blood cholesterol and blood triglycerides, but all fat constituents of the blood were higher in diets containing sugars (low-molecular carbohydrates) than on those containing starches (high molecular carbohydrates).

Recently, Dr. Milton Winitz and associates reported observations from a clinical study, funded by the National Aeronautics Space Administration (NASA), in which 18 young normal healthy adults were given chemical diets (composed of glucose, 18 essential and nonessential amino acids, the required vitamins, the pertinent salts and ethyl-linoleate as the source of essential fat). They observed that substitution of 25 percent of the glucose with an equal weight of sucrose, at the end of the fourth week in the otherwise identical diet, resulted in progressive increase in the total blood cholesterol levels from a mean average of 160 mg percent to a mean average of 200 mg percent at the end of the third week of this particular diet. Finally, the replacement of sucrose by glucose in the latter diet was followed by a precipitous drop in total blood cholesterol levels to a mean average of 175 mg percent at the end of the first week and 151 mg percent at the end of the nineteenth week of the experiment, even though no correlation was observed between weight change and blood cholesterol levels over the 19-week period.

A number of researchers from various institutions have made essentially the same kind of observations, and it appears that we have here not one but two superimposed effects. One is due to the difference between the effect of eating high-molecular carbohydrates (such as bread) and the effect of eating low-molecular carbohydrates such as glucose or sucrose as we saw in the chapter on diabetes. After ingestion, high-molecular carbohydrates such as bread, rice, potatoes, cereals, have first to be broken down into molecules of glucose (which takes a longer time) before they can be absorbed from the gut and consequently, the eating of high-molecular carbohydrates is followed by a mild but prolonged delivery of glucose into the blood stream, stimulating only a moderate impulse for release of insulin from pancreatic islets. Eating low-molecular carbohydrates (that are almost immediately broken down into glucose) such as sugar-sweetened foods is followed by a rapid delivery of glucose into the blood stream, which provides a powerful impulse for release of insulin into the blood.

It was discovered that high blood levels of glucose and of insulin lead to an increased synthesis of fat from glucose and are thus related to high levels of fat (triglycerides) and of cholesterol in the blood. They lead finally to fat storage in the tissues of the body, thus contributing to various undesirable consequences including such chronic diseases as obesity, atherosclerosis and heart disease.

THE VICIOUS SUGAR CYCLE

When a person (or an animal) eats sugar-sweetened foods, his body gradually builds up large amounts of special enzymes geared specifically to get rid of glucose from the blood stream by transforming it into fat. When a person eats sugar-sweetened foods, his body builds up these special enzymes. Then when he stops eating these foods, these special enzymes literally get hungry. The person craves more foods containing sugar to satisfy these special enzymes and their hunger. What is especially tragic is that parents with the best intentions are turning their children into sugar addicts at an early age. Sugar-coated foods dominate the dry cereal market. Dessert snacks come packaged, ready to drop into the lunch bag. Soft drinks and candies are available in vending machines and quick lunch stands. Worse, these products are lavishly advertised on TV in ways coldly calculated to win the interest of children. It is a rare parent who has the determination and the cleverness to outwit the pressure from their own children who want to eat the very foods that will do them so much harm. However, those parents who succeed will win their children's gratitude later on when the children sail through middle age with trim, vigorous bodies and no signs of the chronic diseases that are beginning to plague their sugar-eating peers.

There is an additional bonus to holding firm in a stand against sugar-sweetened foods. How many parents have lost their own battle of the bulge because their cupboards were stacked with sweets for their children? When candies and cookies, canned puddings, and sugar-coated cereals are ready at hand for munching, it takes an iron will to resist them. When these so-called treats are out of the house, resistance is much easier.

Fortunately there are real treats available for both children and adults. One family I know keeps a bowl of mixed nuts and a nut-cracker on their coffee table. Children enjoy cracking open the nuts for their afternoon snack. In the evening the bowl is just as popular with adult guests. Peanuts and soybeans come individually packaged for slipping into lunch bags and shirt pockets. Home-made popcorn is a fine afternoon or evening snack. Pumpkin and sunflower seeds and pine nuts are fashionable eating with the young set, which parents can provide with a clear conscience. And when the woman of the house bakes corn muffins or walnut biscuits instead of pancakes, she will find they make a satisfactory hit.

PENALTIES OF SUGAR ADDICTION

Except for a rare jogger or ditch digger, adults who are sugar addicts are almost invariably overweight. When they try to reduce, they encounter tremendous difficulties because they must overcome not only the normal feeling of appetite or hunger but also the additional, strong craving for sugar-sweetened foods caused by these hungry enzymes. In this sense, sugar is truly a habit-forming substance. Most sugar addicts are unable to resist their craving for sugar-sweetened foods for long; usually after a few days of dieting, they give up and again start eating sugar-sweetened foods. Any person can become a sugar addict.

To lose weight, sugar addicts must break down the hungry enzymes. Dr. Hollifield and Dr. Parson from the Virginia School of

Medicine have shown that the most efficient way to do so is by a 48-hour fast at the beginning of the treatment to reduce weight.

When an obese person complains "everything I eat turns into fat," he refers in his own way to the fact that his body has been tuned up to a faster-paced manufacture of fat.

Unfortunately, this increased enzyme activity can become permanent, if sugar eating becomes a habit—and once it becomes permanent it is very difficult to reverse. Here, then, is one of the main reasons why it is often so difficult for obese people to lose weight even after they stop eating so much. To these people a special approach to weight reducing is needed (see Chapter 13).

What so many overweight and obese people seem to be looking for—and are deeply disappointed when nobody offers it to them—is some kind of a magic weight-reducing diet which allows them to eat sugar-sweetened foods, to indulge in all the other nutritional errors of everyday life, and yet to stay slim without self-discipline or self-control. Absolutely no diet exists that can prevent a person from becoming fat if he keeps eating sugar- and honey-sweetened foods.

Dr. G. D. Campbell from the Department of Medicine, University of Natal, Africa, studied diabetes in Africans in and around Durban and observed that when Zulu people living in rural areas move into permanent residence in town, it takes about 18 to 22 years of "incubation" or exposure to town life and food, in order to develop diabetes. Statistical data showed that the rural Zulu's average annual intake of sugar per person had been below 20 pounds, and only recently had risen to 39 pounds, but for Zulus living in town the average was 89 pounds per person annually.

Dr. Campbell also studied diabetes in Asians. He noted that when an Indian moves from India to Natal, Africa, his chances of developing diabetes increase about tenfold. Here again, the average annual intake of sugar per person in India is 12 pounds, whereas in Natal the probable intake of sugar in all forms by working-class Indians is about 77 pounds yearly, and with higher-class Indians it is in the region of 110 pounds—an intake approaching that of people in England and the United States. Dr. Campbell's studies have not only shown that there is a remarkably constant "incubation period" of exposure to high sugar intake (averaging 18 to 22 years) before diabetes emerges, but also that an average "consumption threshold" of about 66 pounds per person yearly must be exceeded in most racial groups before diabetes becomes "common," that is to say, before the prevalence of diabetes equals or exceeds that found in the United States or in Europe.

Dr. A. M. Cohen, at the Hadassah Medical School in Jerusalem, reported that diabetes is unknown in Yemen but common in Israel, and that when Yemeni Jews move from Yemen to Israel, the diabetic emergence is highest 25 years later. Their careful dietary studies show that fat and protein intakes were the same in both countries and that the only difference lay in sugar consumption. On a daily basis, the sugar (sucrose) consumption of Yemenites in Yemen was 6.6 grams; it rose to 51 grams in new Yemenite settlers, further increased to 63 grams in long-time Yemenite settlers and was highest in long-time European settlers in Israel with 92 grams of daily sugar intake. On a yearly basis, the sugar consumption in Yemen was 8.8 pounds per person, whereas in Israel it is 80 pounds per person. In Israel sugar accounts for 25 to 30 percent of the total carbohydrate consumption, whereas the carbohydrate consumed in the Yemen consisted solely or mainly of starches. At the same time, there is an increase in body weight from the average of 125 pounds in Yemeni immigrants to 143 pounds in Yemeni settlers.

These studies prove that people of any ethnic origin, in any part of the world, even in populations where diabetes is virtually unknown, can develop this disease if their sugar intake reaches high levels and is sustained during the "incubation" period. It should be remembered that many people in the United States daily eat sugar well above the "diabetes-inducing threshold" in the form of candy and other sugar-sweetened foods; this habit begins in early childhood and may become deeply ingrained for the rest of the individuals' life.

Dr. John Yudkin, who pointed out how tremendously the average sugar consumption has increased in England, also analyzed the factors in the wealthier countries which may have contributed to the rise of heart disease, as compared to the factors in poorer countries. He pointed to three major changes: smoking, diminished physical activity, and alteration in food constituents. Of the last, the rise in sugar consumption is far greater than any other change in our major foods, and *Dr. Yudkin drew attention to the startling fact that sugar intake is more closely related than fat intake to mortality caused by heart disease.*

Dr. Yudkin also presented statistical data showing that persons who suffered a heart attack (infarction) had a mean daily sugar intake of 132 grams and persons who had atherosclerosis of peripheral arteries had a mean daily sugar intake of 144 grams, which is almost double the 77 grams daily sugar intake of normal healthy control individuals.

Sugar intake can be stressful to the heart, especially in susceptible middle-aged individuals. Dr. Emanuel Goldberger, Professor of Medicine at Albert Einstein College of Medicine in New York, reported that oral ingestion of 100 gm glucose during a glucose tolerance test is followed by an increased heart rate and changes in the electrocardiogram. Similar observations were made by Dr. Leon D. Ostrander and associates at the University of Michigan, who investigated the relationship of heart disease to high levels of glucose in the blood (hyperglycemia) and observed that many persons with heart disease have a mild or latent diabetes, but their low tolerance for glucose is overshadowed by complaints about heart disease, which is the principal cause of their troubles.

This view is further supported by studies on the distribution of heart disease in a typical sample of the American population done by Dr. F. H. Epstein and associates, also at the University of Michigan. They observed that heart disease is more frequent in individuals who have a low tolerance for glucose and that there is an important association of heart disease with unusually high levels of glucose in the blood after a standard glucose tolerance test. These observations by various researchers indicate that the avoidance of sugar in any form (even in an excess of canned fruit) and its replacement by high-molecular carbohydrates (like bread, rice, cereals, starches) is another basic health measure, especially for middle-aged persons.

The dangers of sugar eating may not be as evident as the dangers of cigarette smoking, but they are no less devastating. It is the honest opinion of the author that a nationwide campaign against sugar consumption is called for. The consequences of such a campaign on the sugar industry in this country would be by far outbalanced by a large-scale, nationwide improvement in health, and a substantial decline in the frequency of death (that is, in morbidity and mortality) from several chronic disease over the entire population of the United States, the monetary value of which could be estimated possibly only in hundreds of millions of dollars of health expenses, wages, and human lives saved.

13 | Strategies to Avoid Overeating and Becoming Overweight

ABOUT HALF OF THE MIDDLE-AGED POPULATION OF THE UNITED States can avoid gaining weight simply by

¶Avoiding larger meals,
¶Avoiding too long intervals between meals,
¶Avoiding sugar-sweetened foods,
¶Avoiding irregular eating habits,
¶Avoiding sedentary life and lack of physical activity.

If you do not lose weight by following these precautions, you will have to put in some additional effort to avoid overweight.

First, what is a "normal" weight? How does a person tell how much overweight he is?

The most frequently used means to estimate or assess the degree of overweightedness and of caloric overnutrition are the measurements of actual heights and weights of persons and their comparison to standard weights for given heights, sex, and body build. Such comparisons are widely used in spite of the fact that they are not the best indication of the degree of overweight. In the United States the standard reference tables for normal weight have been the tables that show the average weights for heights and ages, originally published in 1912, updated in 1959, and summarized in Table 1.

These tables show a gradual increase in body weight between ages 22 and 55, amounting to about 15 to 25 pounds depending on

TABLE 1 AVERAGE WEIGHT OF AMERICAN MEN AND WOMEN[1]

(in pounds according to height and age range)

Height Feet	Inches	Age range 15-16	17-19	20-24	25-29	30-39	40-49	50-59	60-69
Men									
5	0	98	113	122	128	131	134	136	133
5	2	107	119	128	134	137	140	142	139
5	4	117	127	136	141	145	148	149	146
5	6	127	135	142	148	153	156	157	154
5	8	137	143	149	155	161	165	166	163
5	10	146	151	157	163	170	174	175	173
6	0	154	160	166	172	179	183	185	183
6	2	164	168	174	182	188	192	194	193
6	4	..	176	181	190	199	203	205	204
Women									
4	10	97	99	102	107	115	122	125	127
5	0	103	105	108	113	120	127	130	131
5	2	111	113	115	119	126	133	136	137
5	4	117	120	121	125	132	140	144	145
5	6	125	127	129	133	139	147	152	153
5	8	132	134	136	140	146	155	160	161
5	10	..	142	144	148	154	164	169	..
6	0	..	152	154	158	164	174	180	..

[1]Adapted from table on average weights and heights, Build and Blood Pressure Study, 1959, Society of Actuaries, Chicago, 1959, vol. 1.(1)

the height and sex. The most serious drawback of these average weight-height tables is that they are computed to accept a rise in body weight with age.

Increase in body weight with age is not inevitable, is not normal, and there are indications that it may become dangerous to health and to life of persons involved. Statistical data indicate that from ages 35 to 55 the lowest number of deaths or mortality rates (mainly from heart attack) were recorded among men 5 to 10 pounds underweight; from ages 57 to 62, among those 15 to 20 pounds underweight (compared to the average weights of the 1959 updated tables).

The gradual increase in body weight with age as observed in the United States and other Western countries is similar to the situation regarding the gradual increase in blood pressure with age, observed in 95 percent of the population in the United States and other Western countries. In fact, both are dangerous to health and to the life of the persons involved.

Today, authorities believe that middle-aged persons should continue to weigh no more than they did at 25 years of age for men and about 20 years for women, and that any weight gain after 22-25 is likely to be fat. Among relatively primitive populations in Polynesian islands and in the China Sea, there is no increase of average body weight after 25. In three nomadic pastoral tribes in northern Kenya, there is no increase in average body weight, and after age 50, there is even a notable decline. This decline in body weight during the later years of life is physiological and normal.

With this in mind and in recognition of the obvious fact that appropriate weights for the same height must differ according to the skeletal type, new standard tables of "desirable" weights (at first labeled "ideal") for men and women aged 25 and over were compiled, which list body weights for the same height under three headings: light or small frame, medium frame, and heavy or large frame.

They were published in the *Statistical Bulletin,* 1959, and are given in Table 2. Measurements are made with indoor clothing and shoes. These tables are currently recommended for use as standard of "desirable" weights. Unfortunately, however, there is no accepted system for deciding who has a "light" frame, and so on, and no actual evaluations of frame size were made in developing these tables.

It is not surprising that most overweight individuals claim to have a "large" frame when in fact they belong in the "medium" category, or a "medium" frame when they belong in the "small" category. Very few are inclined to assess themselves as having a "small" frame because then they are even more overweight than they would like to admit.

Even though all the height-weight tables and their various modifications continue to have value, it is now widely recognized that they have far less validity than has been claimed for them. For example, many sedentary persons are exceedingly fat without being overweight, while the opposite condition, that is overweight without being fat, is common among people doing heavy physical work. College football linemen are generally overweight, but they are generally not fat.

Jean Meyer, one of the world's foremost authorities on nutrition (and fatness) writes "looking at yourself naked in a mirror is often a more reliable guide for estimating obesity than body weight." And he concludes, "if you *look* fat, you probably *are* fat." Thus, after complete circumnavigation we come back to where we

TABLE 2 DESIRABLE WEIGHTS FOR MEN AGED 25 AND OVER
(in pounds according to height, and frame, in indoor clothing)

Height		Small Frame	Medium Frame	Large Frame
feet	inches			
5	2	112-120	118-129	126-141
5	3	115-123	121-133	129-144
5	4	118-126	124-136	132-148
5	5	121-129	127-139	135-152
5	6	124-133	130-143	138-156
5	7	128-137	134-147	142-161
5	8	132-141	138-152	147-166
5	9	136-145	142-156	151-170
5	10	140-150	146-160	155-174
5	11	144-154	150-165	159-179
6	0	148-158	154-170	164-184
6	1	152-162	158-175	168-189
6	2	156-167	162-180	173-194
6	3	160-171	167-185	178-199
6	4	164-175	172-190	182-204

started. Many an overweight person, alarmed by his looks in the mirror, buys himself a bathroom scale, tries to find out all about the various height-weight tables or even about skinfold measurements, and then may find it hard to believe that the best guide for estimating his fatness is—what alarmed him to begin with: his looks in the mirror.

Most people can avoid overeating and gaining weight without actually counting calories. Only those with special problems need to count calories and then for only a relatively short time.

The best tactic to lose weight without counting calories is to give up the "satiety feeling" which comes after a large meal. This means you must stop eating while you are still a little hungry. It sounds more painful than it really is. At first the impulse to eat more food is strong, but it grows weaker as the days pass. The additional bonus of feeling vigorous and alert after eating less tends to compensate for the hunger feeling experienced in the first few days. In a little while you may find yourself preferring the new regime to the habit of eating until you are stuffed.

For those who need to count calories in the early stages of their

TABLE 2A   DESIRABLE WEIGHTS FOR WOMEN AGED 25 AND OVER
(in pounds according to height and frame, in indoor clothing)

Height		Small Frame	Medium Frame	Large Frame
feet	inches			
4	10	92-98	96-107	104-119
4	11	94-101	98-110	106-122
5	0	96-104	101-113	109-125
5	1	99-107	104-116	112-128
5	2	102-110	107-119	115-131
5	3	105-113	110-122	118-134
5	4	108-116	113-126	121-138
5	5	111-119	116-130	125-142
5	6	114-123	120-135	129-146
5	7	118-127	124-139	133-150
5	8	122-131	128-143	137-154
5	9	126-135	132-147	141-158
5.	10	130-140	136-151	145-163
5	11	134-144	140-155	149-168
6	0	138-148	144-159	153-173

dieting, there are several approaches to choose from. One is to multiply the "desirable" weight of the individual (in pounds) by the number ten. The resulting estimate however must be adjusted for age and activity. Add 100 to 200 calories if you are a young male, and deduct 100 to 200 calories if you are an elderly female. Ordinary light activity requires a 20 to 30 percent increase. Strenuous activity may require as much as 40 to 50 percent increase.

Example: Male, age 35, large frame, height 6 feet, weight 192 pounds, light activity. Ideal or "desirable" weight (from Table 2) is 164-184 pounds; basic caloric allotment is 1640 to 1840 calories, adjustment for age (young male); add 200 calories, adjustment for ordinary light activity (20 percent increase): add 330 to 370 calories. Total calories: 2170 to 2410 calories.

Another approach, which appears quite satisfactory, calculates the daily caloric requirement for moderately active, average young men by multiplying the desirable weight in pounds by 19-20 calories for each pound of desirable weight, and for average young women by 17-18 calories for each pound of desirable weight. For less active persons, the value may be lowered to 16 and for the very sedentary to 12-15 calories per pound. For more active people, like manual workers, the value is increased to 20 calories per pound, and even up to 25 calories per pound of desirable weight for those habitually engaged in strenuous physical exertion.

Those who prefer tables will find essentially the same information in Table 3, which has been published by the Canadian Council on Nutrition, and is just one example of a number of various tables with basically similar information. Maintenance activity is described as that of an unemployed person engaged only in waiting upon himself, and this is estimated to be 133 percent of the basal metabolic rate.

It is a very simple fact, so often disregarded, that as a person grows older he should eat less. This applies especially to middle-aged persons.

As we grow older, all of us experience a decline in oxygen consumption and in the capacity of the body to "burn" calories, discussed on page 49. It is evident, then, that the daily intake of caloric nutrients should be gradually reduced. The important question is: reduced by how much? Differences of opinion occur as soon as more than one agency tries to come up with an answer.

The National Research Council suggests that daily caloric al-

TABLE 3

Daily Caloric Intakes or Allowances Recommended for Adults of Different Body Size and Degree of Activity

MEN	144 lbs.		158 lbs.		176 lbs.	
	Calories	Protein, gm	Calories	Protein, gm	Calories	Protein, gm
Maintenance	2150	46	2300	50	2500	55
A	2650	,,	2850	,,	3100	,,
B	3400	,,	3650	,,	3950	,,
C	4000	,,	4250	,,	4600	,,
D	4600	,,	4900	,,	5350	,,

WOMEN	111 lbs.		124 lbs.		136 lbs.	
	Calories	Protein, gm	Calories	Protein, gm	Calories	Protein, gm
Maintenance	1750	35	1900	39	2050	43
A	2200	,,	2400	,,	2550	,,
B	2800	,,	3000	,,	3250	,,
C	3300	,,	3550	,,	3800	,,
D	3800	,,	4100	,,	4400	,,

lowances be reduced by 5 percent per decade between ages 35 and 55, and by 8 percent per decade between 55 and 75. A further 10 percent decrease per decade is recommended for the years beyond 75. These recommendations are based on the known decreases in basal metabolic rate and the suggested decrements in total energy requirements, published in the report of the Food and Agriculture Organization of the United Nations.

This specific percentages are only suggestions or estimates which vary from one agency to another or from one country to another. The Canadian Council on Nutrition suggests that "maintenance requirements" (daily caloric requirements or allowances) decrease by the following amounts with age: 25 to 35 years, 3 percent of requirements at 25; 35 to 45 years, 5 percent; 45 to 55 years, 9 percent; 55 to 65 years, 13 percent; and over 65 years, 17 percent.

Those who prefer tables will find approximately the same type of information in Table 4, recommended by the Food and Nutrition Board, National Academy of Sciences, U.S. National Research Council; it is designed to maintain good nutrition for practically all healthy persons in the United States.

Often people are overjoyed if they lose a few pounds, only to be saddened when they gain them back. How are these quick losses or gains in body weight possible? Before discussing caloric allowances any further, it may be worthwhile to say a few words about calories and about the caloric value of pounds lost or gained.

Careful experiments have determined that obesity tissue, when burned in a calorimeter, has a value of 3,000 to 3,500 calories per

TABLE 4
Daily Caloric Intake

MEN	Age Years	Weight kg (lbs)	Height cm (in.)	Daily Calories	Daily gm Protein
	18-35	70 (154)	175 (69)	2900	70
	35-55	" "	" "	2600	70
	55-75	" "	" "	2200	70
WOMEN	18-35	58 (128)	163 (64)	2100	58
	35-55	" "	" "	1900	58
	55-75	" "	" "	1600	58
Pregnant (2nd and 3rd trimester [3-month period])				+200	+20
Lactating				+1000	+40

pound. However, a dietary deficit or surplus of 3,000-3,500 calories will not invariably produce a corresponding weight loss or gain of one pound. There are often other factors involved, particularly the loss or gain of body water. During the first few days on a sharply reduced diet, the body tends to lose more water than fat; for this reason, the calorie value of this lost weight is much lower than 3,000 calories per pound.

In experiments with young men who substituted on a carbohydrate diet providing 1,000 calories daily and who followed a fixed schedule of physical activity to make the energy expenditure of 3,200 calories per day, the calorie equivalent of the weight lost during the first three days averaged only 1180 calories per pound lost. Later the calorie equivalent of the weight loss increased: between days 11 and 13, it was 3200 calories per pound; between days 22 and 24, it was 3950 calories per pound. During the first days of heavy eating after a calorically restricted diet, the rapid gain in weight to a great extent is due to the retention of water in the body.

In experiments with young healthy men whose diet was changed from 3500 to 1500 calories daily, the weight loss was rapid at first and decreased gradually with time until calorie equilibrium was achieved and the body weight was about 25 percent less than it had been. If the diet was then changed back to 3500 calories daily, the increase in weight was very rapid at first. Later, in spite of continued eating at the same level of excess calorie intake, no further increase of body weight was detected for some time.

Similarly, in well-controlled experiments, the diets of obese women were alternated between excesses and restrictions at four-day intervals, the observed weight changes corresponded to averages of 980 to 1640 calories per pound lost or gained. Such rapid weight losses (or gains) caused by water losses (or gains) during temporary caloric restrictions (or excesses) are present both in persons on a restricted water intake (800 ml/day) and in persons allowed to drink a larger amount of water (about 1800 ml/day). This means that your weight losses (or gains) while on a reducing diet (or after a "little" excess in food intake) will be the same whether you drink much water or not. And if you gain unwanted pounds, don't kid yourself by blaming it on drinking too much water. Needless to say these rapid weight gains, following a "little" too much food intake, are cause for frequent complaints by overweight persons and also the cause of frustration in their unsuccessful attempts to shed unwanted pounds.

Isn't there some single food, a sort of "ideal diet" a person could take every day, then stop worrying about nutrition? Unfortunately, there isn't. A calorically restricted food intake has to be well balanced in its major constituents (proteins, carbohydrates, fat, and other nutrients) in order to have its full beneficial effect. Vegetarians need to be sure they are giving themselves the indispensible amino acids in the proportions their bodies require. All in all, there are some 50 known nutrients (amino acids, fatty acids, the basic sugar glucose, vitamins, minerals, and water) and perhaps other nutrients not yet discovered. Obviously, no single food can contain all these essential nutrients in the proper combination to nourish us.

In fact, it is difficult, if not impossible, to devise a general food plan that would be just right for everyone. Food values and diet patterns vary. And so also do requirements for each of us depending on inherited (genetic) and enviornmental factors, age, sex, stress situations, etc.

Dietary recommendations of basic nutrients based on the needs of young healthy moderately active adult males, by two American agencies and by Canadian and Japanese agencies, show some surprising differences among their conclusions, even though the committees had access to the same basic information. Differences of opinion existed in regard to practically every nutrient for which requirements or allowances have been recommended by more than one agency. These committees have stated, however, that they have tried to recommend dietary allowances designed "to afford a margin of sufficiency above average physiological requirements to cover variations among essentially all individuals in the general population."

An excellent approach to nutrition as well as to dieting is that provided by the Food Exchange System, discussed in detail in chapter 15.

This system divides foods into seven categories: meat, fat (including bacon and nuts), breads (including all the cereals and potatoes), milk products, fruit, leafy vegetables, and starchy vegetables. It suggests a good balance of these foods for people with various caloric needs. In filling out these seven categories in your own daily eating, a good rule of thumb is: give yourself as much variety as possible. Variety in foods is not only fun, it functions to provide you with all the nutrients you need.

For quite a long time, the medical profession has felt the need for a greater standardization of values on food composition. This need is particularly acute for the dietary management of diabetes, which requires very careful measurements of daily food intake for a given amount of insulin injections. In 1942 the Diet Therapy Section of the American Diabetic Association appointed a committee of leading nutritionists for this task. This committee in cooperation with other groups worked out the Food Exchange System. This system is widely recommended and used in the United States for computing daily menus from a large variety of foods within the limits of a given caloric allowance, not only by diabetics but also by overweight persons who wish to reduce.

14 | Practical Considerations Before Starting Your Diet

BEFORE YOU START A WEIGHT REDUCING PROGRAM, YOU should make an effort, preferably with the help of your physician, to determine the underlying cause(s) of your overweight or obese condition. The success or failure of your weight reducing efforts may depend to a considerable extent on whether or not you discover, identify, and correct the causes which contribute to your overeating, or in any other way distort your energy balance.

Overeating can be due to excessive appetite or innate drives toward eating. It can be intensified by various hormonal, environmental, emotional, or psychological factors. Unless these factors are identified and corrected, your weight reducing efforts may remain relatively unsuccessful. If you have deep emotional problems, it is wise to resolve the problems before a weight reduction program is started.

If you have not been overweight since childhood, if you are emotionally well adjusted, and if you are motivated to lose weight, you are likely to succeed in your program. If you are not motivated or have no meaningful reason to lose weight, your chances for losing weight are poor. Remember, it is wise to set a realistic goal or, better yet, a number of goals, each progressively more difficult. The majority of experienced nutritionists consider that a weight loss of about five pounds in a month, maintained for an additional month, is an ideal rate—unless the dieting person is excessively obese, which calls for a special approach.

In order to lose weight the person must eat fewer calories than he uses. Five pounds of fat lost represents an energy deficit of about 17,000 to 18,000 calories. If this loss is accomplished in one month, it means that the daily caloric intake must average 500-600 calories less than the total calories expended. Some nutritionists even recommend a daily deficit of about 1000 calories, which is roughly equivalent to losing two pounds weekly. General experience indicates that a diet of 1100-1200 calories for women and 1500-1700 calories for men is acceptable and usually will produce the moderate weight loss of 1 to 2 pounds per week. Remember that for most people a diet of less than 1000 calories a day may become insufficient to provide essential nutrients for maintenance of good health.

The lower the caloric intake, the more rapid the weight loss. Too rapid a weight loss in some persons may be attended by weakness, dizziness, and an increased tendency to anginal heart attacks. In elderly persons, rapid weight reduction is especially undesirable. Often, persons who accomplish a steady slow but consistent loss are more likely to maintain this loss, and to weigh less a year later, than those who accomplish a rapid initial loss. The rapid weight losers often tend to be rapid weight gainers.

The diet itself should be practical, made up of ordinary everyday foods, tailored to the individual's social and economic circumstances and should enable him to do his usual work at a satisfactory level. Food fads should be avoided. Whether the Food Exchange System (see Chapter 15) is applied or not, a nutritionally adequate, low-calorie diet can be planned by using one or more of the following simple modifications, depending on the desired calorie level: (a) use skimmed milk and decrease butter or margarine (fat exchanges), (b) reduce the amount of bread, cereal, and/or potato (bread exchanges), (c) include 1 or 2 extra servings of vegetables to replace vitamins and minerals lost with the reduced amounts of bread and cereals.

There is no doubt that the Food Exchange System is a vaulable help in computing amounts of foods in weight reducing diets or meal plans. Many people, however, would follow weight reducing programs more readily if they knew how to do it without having to count calories, even when calorie counting is so simplified as in the Food Exchange System. Fortunately, it is possible for a great majority of these persons (as long as they are not diabetics) to reduce without anything more than a cursory look at the Food Exchange System. Simply learn to resist your appetite, avoid the feeling of satiety, and, if necessary, resist to some extent the hunger feeling as well.

In normal healthy individuals the two main stimuli for eating are hunger and appetite. Hunger is the sensation which makes one want to eat, and is usually associated with appetite but may be independent of it. The opposite of hunger is satiety, which is a pleasant and completely satisfied feeling that comes after eating a great amount of food. Hunger is satisfied and satiety is produced by ingestion of calorie-containing or energy-providing foods.

HOW TO RECOGNIZE REAL HUNGER

Hunger may be recognized in two ways: a generalized weakness and hunger pangs. The weakness may be related to sensory nerve impulses from the alimentary canal, and perhaps to the lowered blood level of sugar glucose; injection of insulin in a normal healthy person lowers blood glucose and is promptly followed by a clear sensation of hunger. Hunger pangs are a more definite perception in the stomach or the stomach region consisting of intermittent sensations of tension or pressure of brief duration and related to increased stomach motility. The physiological basis for hunger pangs appears to be inherited; the fixed pattern does not vary markedly whether the period of abstinence from food is prolonged or short.

Appetite, while often accompanying hunger, may be present without it. One may want to continue an excellent meal after hunger has been satisfied. The sensations of hunger and appetite can vary in degree and they are also interrelated. When we are very hungry we will eat relatively unappetizing food; when we are less hungry we are inclined to eat only appetizing food. If only unappetizing food is available, we are likely to eat less—that is, we only satisfy our hunger. If highly appetizing food is available, we are likely to eat it even though our hunger has been satisfied. One may add that appetite may be satisfied for one food, but still exist for others.

Appetite can be a major cause of overeating. Its components are mainly psychological and often are the result of individual past experiences. Dr. Stanley Schachter, Professor of Psychology at Columbia University in New York, made some very interesting observations with normal (thin) and obese individuals offering appetizing or unappetizing foods under various appetizing or unappetizing circumstances. He reported that obese people ate more than normal (thin) people if food was appetizing, or if it was offered under appetizing circumstances (such as in good restaurants), whereas if food was unappetizing (or offered under unappetizing circumstances) the obese ate less than normal (thin) people. These observations indicate that external clues—taste, sight, or smell of food—play an important part in the appetite of the obese. You will have to learn to resist, in one way or other, the various feelings of appetite and hunger if you want your reducing program to be successful.

Before starting a weight-reducing program, weigh yourself the first thing in the morning for a few days. This will give you an idea of your average body weight during this period. Then, after about a month of eating-without-satiety feeling, compare how much of a difference this relatively small sacrifice on your part has made in your body weight. If, however, you are using the Food Exchange System or counting calories in any other way, during this period set out to eat daily 600 to 1000 calories less (than the amount of calories your body needs for your daily energy expenditure) and be sure to learn to equate a certain degree of hunger with this deficit in your daily caloric intake.

HOW TO LOSE WEIGHT WITHOUT COUNTING CALORIES

The idea is not simply to count calories and food exchanges, but to learn to associate the degree of loss of satiety with a certain amount of body weight loss. During this period and subsequently you should weigh yourself only once a week, preferably at the same time of day. Weighing yourself only once a week will help you to avoid being influenced by the day-to-day gains and losses in body weight, fluctuations that all normal people undergo because of gains and losses of body water.

Soon you can learn to find out, solely from the loss of satiety or from the degree of hunger you feel, just how much less food you should eat in order to reduce or stay slim, without the help of the Food Exchange System or food calorie tables. Actually the Food Exchange System (as well as the food calorie tables) are not much more than a crutch. No doubt, they can be very helpful in the beginning, but you want to be free of cumbersome crutches, and you can be.

You must remember, however, that the relationship between hunger-experiencing and weight loss can change as the weight loss progresses. In other words, while losing the next "five pounds," you may experience a little more hunger and discomfort than you did while losing the previous "five pounds." You may draw a certain satisfaction from knowing that by surmounting the loss of satiety-feeling you will have harnessed the same forces (appetite and hunger) which made you overweight in the first place. These same forces can now work for you and help you against the enemy, which is your natural tendency toward overweight.

It will be easier for you to give up the satiety-feeling if you learn a few helpful "tricks." Learn to eat slowly; as soon as you start to eat, remind yourself that you are going to stop as soon as your need for food is satisfied, that you will resist the desire to eat long before you reach that full, don't-want-another-bite feeling.

Many a person's feeling of satiety after a copious lunch is invariably followed by a feeling of tiredness, lassitude, and sleepiness during a major part of the afternoon (unless he takes a nap after lunch). These same people discover that by eating less at lunch and by giving up the feeling of satiety, they experience in the afternoon a new feeling of freshness and wakefulness.

If after one month of eating-without-satiety feeling your weight has fallen off, keep up this program until your weight stabilizes at a new lower level. Then maintain this weight for another month by rigidly adhering to the eating-without-satiety-feeling. You may long for that feeling of satiety after meals, but you will know that, if you begin to compromise, your weight will go up and you will again feel less alert after meals. Although the satiety feeling once was pleasant, it normally lasted only a few minutes anyway, and having to live without it is a small sacrifice in view of the benefit from its avoidance.

However, if after one month of eating-without-satiety-feeling your weight has *not* fallen off enough, you will have to increase your food restriction and tolerate more hunger. Instead of eating as soon as you are hungry, don't eat until an hour or two after you become aware that you are truly hungry. Then eat slowly and only until the moment you can say, "Now I am not really hungry any more, but I am not completely satisfied either." Stop at this point.

Learn to regard food eaten when you are not really hungry as poison, harmful to your health. There is a true French saying, *L'appe-*

tit vient en mangeant or "Appetite comes with eating;" that is why you should stop eating as soon as you have satisfied your hunger and when, in fact, you would like most to continue. In this way you will learn over the months to estimate just how much hunger it takes for you to maintain a certain level of weight loss, and you will learn to maintain it.

15 | The Food Exchange System: A Way to Compute Daily Calorie Intake

HAVE YOU EVER TRIED TO ESTIMATE IN TERMS OF CALORIES THE amount of food you should allow yourself to eat in one day? Have you ever tried to look up the caloric values of your favorite kinds of food? Many people really have tried and have had difficulty in finding the number of calories for some of the foods they usually eat. Further, they have become quite confused when they found that different books give quite different caloric values for the same amounts of the same kinds of food.

This situation would have remained unchanged if it were not for the very special need of a large group of people for whom an accurate counting of calories may often be a question of life or death. These people who need to count calories so accurately are diabetics, especially diabetics who require daily injections of insulin. If a diabetic who is on insulin treatment eats more food than he is supposed to, his blood level of sugar glucose may rise dangerously high and even lead to what is called a diabetic coma. If the same diabetic eats less food than he is supposed to, his blood level of sugar glucose may drop dangerously low, and result in the equally dangerous hypoglycemic shock.

For a number of years physicians and dieticians have been aware of the need to count accurately the caloric values of the foods that a diabetic person chooses to eat. Finally, the American Dietetic Association, together with the American Diabetic Association, selected a committee of over 20 specialists and charged them with the task of working out a simple method of counting caloric values of foods in order to allow diabetic persons to choose from a great variety of foods and still stay within the narrow limits of daily caloric allowances. After several years of studies, the so-called Food Exchange System came into being.

Very soon it became evident, however, that the Food Exchange System can be valuable in calculating food amounts for various weight-controlling diets.

In the Food Exchange System, all foods are assigned to one of the six or seven food categories or food exchanges. One exchange of a given food may be substituted for one exchange of any other food within that food category; the protein, carbohydrate, and fat intake will remain just about the same. A slice of bread, for example, is defined as that quantity of any food that yields 15 grams carbohydrate and 2 grams protein.

Although the average slice of bread may weigh 25 grams and contain approximately 13 grams carbohydrate, the committee of experts decided that it would be preferable to list all the foods in the bread exchange in amounts that contain approximately 15 grams carbohydrate. A 1/2 cup serving of many cereals, which is an easy quantity to measure, yields approximately this amount of carbohydrate and may be "exchanged" for the slice of bread. Similarly, 1 potato (2" diameter, baked or boiled), 2 Graham crackers, or 5 saltines yield 1 bread exchange, and may be "exchanged" for any other in the bread exchange group. The typical day's consumption of bread exchanges is, therefore, approximately 15 grams of carbohydrate per serving.

A meat portion, such as an egg, can be "exchanged" for another meat portion, such as an ounce of cheddar cheese. During the course of a day an individual who is allowed to consume 1500 calories or 6 bread exchanges, 6 meat exchanges, 3 fat exchanges, 3 fruit exchanges, 2 milk exchanges, and one vegetable B (starchy vegetable) exchange, is likely to select several different foods from the list of bread exchanges, such as potato, cereal, or crackers, several different foods from the meat exchanges, and from other food exchanges as well. He is not allowed, however, to substitute food from one exchange (e.g., meat) for food from another exchange (e.g., bread, milk, fruit, etc.).

There are seven food exchange categories. Each food exchange is characterized by its caloric content and defined by its carbohydrate, protein, and fat contents in grams.

1. *Meat exchanges:* foods with high protein, some fat, and no carbohydrate content. One meat exchange is the amount of food containing about 7 grams protein, 5 grams fat, and about 73 calories. A meat exchange corresponds to one ounce of meat, or to one large egg. One frankfurter (8-9 per lb.), 3 medium sardines, or 5 small shrimps, clams or oysters also correspond to 1 meat exchange. One ounce (or a cube 1" x 1" x 1") of cheddar cheese corresponds to 1 meat and 1 fat exchange; 1-1/2 ounces Edam cheese (or Gruyère, Swiss, Liederkranz) corresponds to 1 meat and 1 fat exchange. More examples of meat exchanges are given in Table 5.

TABLE 5 MEAT EXCHANGES
Per unit: protein, 7 gm.; fat, 5 gm.

Food	Approximate Measure	Weight
Meat and poultry, medium fat (beef, lamb, pork, liver, chicken)	1 oz.	30 gm.
Cold cuts (4 1/2-in. square, 1/8-in. thick)	1 slice	45 gm.
Frankfurter (8 or 9 per lb.)	1	50 gm.
Fish		
Cod, mackerel	1 oz.	30 gm.
Salmon, tuna, crab	1/4 cup	30 gm.
Oysters, shrimp, clams	5 small	45 gm.
Cheese		
Cheddar or American	1 oz.	30 gm.
Cottage	1/4 cup	45 gm.
Egg	1	50 gm.
Peanut butter*	2 Tbsp.	30 gm.

*Limit use or adjust carbohydrate (deduct 5 gm. carbohydrate per serving when used in excess of one exchange).

2. *Fat exchanges:* foods containing mainly or only fat. One fat exchange contains 5 grams fat and 45 calories. One fat exchange corresponds to one teaspoon of butter, margarine, cooking fat, bacon fat, lard, olive or salad oil or one slice crisp bacon. One fat exchange is present in 1 tablespoon (or in three teaspoons) of French or Russian dressing, mayonnaise (commercial or homemade), heavy

whipping cream, or cream cheese. Also, one fat exchange is present in about 10 almonds or 10 peanuts, 6-8 pecans, 5 cashews, 5 halves black walnuts, 5 small olives, or 4 large ripe olives, or 1/8 avocado (4" diameter). More examples of fat exchanges are in Table 6.

TABLE 6 FAT EXCHANGES
Fat-5 gm. per serving

Food	Approximate Measure	Weight
Butter or margerine	1 tsp.	5 gm.
Bacon, crisp	1 slice	10 gm.
Cream		
Light, 20%	2 Tbsp.	30 gm.
Heavy, 40%	1 Tbsp.	15 gm.
Cream Cheese	1 Tbsp.	15 gm.
French dressing	1 Tbsp.	15 gm.
Mayonnaise	1 tsp.	5 gm.
Oil or cooking fat	1 tsp.	5 gm.
Nuts	6 small	10 gm.
Olives	5 small	50 gm.
Avocado (4-in. diameter)	1/4	25 gm.

3. *Bread exchanges:* foods containing about 15 grams carbohydrate, 2 grams protein and about 70 calories. One bread exchange corresponds to: one slice of bread, one muffin (2" diameter), one biscuit (roll, 2" diam.), or one potato (2" diameter, baked or boiled), 2 graham crackers (2-1/2" x 2-1/2"), or 5 saltines (2" x 2"), 1-1/2" cube corn bread or sponge cake (no icing), or 2-1/2 tablespoons of flour. One bread exchange is also present in: 1-1/2 cup puffed rice, popped popcorn; 1 cup Cheerios, canned pumpkin; 2/3 or 3/4 cup dry cereal, corn flakes, Wheaties, Rice Crispies, parsnips; 1/2 cup raisin bran, bran flakes, Cornfetti, grape nut flakes, Krumbles, creamed potatoes, peas or split peas (dry or cooked), lima beans (dry or cooked), canned, drained corn, macaroni, spaghetti, noodles, cooked rice or grits; 1/2 cup vanilla ice cream corresponds to one bread and two fat exchanges; 1/3 cup all bran, grape nuts, corn (or 1/2 ear), 1/4 cup baked beans (no pork), sweet potatoes, or yam. Other bread exchanges are listed in Table 7.

TABLE 7 BREAD EXCHANGES
Per serving: carbohydrate, 15 gm.; protein, 2 gm.

Food	Approximate Measure	Weight
Bread	1 slice	25 gm.
Biscuit, roll (2-in. diameter)	1	35 gm.
Muffin (2-in. diameter)	1	35 gm.
Cornbread (1 1/2-in. cube)	1	35 gm.
Flour	2 1/2 Tbsp.	30 gm.
Cereal		
Cooked	1/2 cup	100 gm.
Dry (flaked and puffed)	3/4 cup	20 gm.
Rice and grits, cooked	1/2 cup	100 gm.
Spaghetti and noodles, cooked	1/2 cup	100 gm.
Crackers		
Graham (2 1/2-in. square)	2	20 gm.
Oysterettes	20 (1/2 cup)	20 gm.
Saltines (2-in. sq.)	5	20 gm.
Soda (2 1/2-in. sq.)	3	20 gm.
Round, thin (1 1/2-in. diameter)	6-8	20 gm.
Vegetables		
Beans and peas, dried, cooked		
(Lima, navy, split pea, cowpeas)	1/2 cup	100 gm.
Beans, lima, fresh	1/2 cup	100 gm.
Beans, baked (no pork)	1/4 cup	50 gm.
Corn, sweet	1/3 cup	80 gm.
Corn, popped	1 cup	20 gm.
Parsnips	2/3 cup	125 gm.
Potatoes, white--baked or boiled		
(2-in. diameter)	1	100 gm.
Potatoes, white--mashed	1/2 cup	100 gm.
Potatoes, sweet or yam	1/4 cup	60 gm.
Sponge Cake, plain (1 1/2-in. cube)	1	25 gm.
Ice cream (omit 2 Fat Exchanges)	1/2 cup	70 gm.

4. *Milk exchanges:* foods containing nearly equal amounts of carbohydrate, protein, and fat. One milk exchange contains about 12 grams carbohydrate, 8 grams protein, 10 grams fat, and about 170 calories; it corresponds to one cup (8 ounces = 1/2 pint = 240 grams) whole milk. Nonfat milk reduces milk fat content by 2 fat exchanges and the value of nonfat milk exchange is 80 calories. One

milk exchange is also present in 1/2 cup (120 grams) of evaporated milk and in 1/4 cup (35 grams, 3 level tablespoons) of whole powdered milk. One cup buttermilk (or 1 cup nonfat skim milk) corresponds to 1 milk exchange less 2 fat exchanges; 1 cup plain yogurt corresponds to 1 milk exchange less 1 fat exchange. Other milk exchanges are listed in Table 8.

TABLE 8 MILK EXCHANGES
Per serving: carbohydrate, 12 gm.; protein, 8 gm.; fat, 10 gm.

Type of Milk	Approximate Measure (cup, 8 oz.)	Weight (gm.)
Whole milk (plain or homogenized)	1	240
Skim milk[*]	1	240
Evaporated milk	1/2	120
Powdered whole milk	1/4	35
Powdered skim milk (nonfat dried milk)[*]	1/4	35
Buttermilk (from whole milk)	1	240
Buttermilk (from skim milk)[*]	1	240

[*]Since these forms of milk contain no fat, two fat exchanges may be added to the diet when they are used.

5. *Fruit exchanges:* foods containing mainly or only carbohydrate. One fruit exchange contains about 10 grams carbohydrate and about 40 calories. One fruit exchange corresponds, for instance, to one apple (2-1/4" diameter), one orange (2-1/2" diam.), 1/2 small grapefruit, mango or banana, 2 dates, figs, plums or dried prunes, 3 fresh apricots, 10 large or 15 small cherries, 12 grapes, 1/2 cup orange juice, grapefruit juice, or apple sauce. Other examples of fruit exchanges are in Table 9.

6. *Vegetable A exchanges* (or free exchanges): foods with very little or no measurable carbohydrates. The following vegetables need not be counted in the diet, unless portions are larger than one cup at one meal, whereas portions larger than one cup should be counted as one vegetable B exchange: asparagus, broccoli, Brussels sprouts, cauliflower, celery, chicory, cumcumber, eggplant, escarole, green beans, greens: (beet greens, chard, collards, dandelion, kale, mustard, spinach, turnip), lettuce, mushrooms, okra, parsley, pepper (green or red), radishes, rhubarb, romaine, sauerkraut, summer squash, tomatoes, turnip greens.

TABLE 9 FRUIT EXCHANGES*

Carbohydrates—10 gm. per serving

Food	Approximate Measure
Apple (2-in. diameter)	1
Applesauce	1/2 cup
Apricots	
Fresh	2 medium
Dried	4 halves
Banana	1/2
Blackberries	1 cup
Raspberries	1 cup
Strawberries**	1 cup
Cantaloupe (6-inch diameter)**	1/4
Cherries	10 large
Dates	2
Figs, fresh	2 large
Figs, dried	1 small
Grapefruit**	1/2 small
Grapes	12
Grape juice	1/2 cup
Honeydew melon (7-inch diameter)	1/8
Mango	1/2 small
Orange**	1 small
Orange juice**	1/2 cup
Papaya	1/3 medium
Peach	1 medium
Pineapple	1/2 cup
Pineapple juice	1/3 cup
Plums	2 medium
Prunes, dried	2 medium
Raisins	2 Tbsp.
Tangerine	1 large
Watermelon	1 cup

*Unsweetened canned fruits may be used in the same amount as listed for the fresh fruit.

**These fruits are rich sources of ascorbic acid. At least one serving should be included in the diet each day.

7. *Vegetable B exchanges:* foods with moderate amount of carbohydrate, small amounts of protein, and no fat. One vegetable B exchange contains 7 grams carbohydrate, 2 grams protein and 35 calories. One vegetable B exchange corresponds to 1/2 cup (or 100 grams) beets, carrots, green peas (fresh or cooked), canned mixed

vegetables, onion, pumpkin, rutabagas, winter squash, turnips, or to 1/4 cup of canned lima beans, canned green peas.

Additional lists of variety of foods for the six or seven food exchange categories can be found in the Expanded Food Exchange Lists on pages 204-269 of the book by Margaret Bennett, *The Peripatetic Diabetic* (1969 Hawthorn Books, Inc.)

You can calculate and select the amounts of daily food intake by using Table 10. For six different levels of daily caloric intake, this table gives the suggested amounts of carbohydrate, protein, and fat in well-balanced proportions, together with the suggested number of food exchanges for all seven food exchange categories.

TABLE 10

Caloric Levels in Sample Plans and the Number of Food Exchanges for One Day

Daily Intake Energy (Calories)	Carbohydrate (Grams)	Protein (Grams)	Fat (Grams)	Meat Exch.	Bread Exch.	Fat Exch.	Milk Exch.	Fruit Exch.	Vegetable B Exch.	Vegetable A Exch.
1200	125	60	50	5	4	1	2	3	1	As desired
1500	150	70	65	6	6	3	2	3	1	,,
1800	180	80	80	7	8	5	2	3	1	,,
2200	220	90	100	8	10	8	2	4	1	,,
2600	260	105	110	9	12	11	2	5	1	,,
3000	300	120	125	10	15	13	2	6	1	,,

16 Special Problems in Losing Weight

"I CAN'T LOSE WEIGHT." THIS COMPLAINT IS FAMILIAR. SO IS the reply: "Stop eating so much and you will." More often than not, cruel as it sounds, this reply closely represents the facts of the case.

But there are a small percentage of truly obese people for whom the usual reducing diets result only in frustration. Typically, people in this group began getting fat as children; in addition to the problems of obesity, they probably have also had to cope with their emotional reactions to years of being teased, shamed, and rejected.

At last dieticians are coming to realize that these people are not merely self-indulgent. They have inherited special problems that make dieting very difficult. They can lose weight, but for them a successful reducing campaign requires special strategy and special attention.

Some obese persons can eat very little or "almost nothing" and still show no weight loss. They lose weight very slowly when simple food or caloric restriction is imposed upon them. Such cases are well known in medical literature and are familiar to every physician who has observed obese persons under carefully controlled conditions.

Two major common factors or causes are nearly always associated with the difficulties of obese people in losing weight. One is excessive water retention, which may reach very large proportions; the other involves metabolic or enzymatic adaptations of body tissues to long-spaced heavy meal eating, or to sugar-sweetened foods.

Some obese women have been observed to continue water retention for many weeks during caloric restriction with no weight loss and often even some weight gain. To understand water retention in obese individuals, it should be pointed out that the burning of 100 grams of fatty acids (the main constituents of fat or triglycerides) yields as a by-product 112 grams of metabolic water. If this water—which weighs, strange as it sounds, more than the fat from which it was formed—is not excreted promptly, it can completely cancel the loss of body weight that would otherwise have occurred from the burning of tissue fat.

Water retention in obese individuals is more likely to occur when the individual is standing in an upright position than when he is resting in a recumbent, horizontal position. This condition has been known for many years. Even normal nonobese individuals sometimes retain water if they spend long hours on their feet. However, the retention of water in an upright position is considerably greater in obese individuals where it may, in some cases, result in an almost complete cessation of urine formation.

Drs. E. S. Gordon and M. Goldberg from the University of Wisconsin Medical School treat this condition. About every 10 to 14 days, they give their weight reducing patients a diuretic to increase water excretion. On the basis of their experience with many overweight patients, they consider mercurial diuretics, such as sodium meralluride (Mercuhydrin) 2 ml injected at bedtime, most effective. If injections are to be avoided, oral diuretics—such as chlorothiazide (Diuril) 500 to 1,000 mg or hydrochlorothiazide (Hydro-Diuril) 50 to 100 mg, also taken at bedtime—may be used. Chlormerodrin (Neohydrin) and methyclothiazide (Enduron) also have been used successfully.

As we know, obese people also have trouble in losing weight because of the enzymatic and metabolic adaptations that their body tissues have made to long-spaced heavy meal eating and to the eating of large amounts of sugar-sweetened foods. Drs. G. Hollifield and W. Parson, from the Virginia University School of Medicine, have shown in experiments with obese animals that such enzymatic adaptations can be broken most easily by imposing a 48-hour fast at the beginning of the obesity treatment. The 48-hour fast is then followed by a "nibbling type" eating pattern (5 or more small meals a day) which leads to a normal low level of fat synthesis, accompanied by a reduction of the previously hyperactive enzyme systems.

Many dieticians now recommend starting the treatment of "entrenched" obesity with this 48-hour total fast. The fast is not designed to produce spectacular losses of weight but rather to break the enzymatic and metabolic adaptations of body tissues, which have been overactive toward an increased fat synthesis. Dieticians differ, however, about what regime their patients should follow after the fast.

Drs. E. S. Gordon and M. Goldberg, from the University of Wisconsin Medical School, give after the 48-hour fast a high-protein, low-calorie diet, containing 100 grams protein (400 calories), 50 grams carbohydrate (200 calories) and 80 grams fat (720 calories), totaling 1,320 calories a day. Their basic concept is that the carbohydrate content of the food should be low. They recommend moderately high protein content for its high satiety value. The fat content of their diet is moderate and cannot be considered either high or low. They add a supplement of polyunsaturated fatty acids, the caloric content of which is calculated as part of the fat content. The salt content of their diet is low (between 2 and 3 grams daily). The total caloric value of their diet is quite high in terms of reducing diets, but its success provides excellent evidence that severe caloric restriction is not necessary for successful and even rapid weight reduction.

THE ALL-PROTEIN DIETS

All-protein diets probably are most suitable for healthy adult obese individuals who are forty or more pounds overweight, want to get rid of their pounds quickly, and have been unable to do so with any other weight-reducing diets. The particular advantage in an all-protein diet is the convenience of not having to count calories; certain foods may be eaten as desired to satisfy hunger.

Perhaps the best known of the all-protein diets for many years has been the so-called Mayo diet (no connection with the famous Mayo Clinic) in which the person is allowed to have all the steak he desires, but nothing else. Another version consists of nothing but grapefruit, eggs, and bacon—all you want to eat. If a person sticks to the Mayo diet for any length of time, he will indeed lose weight quickly, but soon he will also begin to crave other foods and a more balanced menu. He will be so tired of the limited selection of foods that he just won't be able to eat much of them.

A good description of a similar situation—in which people had all the meat they wanted but craved other foods, particularly bread —comes from the people who settled the North American continent. As they traveled across the great plains, they had an abundant supply of meat in the form of freshly killed game, but after their supply of flour ran out, they were miserably hungry, even though they had all the meat they could eat.

A diet deficient in any of the four basic varieties of food— carbohydrates, protein, fat, and fruit—will not satisfy hunger and will soon become so disagreeable that the person would rather have nothing at all than any more of the "one-food" diet.

There are a number of variations of the all-protein diet in which the dieter is allowed unlimited amounts of certain protein foods. Of these the so-called "quick-weight-loss-diet" of Dr. I. M. Stillman, has received great publicity. The quick-weight-loss diet consists primarily of protein foods; lean meats, lean fish, eggs, and cottage cheese plus no less than 8 glasses of water each day.

In this diet one can eat as much as one desires to satisfy one's hunger from a great variety of lean meats, beef, veal, lamb, chicken, turkey, fowl, fish, game, and seafood; one can eat these lean parts roasted, broiled or boiled, and with no fats, oil, butter, or margarine added.

All kinds of lean fish, broiled, baked or boiled, like carp, cod, flounder, haddock, whitefish and white perch are permitted but no fish rich in fat, like salmon, sardines, tuna fish, and no smoked or fried fish. One can eat broiled, baked, or boiled seafood like clams, crabmeat, lobster, mussels, oysters, scallops and shrimp, but no smoked or fried seafood.

One can eat skim-milk cheese, cottage cheese, farmer cheese, and other cheeses made with skimmed milk, but no cheese made with whole milk. One can eat eggs fried in nonsticking pans without fat, oil, butter, or margarine.

Eight to 10 glasses of water (10 ounce glasses) daily are recommended and all the coffee or tea one wants but with no cream, milk, or sugar. Taking daily vitamin and mineral tablets of the common available multivitamin preparations is also recommended. In moderation, one may use common seasonings, such as salt, pepper, horseradish, cloves, thyme, garlic, and other spices or herbs, catsup, cocktail sauce, tabasco sauce. However, no mayonnaise, salad dressings, creamy or oily sauces are permitted.

Here are categories and examples of foods which are proscribed:

Bread, rice, potatoes, crackers or cookies in any form, commercial cereals
Fruit of any kind, fruit juices
All vegetables
Whole milk, sugar in coffee or tea, and candy
Ice cream, sherbets of all kinds
Alcohol

Experience has shown that the overweight and obese people who desire to lose weight do not find these restrictions too hard to follow, because they realize that they are on an all-protein diet only for a limited time and that, as soon as they lose their excess weight, they can allow themselves to again enjoy a well-balanced diet of other foods.

It is not unusual on the all-protein diets to lose 10-15 pounds (and even more) during the first week, 8-10 pounds during the second week, and 5-7 pounds each consecutive week until within reach of desirable weight. There have been many reported cases of obese people on the all-protein diets who have lost over 100 pounds in 15-20 weeks. It should be pointed out, however, that such spectacular losses of pounds are not and cannot be due only to some mysterious "melting fat away," but to a great extent are due to the loss of body water, as discussed above.

Once the weight is within 10 or 15 pounds of the desirable weight, it is recommended to switch from the all-protein diet for a few months to the "eating-without-satiety feeling" diet that is well balanced in foods from all four major food groups (that is, carbohydrates, proteins, fats and fruit). After a few months of a well-balanced diet eaten without-satiety feeling, if the person is still above his desirable weight, he can take off the excess pounds by another week or two of the all-protein diet. When his desirable weight is achieved, he will go back to a well-balanced diet and to eating-without-satiety feeling.

It must be noted that Dr. I. M. Stillman's book, *The Doctor's Quick Weight Loss Diet,* has been included in the *Not Recommended* section of the list *"Nutrition Books: Recommended and not Recom-*

mended" published by the Chicago Nutrition Foundation, together with the following comment by Dr. Philip L. White, Secretary of the Council of Foods and Nutrition of the American Medical Association: "Dr. Stillman's Quick Weight Loss Diet is simply one consisting, as much as possible, of protein, very little fat, and no discernible source of carbohydrate. . . . This diet is an intentional nutritional imbalance. Anyone with kidney trouble or with a proclivity for gout, diabetes, or any medical problem in which urea nitrogen, ketone bodies, or electrolyte balance are poorly handled, could be a candidate for sensational trouble. One should be conserned about the possibility that individuals might stay on such a diet for too long a period of time or return to it too frequently. Extreme caution should be used in adopting the all-protein diets. Only the most limited use in conjunction with the help of your physician is recommended."

Careful experimental studies with humans and with animals have revealed a number of health dangers associated with high-protein diets. Observations keep accumulating to indicate that high-protein diets contribute to the development of high levels of cholesterol and fat in the blood. This is indicated by the drop in blood cholesterol levels following substitution of proteins for carbohydrates in the diet.

Dr. R. H. Furman from the University of Oklahoma Medical Center has found in experiments with human subjects that substitution of glucose for protein in the same caloric amount resulted in a 25 percent reduction in blood levels of cholesterol and fat, as compared with the values observed during the period of conventional diet, which was rather high on protein. Similarly, Dr. R. E. Olson and associates in Pittsburgh observed in experiments with human subjects a decrease in blood cholesterol levels during a seven-day period of low-protein diet (25 grams daily, mainly protein of vegetable origin).

Other studies with animals indicate that high-protein diets shorten life span and contribute to the development of atherosclerotic lesions in coronary heart arteries. Dr. R. J. Jones of the University of Chicago found that rats on a high-protein diet have a shorter lifespan than control animals receiving a well-balanced diet. They also observed that rats receiving a high-protein diet manifest an increased incidence of atheromatous lesions in coronary heart arteries and unusually high blood cholesterol levels, despite a normal or low caloric intake (though the protein intake was high) and a low fat content in their diet.

It is of interest in this connection that high-protein content in the diet worsens fat accumulation in the body because of long-spaced, heavy meal eating, discussed in previous chapters. This has been well documented by Dr. Clarence Cohn, Director of the Division of Nutritional Sciences at the Michael Reese Hospital in Chicago, who observed in experiments with rats fed only two meals a day that a stepwise increase of protein content in their diet was followed by an additional and stepwise increase in fat content in the body of these rats, as compared to control rats, eating the same diet, but at their leisure as they choose (nibbling).

The above observations are of particular interest because they indicate that high-protein diets, combined with the pattern of eating one to three large meals, in Western countries and in the United States, may be one of the factors contributing to the high incidence of coronary heart disease and obesity in these countries. Also, these observations leave little or no doubt that high-protein diets and especially their all-protein varieties should be applied with great caution and that, whenever in doubt, one should not hesitate to consult one's physician.

THE KETOGENIC DIET

It is not the aim of this book to discuss all the existing varieties of the all-protein or high-protein diets and even less the numerous "one-food" diets. But it is worthwhile to say a few words about the so-called ketogenic diet, which is a low calorie diet (of 800 or 1,000 calories) that contains approximately 70 percent fat calories, 20 percent protein, and 10 percent carbohydrate. The expression "ketogenic" indicates that there is an increased production of the so-called ketone substances (such as acetone) by the body of the person on this particular diet.

First of all, during the ketogenic diet laboratory tests for ketone substances in urine, or ketonuria are done (or should be done) routinely four times a day. Within three to four days after the initiation of the ketogenic diet, ketone elevation is readily measurable in blood and urine and discernible in the breath by a fruity odor. This elevation, called ketosis, results from a shift in energy source from glucose to free fatty acid. The absence of a positive reaction for ketone in the urine while an individual is undergoing ketogenic weight reduction implies a failure in the program. If ketonuria does not appear or if it decreases during the "total fast," this serves as reliable proof that food has been consumed by the patient in addition to what he was allowed in the prescribed diet.

Parallel experiments were done; one group of overweight persons was placed on 800-calorie ketogenic diet and another group of overweight persons was placed on 800-calorie high carbohydrate (65 percent) diet. The results of these experiments have shown that the rapid weight loss over the period of the first 7 to 10 days in both groups was almost identical. Such experiments demonstrate that ketogenic dieting offers no particular advantage in the amount of weight loss obtainable, and that ketogenic diet has no special advantage in producing weight loss over and above any other diet.

The only advantage of ketogenic or high-fat diet is that the person accepts this form of dieting without severe side effects. Uniformly and without exception, persons who undergo this dieting find that the satiety value of the ketogenic diet is far superior to that of a mixed or high-carbohydrate diet, even though the food selection is minimal.

The increased production of ketones is associated with a decrease in hunger, but also with a decrease in physical energy and mental alertness, so that the person on a ketogenic diet would rather take it easy and watch television than engage in any strenuous physical or mental activity. Many people do not seem to be bothered by this loss in physical and mental alertness, whereas others consider it a positive disadvantage of the ketogenic diet.

In addition, there are indications that high-fat diets shorten the life span. Dr. C. F. French and his co-workers in the Department of Nutrition of Pennsylvania State College observed some 15 years ago in experiments with rats that fat-enriched diet (23 percent of fat, in the form of corn oil added to the food mixture) decreased the life span of the rats by about 11 percent (from 752 ± 25 days to 676 ± 19 days). Further, they reported that the life-span-shortening effect of fat-enriched diet can be reduced by a carbohydrate-enriched diet, even though the total caloric intake in the fat-enriched diet was less.

CUT OUT ALCOHOL FOR FAST WEIGHT LOSS

If you want to lose a lot of weight fast, you will have to avoid all alcohol rigorously. No other food contains more calories than alcohol, except fat itself. Alcohol provides 7 calories per gram (as compared with 4 grams for both protein and carbohydrate and 9 grams for fat) which means that one ounce of 100-proof whiskey or gin averages 105 calories. Thus a highball with 2 ounces of whiskey furnishes over 200 calories. One dry martini (meaning no vermouth) made with two jiggers (3 ounces) of 86-proof gin or vodka amounts to about 214 calories.

Sugar is another but a less-important source of calories in some wines, vermouths, and cocktails.

Whiskey sour, 4 ounces, contains about 211 calories; Manhattan, 4 ounces, about 188 calories; one 12-ounce can or bottle of beer (4.5% alcohol by volume) amounts to about 171 calories. Dessert or sweet wines (4 ounces, 18.8% alcohol by volume) amount to about 156 calories; table or dry wines or champagne (12.2% alcohol by volume) amount to about 97 calories. Calorie values of a few other alcoholic and nonalcoholic beverages are given in Table 11.

The alcoholic content of a beverage is usually given in terms of what is called "proof"; proof divided by two equals percent alcohol by volume. Thus, a gin or whiskey of 90 proof is 45 percent alcohol. Since one ounce of gin or whiskey is approximately 30 grams, 1 ounce of 90-proof alcoholic beverage contains about 13½ grams of alcohol, and this times 7 calories equals about 95 calories per ounce. So, if one has 2 ounces of 90-proof gin in a cocktail, the calories from the alcohol approximate 190.

Alcohol provides no dietary essentials except calories. For instance, two drinks before a meal supply the same number of calories as a rich dessert. So you have to add your alcohol calories in with the rest, just as if they were food calories. If the total number of calories you eat and drink in a day exceeds the number you burn up, your body uses the alcohol calories for energy and stores the excess food calories as fat. Those who are trying to lose weight or are having trouble in maintaining their weight should keep in mind that they will continue having trouble in maintaining weight if they do not cut down on alcohol, in whatever form they take it. In fact, they may even be eating less than they did years ago. There is no secret magic about it: one cannot diet successfully and stay slim without cutting alcohol down or out. It is as simple as that.

Only a few years ago not one doctor in a thousand would have allowed for a cocktail in the reducing diet he prescribed. Nowadays an increasing number of doctors suspecting their patients will drink

TABLE 11
The Drinkers Guide to Alcoholic Drinks

	Calories
Beer (12 ozs. can/bottle)	171
(3.6% alc. by weight, 4.5% alc. by volume)	
Wines (3-1/2 ozs.)	
Dessert or sweet (includes muscatel, sherries, port, tokay, aperitifs, vermouths; 15.3% alc. by weight, 18.8% alc. by vol.)	137
Table or dry or champagne (includes burgundy, chianti, cherry, peach, berry, etc., 9.9% alc. by weight, 12.2% by volume)	85

Mixed drinks	Calories
Alexander, 3 oz.	228
Daiquiri, 3-1/2 oz.	122
Eggnog, Alcoholic, 4 oz.	335
Gin Rickey, 4 oz.	150
Gin and Tonic, 8 oz.	105
Grasshopper, 3 oz.	254
Highball (Scotch)	140
Manhattan, 3-1/2 oz.	164

	Calories
Martini, 3-1/2 oz.	221
Mint Julep, 10 oz.	212
Old Fashioned, 4 oz.	179
Planter's Punch, 3-1/2 oz.	175
Rum Collins, 10 oz.	180
Stinger, 2 oz.	164
Vodka Gimlet, 3 oz.	203
Whiskey Sour, 4 oz.	211

Alcohol (1 jigger or 1-1/2 ozs.)
Gin, rum vodka, whiskey, brandy, cordials, and liqueurs:

	Calories
80 proof (33.4% alc. by weight)	99
86 proof (36.0% alc. by weight)	107
90 proof (37.9% alc. by weight)	113
94 proof (39.7% alc. by weight)	118
100 proof (45.2% alc. by weight)	127

(Proof divided by two equals percent alcohol by volume. Example: 80 proof whiskey = 40% alcohol by volume) regardless of advice to the contrary permit a cocktail or a highball, a few glasses of wine or beer with the diets they prescribe for not-too-much-overweight patients who cannot do without alcohol.

Quite a number of people have acquired the habit of doing a certain amount of business drinking, or social drinking, while still keeping a slim waistline. Here are some of the strategies you can apply:

Instead of the martini, ask for a glass of dry wine. You will be trading the 220 martini calories for only 85 calories in a 3½ ounce serving of table or dry wine.

Limit yourself to seven drinks a week. It does not matter when you drink them. You can have one each day, or save them all up for the weekend. If you have been having two drinks a day, you will be eliminating half the calories you once took in from liquor.

If you are ordering cocktails when you dine out, have the cocktail but skip the first course—the appetizer or the soup. Or substitute wine for the cocktail, perhaps one glass before dinner and one with the meal. Two glasses of table wine have fewer calories than only one drink of most mixed cocktails (see Table 11).

Keep counting your drinks and calories. There is a universal tendency to stop counting them when you begin to feel guilty about how many you've had. There is a virtue in keeping count. As long as you keep count, you have not given up.

The best strategy of all, however, is to cut out all alcoholic drinking entirely.

PHYSICAL ACTIVITY AND EFFORTS TO LOSE WEIGHT

The daily routine of millions of modern urban dwellers is so low in physical activity that it is below the activity-threshold needed for the appetite to function normally. Often we have appetite for food without being hungry, which is an additional reason why many people overeat and become obese. Lack of physical activity is possibly the most important factor in both the overeating and in the "creeping" overweight of so many people in modern urban societies.

The regulatory mechanisms of food intake in our bodies were just not designed for the sedentary, highly mechanized conditions of our modern life. This type of life appears to be particularly difficult for the persons with large components of mesomorphic and endomorphic types, in their body build. Such persons, in order to adapt to the conditions of sedentary life without developing obesity, basically have two choices: either they have to step up their physical activity and include exercise in their daily routines or they have to curb their appetite and go around mildly or acutely hungry all their lives.

The first solution may be very difficult, particularly in cities with their poorly organized or nonexistent facilities for adult exercise. But the second alternative is so much more difficult that, when you rely on it exclusively for weight-control, you may only continue to have a succession of failures in weight-controlling efforts. That is why in any weight-controlling program it is highly advisable to reorganize your life to include physical activity and regular exercise in the daily routine.

PART III:
Exercise

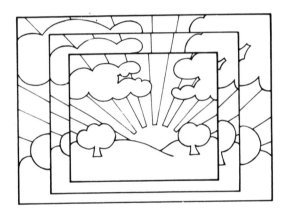

17 | Benefits of Exercise

IF WE DO NOT USE OUR BODIES, WE LOSE THEM THE STATE-ment sounds dramatic, but a growing mass of experimental evidence is leading doctors to conclude that it is close to the blunt truth.

As we know, all the components of the body are continually being repaired and replaced by the manufacturing activity of the tissue cells. An impressive number of recent studies indicate that those components of the body that are used more are also replaced more efficiently and more quickly than those components that are allowed to remain inactive.

The muscle fibers in groups of muscles that are exercised are replaced in larger amounts. The muscle fibers in unexercised muscles are replaced only sparingly.

This relationship applies not only to muscles but to other components of the body that are involved in the exercise such as the bones supporting the muscles, the blood vessels supplying them with blood, the lungs aerating the blood, that is, supplying the blood with oxygen, and the list could continue.

The differences between those body tissues that have enjoyed activity and those that suffered its loss are sometimes almost unbelievable. It has been observed that complete bed rest for two or three weeks has characteristically resulted in calcium losses from the bones, tissue loss from muscles, and a significant decrease in heart and lung function. Just being allowed to engage in the usual daily activities brought about important improvements in heart and lung function, an increase in muscle strength and physical working capacity, and a remineralization, or strengthening of the bones.

These improvements, *achieved by nothing more than getting out of bed and engaging in usual daily activities,* can be further enhanced by regular physical exercise.

Improvements through increased physical activity and exercise have definite effects not only in the heart and lung function and muscle strength, physical working capacity and remineralization of bones, but also in the physiological functions of other organs and tissues of the body. The beneficial effects of increased physical activity even result in changes in the chemical composition of the organs and tissues of the body which are opposite to the changes in the chemical composition as they occur during aging.

For a number of decades the antiaging or rejuvenating effects of physical activity and exercise have been overlooked, and it is only recently that they have begun to be recognized and further analyzed. In fact, physical activity and exercise represent the only efficient therapy for old age available at the present time. Of all the remedies of old age discussed in the first part of this book, such as the hormone therapy or the cell therapy, none are able to achieve better results than regular physical activity and exercise.

However, there are various kinds of exercise, and not all of them have the same anti-aging or rejuvenating effects. For the same amount of effort that a person is willing to put into daily physical exercise, some kinds of exercise result in smaller antiaging or rejuvenating effects than others. Probably the best results are obtained by rhythmic, dynamic, or steady-state exercises such as walking, running, jogging, bicycling, or swimming.

Probably the most frequently praised effect of physical activity and exercise is the prevention of heart disease and heart attack. There are now an increasing number of medical reports indicating a measurable improvement of the heart in patients with heart disease following a period of physical training and exercise. Even the sceptics agree that regular physical exercise may improve the heart and lung function.

Statistical data indicate that heart attacks are more than three times as frequent in sedentary persons than in persons who do regular physical activity and exercise. The number of persons who survive a heart attack is more than four times greater among those who in the weeks and months preceding the heart attack were doing regular physical exercise.

Furthermore, it has been reported that regular physical exercise brings substantial improvements in other chronic diseases of middle age, such as diabetes and high blood pressure. For instance, diabetics needed less insulin each day after they had undertaken regular daily physical exercise. It has also been reported that persons living in the city and suffering from high blood pressure showed a sustained lowering of their blood pressure levels after only a few days of regular physical exercise, especially if combined with a change to rural or mountainous environment.

Regular physical activity and exercise also have important beneficial effects on staying slim and losing weight. Any diet has a much better chance to succeed if accompanied by regular physical exercise.

There has been a good deal of bickering about the helpfulness of exercise in weight control. Despite gloomy comments on the number of miles that must be walked to lose a pound, common sense spotlights the importance of exercise in keeping slim. The caloric expenditure required for maintenance and repair is relatively low. Aside from this small daily expenditure and storing them as fat, the *only* way to get rid of the caloric nutrients we eat is by burning them in our physical activity. The more we exercise, the more calories we can permit ourselves; it is as simple as that. Exercise as a method of increasing our caloric allowance is especially helpful after we have entered the thirties and our bodies are burning their fuel less efficiently. Exercise will permit us to be a little less Spartan in our eating. With few exceptions, those who leave their twenties and neither cut down on their food budget nor increase their exercise are going to become pudgy as well as flabby.

Many people deny being sedentary. They feel busy and they know they are tired at the end of a long day at the office. But tiring activity is not necessarily synonymous with hard physical work. Working at a desk for six to ten hours a day does not use up large amounts of calories. Neither does driving a car, even through hectic freeway traffic. Nor does hassling important matters with a committee of sincere but stubborn members.

Our brains are very good machines for mental work, and they "work" all the time. Nevertheless even the most intense thinking uses up only small amounts of sugar glucose at a time. Thinking makes us tired and tense, but it does not make us slim. A century ago, after a hard day's work, most men needed to rest. Today, they need exercise. Exercise will act to reduce both their tension and their weight; and exercise will function to help their bodies withstand the emotional stresses they must endure on their jobs.

Most Americans need more exercise in their daily routine. Such simple additions as walking a few extra blocks or climbing three or four flights of stairs each day would take little time to accomplish a significant health benefit.

Admittedly, it is more difficult to get into shape when we are middle aged than when we were young. It takes longer. We ache more. We have to be cautious about pacing ourselves. Family and business commitments steal our recreational time. Furthermore, as is the case with some of us, if at our peak we had less physical strength, less stamina, and muscle flexibility than those that made the team, the effort involved is of discouraging proportions. And worse, our first feeble efforts may be greeted by gales of laughter and clever remarks.

On the other hand, regardless of our natural endowments, getting and staying fit is more important after thirty than before. And there are rewards that make the efforts worthwhile. We look better. We feel better. And there is good indication to believe we think better, too. Exercise has anti-aging effects on the brain as well as on the rest of the body. We are better able to cope with our jobs, with vigor and pleasure, and we still have enough energy left when we return home to enjoy our families and have a little fun.

18 | Exercise: Rx for Rejuvenation

EXERCISE IS THE CLOSEST THING TO AN ANTI-AGING PILL NOW available. The time may come when we can stay young effortlessly, but we had better face the fact that staying young and vigorous today requires self-discipline. This self-discipline, if we acquire it, will tend to make up for an unlucky shake of the genetic dice, since we have no control over the inborn strengths and weaknesses of our bodies. We can, however, control what our bodies become, and we can make them surprisingly strong and long lasting.

It is not that old men sit around most of the time, it is that sitting around ages men before their time. Only recently at the USC Gerontology Research Center, Dr. Herbert A. DeVries, Professor of Physiology at the University of Southern California, pointed out that the changes in function of various organs in the human body that we associate with age are very similar to the changes that can be produced in young men simply by keeping them inactive. Dr. DeVries reported that increased physical activity alone without any other therapeutic procedure reversed the aging process and over a period of time restored the characteristics of youth to the bodies of middle-aged men.

Dr. DeVries found that the heart and lungs functioned better and muscle strength and physical working capacity increased with increased physical activity. Apparently, our bodies thrive on use. Even the body's ability to carry oxygen from the air to its tissues, probably the best measure of vigor that we have and obviously one of our most vital life lines, was significantly improved. It is encouraging to note that older men were as able to achieve similar percentages of improvements by exercise as young men. Dr. DeVries's results suggest that a proper regimen of exercise also relieves nervous tension, reduces joint stiffness, lessens the fatigue level resulting from a day's work, lowers the blood pressure, and reduces the amount of fat in the body tissues. It acts like a miracle drug, and it's free for the doing.

The idea that physical activity and exercise might have antiaging and rejuvenating effects was initiated several years ago with the chance observation that prolonged bed rest produced harmful effects. Research into the benefits of exercise began for several apparently unrelated reasons:

1) Hospital personnel noted that patients leaving their beds after prolonged bed rest showed serious signs of weakness and dysfunction that seemed to be unrelated to their previous sickness or injury. The doctors and nurses began wondering if the bed rest itself were harming their patients.

2) Often doctors wished to prescribe physical activity for convalescing patients, but they needed to know how much exercise a bedridden patient could safely tolerate.

3) The armed forces during World War II became interested in methods of speeding up the rehabilitation of disabled soldiers. This focused interest on the possibility that exercise during bed rest might be useful.

Dr. Ancel Keys, a professor at the University of Minnesota, carried out some studies on healthy young men from 20 to 32 years of age. He observed that after only a few weeks of bed rest, these men in the prime of life developed a generalized weakness and marked atrophy of the muscles. Furthermore, they suffered significant loss in blood volume. Their bones showed a loss of calcium. Their muscle protein lost nitrogen, vitamins, phosphorus, total sulphur, sodium, and potassium.

Dr. John E. Dietrick, professor at the Cornell University Medical College in New York, confirmed these findings with his study. He immobilized healthy young adult volunteers in plaster casts of the pelvic girdle and legs for 6 to 8 weeks. His subjects developed the same generalized weakness, muscle atrophy, calcium loss from the bones, and nitrogen loss from the muscles as had the subjects in Dr. Keys's experiment.

Dr. Dietrick's study documents the melting away of the muscles in considerable detail. By measuring the nitrogen excretion in the urine, he observed that the melting away began on the fifth to sixth day of inactivity and reached its peak during the first half of the second week. Total nitrogen losses, which came mainly from the skeletal muscles, ranged from 29.8 to 83.6 grams and averaged 53 grams per person. This corresponds to a loss of about 9 pounds of muscle per person. Anyone who has ever bought a nine pound rump roast knows that this is a good-sized amount of tissue.

Interestingly enough, Dr. Dietrick's immobilized subjects did not lose nine pounds of weight when measured on the scales. Their loss of muscle tissue had been equalized by an approximate average nine pounds gain in fat. The immobilization also resulted in a deterioration of the mechanism essential for adequate blood circulation in the erect position, as indicated by an increased tendency in the subjects to faint while taking their tilt table tests. This study highlights the fact that even in young people the gross deteriorating effects of inactivity are hidden beneath the skin. The outline looks more or less the same, the weight may remain the same, but good tissue has been replaced by fat and after six weeks of bed rest, even a young man is not the man he had been.

The study also found the same increased excretion of phosphorus, and other constituents of the body, such as total sulphur, sodium, and potassium that Dr. Keys had observed. By measuring the calcium excreted both in the urine and in the feces, Dr. Dietrick was able to estimate that maximum damage to the bones was occurring by the fourth to fifth week of immobilization. Total calcium losses from the bones ranged from 9 to 24 grams. These findings have serious implications for the weekend or summer athlete. Since an unexercised bone is less dense and more vulnerable to stress, sudden fits of physical exertion are more likely to result in broken bones than a regular program of exercise.

After the casts had been removed from the subjects' hips and legs and they were again allowed to exercise, nitrogen, calcium, sulfur, phosphorous and potassium again were retained by the body. However, the young men were slow to recover the level of metabolic function they had enjoyed before the experiment began. More than six weeks elapsed before their calcium metabolism was stabilized.

Probably the most important aspect of the overall deterioration that takes place with inactivity is the decline in what is called the maximal oxygen uptake.

Maximal oxygen uptake measures the delivery of oxygen from the air we breathe to all the cells inside the body. Oxygen is absolutely necessary for the burning of the fuels, sugar glucose and triglycerides, which burning provides the required energy for all the processes and functions of the body. The transportation of oxygen from the air to our body tissues requires the combined efforts of the lungs, heart and blood vessels; the maximal oxygen uptake measures the efficiency of this team of organs. In a way, it is the equivalent of what is called the aerobic work power of the body. If a person does hard physical labor or if he runs as fast as he can, he will soon be out of breath and panting heavily. Some persons get out of breath very easily, after the smallest physical effort. Others can exert themselves harder and longer before they reach the point of panting.

The largest amount of oxygen which a person is capable of taking in while engaged in maximal physical exercise is called the maximal oxygen uptake. It is the highest amount of oxygen a person is able to retain in a unit of time. This is by far the best yardstick of a person's vigor. Measurements of maximal oxygen uptake are used to compare physical condition and to provide an indication of the person's capacity to perform strenuous physical work. This measuring device has been used to demonstrate the decline in vigor with age and the similar decline in vigor with physical inactivity.

Possibly one of the most important observations in this area was made only a few years ago by Dr. Carleton B. Chapman, Professor of Medicine, and a group of ten physicians, co-workers at the Department of Medicine, University of Texas, in a joint study of the effects of a 20-day period of inactivity during bed rest in 5 young adults, followed by a 55-day period of physical training. In this study, Dr. Chapman and his co-workers were particularly interested in the problem of oxygen transportation from the air to the cells inside the body because this problem is central to the understanding of the mechanisms through which man adapts to physical activity.

At the end of their study, Dr. Chapman reported that the most striking effect of the 20-day inactivity was a pronounced decrease in maximal oxygen uptake, which averaged 28 percent, or 0.96 liter per minute (from 3.39 to 2.43 liter per minute).

There are various factors which influence the maximal oxygen uptake, such as the volume of the blood moved by one heart stroke, called the stroke volume, or the volume of blood moved by the heart in one minute, called the cardiac output. Dr. Chapman reported that inactivity through bed rest resulted in about 30 percent decrease in stroke volume and about 15 percent decrease in cardiac output.

On the other hand, when the period of inactivity in bed was replaced by physical exercise, maximal oxygen uptake again increased by 33 percent. There was again an increase in cardiac output and in stroke volume, indicating that the 33 percent increase in maximal oxygen uptake due to exercise was due equally to an increase in arterio-venous difference, an increase in cardiac output and an increase in stroke volume.

On the other hand, the replacement of inactivity in bed with physical exercise had no effect on total lung capacity. Even these so-called negative results have their importance in that they show where not to look for undesirable changes due to inactivity. For instance, one would be inclined to expect that the total lung capacity would decline due to inactivity and yet this does not happen.

Compared to maximal oxygen uptake, which in young healthy men is about 3 liters per minute, the minimal oxygen requirement (as it takes place when one is at complete rest) is only about 0.26 to 0.30 liter per minute, which is about 10 times less. This difference between minimal and maximal oxygen uptake is due to the difference between minimal and maximal physical activity.

Any activity of our body requires energy which the tissue cells produce by burning caloric nutrients like carbohydrates and fat. As in all other combustions the burning agent is oxygen, and the problem is to get enough oxygen to all the cells of the organs and tissues of the body. Because the caloric nutrients are usually in sufficient supply, the maximal working capacity of an individual, or his vigor, depends entirely on the amount of oxygen his lungs, heart, and blood vessels can supply to the cells of the body in a given unit of time.

If you do some heavy physical work or exercise, sooner or later you will need more oxygen than your lungs, heart, and blood vessels are able to provide. You will breathe heavily and may need to slow down. Even if you breathe as fast as you can, your cardio-respiratory system is not able to supply more than a certain limited amount of oxygen, which very often is less than necessary for the increased need of your working muscle cells. In fact, you incur an "oxygen debt." After resting, while continuing to breathe heavily, you work off your oxygen debt, which seems to be related only to the intensity of exercise. This is what catching your breath really means.

The maximal oxygen uptake of an individual, his vigor, declines in heart disease, but it also declines during aging. If maximal oxygen uptake drops below the minimal oxygen requirement, the situation becomes incompatible with life and leads to its end. This is what we try to avoid, or to postpone as long as we can, and it can be done by regular physical exercise.

When Dr. S. Robinson investigated maximal oxygen intake, he chose 95 normal, nonathletic males ranging in age from 6 to 91 years. He reported that up to the age of 25 years, the average of the highest recorded oxygen uptake ranged from 47 to 53 milliliters per kilogram body weight per minute, but after that age there was a consistent trend of a continuously decreased aerobic capacity.

Thus, the maximal oxygen uptake for the 40-year old men reached about 41 ml per kilogram body weight per minute, the 50-year old men, 39 ml, the 60-year old men, 35 ml and the 70-year old men, 30 ml/kg/min. Or to put it differently, the 40-year old men can take up only 82% as much oxygen as a twenty-year old; the 50-year old men only 78%, the 60-year old only 70% and the 70-year old only 60% of the younger man's oxygen uptake. For comparison, the minimal oxygen requirement (that is, in recumbent, resting position) per kg body weight and per minute, is about 4 ml, increases to about 5.5 ml in standing, but still resting position, and to about 15 ml while walking at 3 miles per hour.

Similar observations were made by others. Recently, Dr. Kenneth H. Cooper, in his book entitled *The New Aerobics,* presented a table with data for maximal oxygen uptake by men in five categories of physical condition: excellent, good, fair, poor, and very poor. In his table, men under 30 years of age and in good physical condition present maximal oxygen uptake with the range from 42.6 to 51.5 milliliter per kilogram body weight per minute.

Men with maximal oxygen uptake over 51.5 ml/kg/min are rated to be in excellent physical condition, whereas values below 42.6 categorize men in fair (or poor) physical condition. In general, maximal oxygen uptake which is under 25 ml/kg/min is rated to be very poor at any age, and values between 25 to 30 ml/kg/min still fall mostly into the poor category. Dr. Cooper points out that the value of maximal oxygen uptake marks man's aerobic capacity, and that this maximal oxygen uptake or man's aerobic capacity is his fitness index.

In Dr. Cooper's table, after the age of 30 there is a continuous decrease in aerobic capacity, that is in maximal oxygen uptake. Thus, men in good physical condition but between 30 to 39 years of age reach maximal oxygen uptake of only 39.2 - 48.0 ml/kg/min, men between 40 to 49 reach only 35.5 - 45 ml/kg/min, and men over 50 years of age reach only 33.8 - 43 ml/kg/min. In other words, the maximal oxygen uptake decreases on the average by about 8 to 9 percent for each ten years of life, whether estimated from data by Dr. Robinson or from the table by Dr. Cooper. This decline with age in man's maximal oxygen uptake, his aerobic capacity or his fitness index, must be kept in mind when developing an exercise program for persons over 40.

If you still have some doubts about the antiaging effects of physical exercise, look at the above results reported by Dr. Robinson or the data from Dr. Cooper, and try to figure out how many decades of life it would take from one's life expectancy, if one's maximal oxygen uptake were reduced by about 28 percent through complete inactivity, which was the average reduction in maximal oxygen uptake observed by Dr. Chapman in 5 young men after several weeks of inactivity during bed rest. Or try to figure out how many decades would be added to one's life expectancy by a 33 percent increase in maximal oxygen uptake, which was its average increase observed by Dr. Chapman in the same five young men when the period of inactivity in bed was replaced by physical exercise. And now also ask yourself these two questions: what is the degree of your daily physical activity, and how many years of life could you possibly add to your own life expectancy by including some more physical exercise in your daily routine?

The overall decline with age in man's vigor, that is, in his maximal oxygen uptake, is the sum of age declines in a number of factors affecting at various levels the transport of oxygen from the air we breathe to the tissue cells of the body. There is a gradual decline with age in the maximal breathing capacity of the lungs. There is an age decline in the diffusing capacity of the lung, by which is meant the volume of oxygen which is capable of moving from the lung alveoli to the pulmonary capillary blood.

Once the oxygen has moved to the pulmonary capillary blood, it has to be taken up by hemoglobin of red blood cells. The amount of oxygen which can be taken up by hemoglobin (or hemoglobin saturation) decreases with the age of the individual. Other factors which contribute to the age decline in maximal oxygen uptake include the age decline in the "stroke volume" which is the amount of blood moved by one stroke of the heart, and the age decline in the "cardiac output" which is the amount of blood moved by the heart in one minute. There is also a significant slowing down with age in the speed of circulation of blood as measured by the mean transit time of dyes injected for the estimation of cardiac output.

Only recently we have had confirmation that the same type of premature aging in the heart's ability to function occurs among sedentary persons or those who have been immobilized for prolonged periods. In fact, exercise has a rejuvenating effect on heart function.

Certain types of exercise, regularly performed, increase the formation of the blood vessels supplying the heart muscle. This increased vascularization of the heart was studied in experimental animals made to perform regular amounts of rhythmic, dynamic exercise (such as running in a training wheel).

Although the major heart arteries did not increase in size, the number of smaller arteries and blood vessels increased. This increased collateral circulation of the heart is an important emergency back-up system. It has been observed both clinically and experimentally that persons and animals who have the advantage of an increased collateral circulation are more likely to survive an infarction, an obstruction of a major artery caused by a blood clot. During an infarction the heart muscle, deprived of its continual delivery of blood, is literally starved of oxygen and often dies for lack of it. If the collateral circulation in the heart is sufficiently developed, it is able to deliver enough blood to the heart muscle to keep it from dying until the heart's normal blood supply is restored.

Coronary heart disease represents the greatest threat to life of the American male. Sudden dysfunction of the two coronary arteries supplying the heart is responsible for more than one-half million deaths in the United States each year. Coronary heart disease is now of epidemic proportions in the United States; it is far and away the number one threat to the lives of adults and older adults in most of the highly developed countries of the world. Many possible explanations have been offered for the causes of coronary heart disease, among which the most frequently mentioned are: too much rich food and too little physical activity.

According to some enthusiasts of exercise, increased physical activity promises to be a sovereign preventive of heart disease, heart attacks, and cardiovascular disorders. Even skeptics agree that regular physical exercise of more than token intensity and duration may be beneficial to the heart and blood vessels.

The businessman is usually sedentary, but in addition he often tends to be overweight, to smoke heavily, to eat foods rich in fats, and to live in a state of tension. It seems reasonable to advise him to change his ways of life and to include more physical exercise in his daily routine, but many researchers consider that there is remarkably little solid evidence that such steps will actually contribute to the "health" of his cardiovascular system. However, now an increasing number of reports suggest a measurable improvement of the heart condition in patients with coronary heart disease following a period of physical training.

Another important reason for doing more exercise is that regular physical exercise helps efficiently to prevent the development of high blood pressure or hypertension, and also helps to reduce the already existing hypertension.

Several investigators have reported that regular physical exercise, especially if combined with an improvement in environmental influence (such as a change to a rural or mountainous environment), resulted in a sustained lowering of the blood pressure in city dwellers. These investigators pointed out that the sooner a person begins to take positive steps to lower his blood pressure, the better. Those with juvenile, labile high blood pressure, as it is called in its early stages, were more successful in lowering it by the application of these methods than those with advanced, fixed high blood pressure.

In a detailed study Dr. Jiří A. Král, a Professor at the Charles University in Prague, reported a fall of the systolic blood pressure and, to a lesser extent, of the diastolic blood pressure within 15 to 20 minutes after physical exercise. Dr. Král repeatedly observed that the fall in blood pressure is usually more marked in those suffering from high blood pressure than it is in those with normal blood pressure. He concluded that exercise plays a valuable role in the prevention and retardation of hypertension.

Researchers theorize that inactivity creates a disturbance in the adaptation of blood vessels to subsequent physical activity. In other words, the less you exercise, the less you are capable of physical activity. No matter what a person's age, exercise should be a part of his daily life.

An 80-year old man, if he wants to live to be 90, needs to exercise. A 90-year old woman, if she wants to live to 100, had better keep exercising. Of course, past 30 we need to avoid putting too much stress on the body. Simple walking and puttering around the house is the best exercise in our eighties and nineties.

Before the rejuvenating effects of physical activity had been recognized, there seemed to be no reason beyond personal inclination to encourage people over 70 years of age to move around. And many, fearing a fall, discouraged older people from walking more than absolutely necessary. Today gerontologists emphasize that it is never too late to be benefited by exercise.

It is never too early to begin, either. A baby who is allowed to move around in his crib is healthier than one who is kept immobile. An active child is healthier than a sedentary one. But once we pass our physical prime, it takes us longer to recover from inactivity. Unquestionably, the older we get, the more important is this miracle medicine, exercise, the rejuvenator.

19 | What Types of Exercise are Best in Middle Age?

PHYSICAL EXERCISES CAN BE DIVIDED INTO TWO MAJOR CATegories, passive and active, with various specific types in each category. Passive exercises include massage, which may be used to stretch tight muscle tissue and to relieve spasm, or to relax. Active exercises may be used to build up endurance, to develop muscle strength, to increase range of motion, to overcome lack of coordination, or to develop and increase control of fine motions. If it is desirable or necessary, some types of active exercise can be made more active by offering resistance to the movement or by doing exercise against resistance, which helps to attain specific results more rapidly.

There are basically two types of active exercises, efforts and muscular contractions. One type consists of rhythmic, dynamic, or steady-state exercises; typical examples of this are walking, running, jogging, and bicycling, which are often done for long periods of time. The other type consists of isometric, static, or sustained kinds of exercise; typical examples of this are lifting, holding, pushing, and moving heavy weight. These are usually done for short periods of time.

Physical activity and exercises aimed at achieving or sustaining physical fitness are different from those used in preparation for participating in sports. Furthermore, each sport category has a different kind of preparatory exercise. For instance, exercises to prepare for skiing are different from exercises for boxing, or for long-distance running.

There are also therapeutic exercises, used for treatment of a variety of conditions: to maintain muscle strength, to improve circulation, or to increase metabolism through physical activity. In order to prevent deconditioning or to achieve reconditioning, all the muscles of the body capable of activity and not affected by disease or injury should be kept active through exercise. Such exercises are basic needs when people are ill, when they have sustained an injury, and also when they grow older. Especially in the more advanced years of life, regular daily activity is vital.

While a great variety of exercises may be included in a list of those used to promote physical fitness, the ones used should be chosen with careful consideration of the person's age, because each person's vigor, or aerobic work power, or capacity to perform a given exercise with a certain intensity, gradually declines as the years pile up. This again is particularly important in the later years of life, when resistance to stress reaches very low levels and the person's vigor becomes very low. Thus, the same intensity of exercise, which was well tolerated and was not stressful several years ago, would become stressful and even harmful, and has to be reduced as the years advance.

When a middle-aged or older person finally comes to the conclusion that he should do regular, daily physical exercise, he may have a difficult problem to solve: what kind of exercise to choose for his future exercise program? This problem is not an easy one. For the same amount of time and effort some types of exercise give less results than others, some actually do more harm than good, and some may even become downright dangerous to the unsuspecting middle-aged person.

Among the kinds of exercise which are of little help and can become dangerous are the isometric static exercises. Unfortunately, there are a number of books extolling the merits of the isometric exercises, pointing out that a person can do these exercises at any time of the day whenever he can spare a few minutes, even while sitting at his desk in the office, or lying down on the sofa, or in bed.

The isometric, sitting-at-your-desk or lying-down exercises promise superlative conditioning without moving a muscle. They are what may be called "internal stress" exercises. In this type of exercise the person's muscles are made to push against one another or against some opposing force like pushing against the wall. They result in muscle contractions and leave the person overstressed, but the heart, lungs, and blood vessels remain unimproved—precisely the organs middle-aged persons most need to improve.

Isometric exercises should be recommended only for young invalids or for persons whose movements are necessarily limited. In such situations, isometric exercises may help to prevent muscles from becoming atrophied. But persons who can get up and move around would do much better to avoid isometric exercises entirely. It is regrettable that books on isometric exercises do not tell anything about the possible dangers of the isometric efforts; helping to develop high blood pressure in middle-aged and older persons, and even provoking a heart attack. Another kind of isometric, sustained or static exercise is weight-lifting, which also gives very fine results in building muscles, but again leaves the person's heart, lungs, and blood vessels unimproved.

Exercises which are best suited and highly recommendable for middle-aged and older persons all belong to the dynamic, rhythmic, or steady-state category. Exercises of this type give best results.

Books on exercise are usually slanted in favor of one or another exercise, ignoring the rest. For example, two books written by a colonel in the U.S. Air Force Medical Corps, with an exercise plan built around the distance a person can run in 12 minutes, claim that this plan is the most effective physical fitness plan ever offered. There is also a book produced by a team of doctors, physical education specialists and artists, which offers an 11-minute-a-day plan for men consisting of 5 basic exercises, and a 12-minute-a-day plan for women consisting of 10 basic exercises, with the aim of achieving and maintaining desirable levels of physical fitness. However, all that these books, and others, prove is that there are various possible approaches to physical fitness, and not just one unique approach which should be rigidly followed.

There are, of course, many other kinds of exercise, like gymnastics or calisthenics, or sports, like tennis and golf; none of these, however, are among the best suited exercises for middle-aged or older persons. They are useful activities and beneficial in some respects and they should be enjoyed to the fullest. The famous heart surgeon, Dr. Paul Dudley White, has said that "golf is a grand way to ruin a good walk." As for calisthenics, the original meaning of the word, "strength for beauty," suggests that it is not exercise designed to promote health. Surprising as it may be to some persons, even tennis does not qualify among the best-suited exercises for middle-aged persons, especially if they have never played tennis before. It may overstress the heart before the oxygen intake systems have had the opportunity to improve.

The everyday activity of most adults, no matter whether they are sedentary or physically active, consists of a mixture of both rhythmic (dynamic, or steady-state) and static (isometric, or sustained) activity, where rhythmic muscular activity usually prevails, and static efforts come rather infrequently and often unexpectedly. Each of these two types of muscular activity puts a different kind of demand on the individual's heart, lungs, and blood vessels. This demand is particularly stressful and even dangerous to the individual's life in the case of strong, static muscular efforts of short duration.

In order to find out what makes the static muscular efforts so dangerous, Dr. A. Lind in Edinburgh, Scotland, investigated for a number of years the circulatory adjustments to static muscular activity. He demonstrated the existence of a powerful cardiovascular reflex which takes place in response to strong static muscular contractions of short duration. This reflex originates in the contracted muscles themselves and causes an unexpectedly high rise of blood pressure and an acceleration of heartbeats.

Dr. Lind found that at low tensions, below about 15 percent of the maximal voluntary muscle contractions, the increase in blood pressure, heart rate, and cardiac output is only small, and does not keep rising but reaches a steady state during the contraction; after the contraction ends, the blood pressure, heart rate, and cardiac output all return quickly to normal values. In contrast, at tensions above 15 percent of the maximal voluntary muscle contraction, the blood pressure and all the other measurements showed no steady state during the contractions but continued to increase until fatigue intervened.

Holding a 40 pound weight (equivalent to a moderately heavy suitcase) produced in each of four persons (who served as guinea pigs) significant increase in blood pressure and a heart rate increase of 24 beats per minute after only 2 minutes; and the response was still rising when the weight was released. Still heavier muscular exertions may lead to even higher increases in blood pressure and to higher increases in total heart load, which may lead to dramatic consequences such as a heart attack or a brain stroke.

Instances are not uncommon where previously fit adults have fallen into an acute heart failure (that is, a failure of the left heart ventricle) after a maximal static exertion, such as pulling a boat to a buoy against a fast tide, or giving a push to a car on a muddy, isolated, country road. In static muscular efforts the greatest part of the oxygen uptake and of the estimated cardiac output occurs *after* exercise, whereas in rhythmic muscular activity oxygen uptake and cardiac output are much more evenly distributed.

The increase in the work load to the heart from rhythmic exercise like walking, jogging, or running, is much more gradual and is due mainly to an increase in blood flow, with only little elevation of blood pressure. In contrast to rhythmic exercise, the static muscular efforts result in only a small increase of blood flow, but in a great increase of blood pressure and an increase in heart rate which present a very heavy load to the heart.

This difference is particularly important because the increase in blood flow caused by rhythmic exercise is tolerated by the heart muscle far better than the increase in blood pressure caused by static efforts. In this regard, even a moderate isometric effort by a localized group of muscles can cause an abrupt increase of blood pressure and an increase of heart load.

This sudden load to the heart, and the increase in blood pressure, is much higher in sedentary individuals who are not accustomed to physical exercise than it is in those who do regular physical activity or exercise. Such an unexpected, sudden load to the heart can become even more dangerous to a sedentary person whose heart and arterial walls are weak or injured.

Many persons who were physically very active in their teens, but who took a sedentary job and failed to exercise regularly, may still feel a great inner pride in their past athletic achievements. Although middle-aged, they may still consider themselves to be as strong as they used to be 20 or even 30 years ago. When an unexpected emergency or need for sudden muscular effort arises, such as pulling a boat to a buoy, giving a push to a car, moving heavy furniture, or lifting and carrying a heavy suitcase, they rise to the challenge with all the determination of their inner pride, not realizing how dangerous such a determination may be.

Sudden muscular efforts of maximal strength and short duration performed by stocky, well-nourished but physically unexercised, middle-aged and older individuals, are particularly dangerous.

Older adults who are not accustomed to regular physical exercise and who have no intention to exercise regularly will usually tend to avoid rhythmic efforts, like walking fast uphill, because they know from past experience that a few minutes later they will be panting uncomfortably and will be having to slow down anyhow. But with static efforts the danger is hidden, because they do not make one breathe uncomfortably. Static efforts occur suddenly and unexpectedly in everyday life. Because even the older persons can do them without panting, they are not aware that they may be flirting with a dangerous overload to their heart and a possible heart attack.

An episode from Sir Winston Churchill's life may be evoked, as described in Lord Moran's book, *The Struggle for Survival: 1940–65* (Constable, London, 1966) which illustrates the problem. The episode happened in Washington on December 27, 1941, when Lord Moran called on his eminent patient. "I am glad you have come," Sir Winston Churchill began. He was in bed, looking worried, and continued, "It was hot last night and I got up to open the window. It was very stiff. I had to use considerable force, and I noticed all at once that I was short of breath. I had a dull pain over my heart. It went down my left arm. It didn't last very long but it has never happened before. What was it? Is my heart all right? I thought of sending for you but it passed off . . ." On hearing this, Lord Moran had no doubt that whether the electrocardiogram showed evidence of coronary thrombosis or not, Sir Winston Churchill's symptoms were those of coronary insufficiency.

Sir Winston was lucky he did not suffer an incapacitating heart attack. But hundreds of thousands of middle-aged, healthy Americans each year are less lucky—they die from a heart attack, which they have unwittingly provoked by a sudden outburst of static (isometric, or sustained) muscular effort of short duration. They could easily have avoided the attack had they learned to resist the temptation of such sudden efforts.

20 How to Exercise Your Heart

THE HEART WHICH BEGINS BEATING BEFORE YOUR BIRTH AND does not stop until death is the archetype of the endurance muscle. It is not surprising, then, that the best way to improve its function is with exercises calculated to increase physical endurance. Any rhythmic or dynamic exercise which emphasizes an even, constant, low level of physical exertion will do.

However, in order to fully achieve their beneficial effects on the heart, the endurance exercise must be performed for at least six minutes to allow the heart, lungs and blood vessels (that is, the entire cardiorespiratory system) to adjust to this new level of energy expenditure. The time span to be measured begins after the exerciser starts huffing and puffing a little with exertion. Then at least six more minutes of huffing and puffing is needed.

Whether you walk or jog, swim or bicycle, is unimportant. But at least six minutes of panting is crucial to the heart in order to achieve the beneficial effect. This type of self-powered motion has produced measurable improvements in the heart condition in sedentary persons or in patients with coronary heart disease.

One of the best features of this type of exercise is that it can easily be adapted to the needs and abilities of almost anyone. An 80-year-old can walk around the block a few times. Young men can perform such feats as long distance running, in which they sustain relatively high levels of physical activity for hours at a time, or short distance running, where they achieve peak levels of thrust and exertion for a few minutes or seconds. In between are numerous gradations of difficulty, energy output, and time consumption that can be had with little or no financial outlay. The rhythmic dynamic exercises fit easily into anyone's life style and pocketbook. And all of them are beneficial.

Unfortunately, however, even they can be harmful if done in too large spurts. Regularity is better than single or rare efforts. Each of us has his own limit. The most vigorous young athlete has a point beyond which exercise will stress his body and heart. Too many exercise programs fail to note these stresses. As a result people have unknowingly done themselves injury.

How much exercise is too much still has not been answered fully. Even heart specialists do not agree about this point, although they all do agree that some regular exercise is vital to good heart function.

Dr. Jeremiah Stamler, Assistant Professor of Medicine at the Northwestern University Medical School, Chicago, in his book *Your Heart Has Nine Lives,* quotes the famous cardiologist, Dr. Paul Dudley White, as saying that "Hard work never hurt a healthy human heart." Dr. Stamler adds that this heart specialist religiously follows his own advice and takes vigorous daily exercise.

Dr. Stamler also noted that "any established myth dies stubbornly" and he gives example of a recent health fair where the public could answer questions about the heart as true or false. A majority said it was true that vigorous activity hurts the heart. "Many people are aghast that a middle-aged man should exercise and voice a protest," he reports. It is his belief that middle-aged men should exercise vigorously.

Such statements may be quite misleading to some lay persons. How many middle-aged men in our affluent, sedentary society have a healthy heart which can take vigorous exercise? And what about those middle-aged men who do *not* have a healthy heart, or who only think they have a healthy heart? How less vigorously should they exercise? How much exercise would be too much for them?

On the other hand, it is well known that men whose occupations involve a great amount of physical work, even hard physical work, proceed in their efforts on the job at a much more leisurely pace; they almost never hasten their efforts to the point where they would be out of breath. Obviously, it is impractical to advise people in sedentary jobs to put in 40 hours a week walking or lifting or carrying loads at a level of energy expenditure below the point of producing an oxygen debt. A compromise has to be found but at what level of physical exertion?

It is relatively easy to propose new exercise programs, even strenuous exercise programs, or methods on how to achieve physical fitness, but a careful, objective evaluation of such programs through research is much more difficult and time consuming. If you are one of the millions of middle-aged, sedentary people who never did much rhythmic dynamic physical activity try to avoid strenuous exercise programs as much as you can.

Do not allow anyone to talk you into running as far as you can go. If you undergo maximum exercise testing be sure it is recommended by a heart specialist and not by just any exercise enthusiast who is inexperienced in heart disease problems. Especially, avoid crash exercise programs. Like crash diet programs, such exercise regimes are usually ineffective. A crash exercise program or the exercise testing of individuals who are not accustomed to regular physical exercise may cause a heart attack. Also, vigorous, regular physical activity does not necessarily prevent coronary heart disease, *especially if it is not accompanied by moderation in food intake and by regular eating habits.*

Many heart specialists are much more cautious in advocating vigorous physical exercise for middle-aged persons. In his book *Your Heart and How to Live with It,* Dr. Lawrence E. Lamb writes that "physical activity if used properly improves the functional capacity of the heart and circulation," and he immediately adds that the important phrase is "if used properly." Then he continues, "similar to many lifesaving medicines, exercise can be a killer if used carelessly. Some heart patients should exercise only with extreme cautiousness."

However, if correctly used, exercise may help to prevent a heart attack or improve your chances of survival if you have one. The stakes are too high for you to be an uninformed exercise enthusiast. Despite current enthusiasm, it is well to remember that exercise can kill you.

Dr. L. E. Lamb illustrates this statement with the case on one of his former patients, a physiologist, who had been a college athlete record holder and had continued to maintain high levels of physical activity, carefully controlling his body weight. By the time he reached 50 years of age he was still exercising vigorously, running as much as six miles a day. His endurance runs at a relatively fast jog were interspersed with short bursts of top speed. During one morning exercise period, his running partner noticed that the patient was no longer with him. The running partner turned back to see what had happened to him and found him lying at the side of the road. He had apparently suffered a heart attack, collapsed, and died instantly.

An examination of his heart showed extensive atherosclerosis of all major coronary arteries, even though the heart muscle presented the features of an athletic heart. The muscle appeared strong and the ventricular cavities were of adequate dimensions. As anticipated, careful examination of the heart muscle showed an acutely damaged area caused by infarction which brought about his death.

This person, who regularly engaged in a high level of vigorous physical exercise and maintained the capacity of an endurance athlete, had extensive coronary heart disease and died during exercise from an acute heart attack. There have been many other instances where accidents leading to the death of young individuals have provided an opportunity to note the presence of an extensive atherosclerosis of coronary heart arteries in young fit individuals who did not suspect their heart arteries were atherosclerotic.

21 | How to Start an Exercise Program in Middle Age

AN AVERAGE, SEDENTARY, MIDDLE-AGED PERSON, WHO WANTS to start his regular daily exercise program, encounters a number of difficulties which may appear small or unimportant to exercise enthusiasts, but which nevertheless are large and important to him.

If he does not start with a suitable kind of exercise and with the right approach, specifically tailored to his needs and possibilities, he may become discouraged and simply give up.

He is going to need to know how much time to spend on his exercise program. As we have seen, in order to fully achieve beneficial effects, these exercises must be performed for at least six minutes in order for the training effect to set in.

Training effect is the name for the collective changes induced by physical exercise of longer duration in the various organs and systems of the body: the capacity of the body to utilize oxygen for improving the strength and pumping efficiency of the heart, strengthening the respiratory muscles, reducing the resistance to air flow in the lungs, improving the blood circulation in blood vessels, toning up muscles throughout the body, and increasing the total amount of blood circulating through the body.

It may satisfy the ego, but walking six or ten flights of stairs for a little extra exercise doesn't condition the circulatory system, simply because the time interval is too short. Climbing the flights of stairs may leave you breathless because you've created a large oxygen debt during your climb. But the climb didn't last long enough for the training effect to set in. That is why the exercise should be continued for at least six minutes or more, to allow the heart, lungs, and blood vessels to adjust to an increased demand for energy.

In a nutshell, here is the basic scheme of physical exercise for adult, middle-aged and older persons: perform endurance exercise for at least six minutes and possibly more, at an intensity low enough to be well tolerated by the person, but high enough to increase pulse rate and make you somewhat short of breath. If they are valid, all the various exercise programs for adult, middle-aged and older persons are nothing else but variations of this basic general approach to endurance exercises.

A good rule of thumb is to exercise until somewhat short of breath. Both shortness of breath and an increased pulse rate are necessary.

The beneficial effect of endurance exercises on the heart, lungs, and blood vessels starts not from the moment the person begins to exercise, but from the moment he begins to be somewhat short of breath and his pulse rate speeds up. Persons who have only a very limited time to do their exercise—only 10 or 12 minutes in the morning, and desire to draw the greatest amount of benefit from their time for exercise, can profitably use the so-called warming-up exercises in order to become somewhat short of breath a little faster.

Basically, any kind of indoor exercise, such as push-ups, sit-ups, leg lifting or leg raising, knee raising, toe touching, arm circling, bending and others—which achieve shortness of breath faster (than the dynamic, rhythmic, or steady-state exercises performed at a usual pace)—can be used as warming-up exercises.

One of the main purposes of the warming-up exercises is to shorten the time necessary to achieve a certain level of shortness of breath, which would take longer time to attain by dynamic exercises alone. Once a desired level of shortness of breath is attained by the warming-up exercises, it should then be maintained by dynamic, rhythmic, exercises, such as brisk walking, jogging or running for at least six minutes or possibly more.

CHOOSING THE EXERCISE PROGRAM

If a person has never exercised before, he should start his exercise program first by walking at a brisk pace for about 10 minutes. If he has an opportunity to exercise outdoors, the brisk walking program can be extended gradually by jogging 50 steps, then walking 5 minutes and jogging another 50 steps, then walking another 5 minutes. Working up slowly from a moderate stress to more strenuous effort is important not only to accustom the heart to the new demands, but also to let tendons and muscles adjust themselves to the new activity.

Another approach to dynamic exercise, particularly if the person must do his exercise indoors, is to run in place. The first few days he should run at a very slow, comfortable pace and only about one hundred steps, counting one step each time the right foot hits the floor. After a few days he may increase to 200, 300, or more hundred steps. The purpose of rhythmic exercise is not to run as fast as you can or as long as you can, but to do it regularly, seven days a week for at least 15 minutes. You can do this form of exercise (running in place) wherever you are, in your home, or on travels, whether it rains, snows, or shines.

People should be discouraged from starting directly on a strenuous running program (without walking and jogging first) unless they have been exercising regularly. Do not expect to accomplish miracles in a single exercise period. Give your heart muscle a chance to develop capacity to ensure that you are not overworking them. The aim is to gradually step up heart action and sustain it at an even, rhythmic pace, sending a rich blood flow to the muscles, to raise the exertion level to a steady state of oxygen intake and to keep it there.

The rule to follow in order to avoid being killed by exercise is this: increase the amount of exercise you take above your daily level only gradually. Many books and pamphlets on exercise contain recommendations that are worse than useless—they are dangerous. *Do not allow anyone to talk you into running as far as you can go.* If you undergo maximum exercise testing, be sure it is recommended by a heart specialist and not by any exercise enthusiast who is inexperienced in heart disease problems and who may be trying to sell you a membership in a franchised gym.

The capacity to perform physical exercise varies widely from one person to another, even among persons of similar age and physical appearance. That's why each person's physical exercise program should be tailored to his own tolerance for exercise, and be based on the results of his personal testing, rather than on what kind of physical exercise others may be doing, or on what exercise he *thinks* he should be able to perform. In testing your tolerance for physical exercise, it is always advisable to start with the least strenuous tests first. Then, after a good rest before the next test, proceed to the more strenuous ones.

The *Walk Test* is possibly the easiest. It's aim is to determine how many minutes (up to ten) a person can walk at a brisk pace without undue difficulty or discomfort on a level surface. In this regards, there are walking programs of various intensity, depending on whether the person can walk for less than five minutes, whether he can walk for more than five minutes but less than ten, or whether he can walk for more than ten minutes.

The walking programs consist of walking at a brisk pace for 3, 5, or 8 minutes (or for a shorter time if the person becomes uncomfortably tired), followed by walking slowly for 3 minutes and then again walking briskly for 3, 5, or 8 minutes (or until he becomes uncomfortably tired). The next week the person can increase the pace as soon as he can walk 3, 5, or 8 minutes without fatigue or discomfort.

The *Walk-Jog Test* is for persons who can walk without difficulty at a brisk pace for more than ten minutes. In the walk-jog test the person alternately walks 50 steps (his left foot strikes ground 25 times) and jogs 50 steps for a total of 10 minutes. Then again, there are walking-jogging programs of various intensity, depending on whether the person can walk-jog for less than five minutes, or for more than five minutes but less than ten, or whether he can walk-jog for more than ten minutes.

There can be all kinds of variations of the walking-jogging programs (tailored to the person's tolerance for exercise), one of which consists of walking for one minute (100 yards) followed by jogging for 10 or 20 seconds (25 or 50 yards) which can be repeated 10 to 15 times or more. The following weeks the person can jog for 40 seconds or 1 minute (100 or 150 yards) between walks for 1 minute (100 yards), and the next weeks he can gradually increase the jogging periods to 2, 4, 6, 8, or 10 minutes of jogging between 1 or 2 minutes of walking, as his tolerance for exercise increases.

While jogging, keep the back straight and don't look down at your feet. It is best to land on the heel of the foot and rock forward. If this proves difficult, try a more flat-footed style. Jogging only on the balls of the feet, as in sprinting, may produce leg soreness. Keep steps short, letting the foot strike the ground beneath the knee. If for any reason you become unusually tired or uncomfortable, slow down, walk, or stop.

12-Minute Test. This test was introduced by Dr. Kenneth H. Cooper, Lieutenant Colonel, U.S. Air Force Medical Corps. In this test you walk and run as far as you comfortably can in 12 minutes. The emphasis is on "comfortably." If you get short of breath, slow down awhile until you get your breath back. The idea is to cover the greatest distance you can in those 12 minutes. Dr. Cooper has found by measurements on the treadmill that the distance covered in these 12 minutes correlates very accurately with the measurements of oxygen consumption, or what he calls the aerobic capacity, which is practically equivalent to the maximal oxygen uptake.

Dr. Cooper is an enthusiast of running exercises. He calls these exercises "aerobics" (because they demand oxygen without creating a large oxygen debt) as opposed to "anaerobics" (which create a large oxygen debt by demanding so much oxygen in so short a time that the heart and lungs can't possibly supply it, and the only way to repay it is to stop and recover). The main objective of an aerobic exercise program is to increase the maximal amount of oxygen that the body can process within a given time. Dr. Cooper calls it the "aerobic capacity."

The aerobic capacity (or the maximal oxygen uptake) depends upon a powerful heart, efficient lungs, and good blood vessels. Because the aerobic capacity reflects the conditions of these vital organs, it is the best index of the person's vigor, and of his overall physical fitness. A 12-minute run determines one's fitness category.

Thus, people who in a 12-minute run are able to cover:

(1) less than 1.0 mile have less than 25 milliliters/kg/minute of max. oxygen uptake;
(2) between 1.0 to 1.24 miles, have between 25.0 to 33.7 ml/kg/min. of max. oxygen uptake;
(3) between 1.25 to 1.49 miles, have between 33.8 to 42.5 ml/kg/min. of max. oxygen uptake;
(4) between 1.50 to 1.74 miles, have between 42.6 to 51.5 ml/kg/min. of max. oxygen uptake;
(5) more than 1.75 miles, have more than 51.6 ml/kg/min. of max. oxygen uptake.

The size or numeric value of the maximal oxygen uptake is a very important factor in your life. In the previous chapters it is shown how much the maximal oxygen uptake declines with age. It is pointed out that if the maximal oxygen uptake declines too much (that is, if it falls below the person's minimal oxygen requirements), the person simply dies from lack of oxygen. Also, observations by Dr. Chapman have been highlighted, because they show that maximal oxygen uptake declines as much as 29 percent during physical inactivity of longer duration, such as bed rest of several weeks, and that maximal oxygen uptake increases as much as 33 percent through physical exercise after the person gets up.

All these observations help to illustrate the tremendous life-saving and life-prolonging potential of endurance exercises, which result in such increases of the maximal oxygen uptake. At some time in your life, your maximal oxygen uptake will approach the minimal oxygen requirements, and eventually it will drop below these requirements. This is the definition of death from old age, and it can be postponed if you've been exercising regularly.

An increase in maximal oxygen uptake of about 33 percent (and even larger increases are possible through regular, daily endurance exercises) may finally result in prolonging life by several decades. Truly, regular daily endurance exercises can make the difference between whether a person dies around the age of 75, let us say, or whether he lives up to 100 years of age and over.

For a long time the maximal oxygen uptake test has been too expensive for the average middle-aged person to take casually, because expensive equipment has been necessary to measure it. Now, based on Dr. Cooper's observations, any middle-aged person can easily estimate his maximal oxygen uptake, simply by measuring the distance in miles which he can cover by running as fast as he can for 12 minutes. Also, he can estimate how much his maximal oxygen uptake has increased after a period of physical exercise, simply by measuring the increase in the distance in miles which he can cover in 12 minutes.

Measure the time and the distance accurately. If you have no other way to measure the distance you have covered in those 12 minutes, drive the same stretch of road in your car and read the distance covered on the odometer. This inconvenience is alleviated to some extent in the 1.5 mile test, which Dr. Cooper developed subsequently to the 12-minute test. In the 1.5 mile test, all the distance you need to measure accurately is the 1.5 mile distance. Besides this, however, you need a stop watch to measure exactly the time you need to cover the 1.5 mile distance.

1.5 Mile Test. Dr. Cooper developed new standards for physical fitness based on the time required to run 1.5 miles, when he was asked to evaluate the physical fitness of more than 15,000 members of the Air Force. In this test, a person between 40-49 years old may fall into the following categories of fitness, depending on how many minutes he needs to run a 1.5 mile distance:

(1) Very poor, if he needs more than 18-1/2 minutes;
(2) Poor, if he needs 16-1/2 to 18-1/2 minutes;
(3) Fair, if he needs 14 to 16-1/2 minutes;
(4) Good, if he needs 11-1/2 to 14 minutes;
(5) Excellent, if he needs less than 11-1/2 minutes.

For persons over 50 years of age, add half a minute to the running time in each category of fitness. A person over 50 years of age would fall into the fair category if he runs the 1.5 mile distance in 14-1/2 to 17 minutes.

For persons between 30 to 39 years old, Dr. Cooper withdraws *one* minute from the running time in each category of fitness. Thus, a person between 30 to 39 years old falls into the fair category if he runs the 1.5 mile distance in 13 to 15-1/2 minutes.

For persons under 30 years of age, withdraw 2 minutes from the running time in each category of fitness. Thus, a person under 30 years of age falls in the fair category if he runs 1.5 mile distance in 12 to 14-1/2 minutes.

The 1.5 mile test has certain advantages compared to the 12-minute test, but the tables of the 1.5 mile test have a certain shortcoming in their present form in that they do not indicate the values of the corresponding maximal oxygen uptake, as they are indicated in the 12-minute test values.

22 | Review and Evaluation of Various Exercise Programs

EXPERIENCE SHOWS THAT ADULT, MIDDLE-AGED, AND OLDER people, can recapture a high degree of physical fitness even after years of sedentary life or inactivity. But they need to do it gradually and they need an exercise program that begins at their present level of physical fitness. The program should be tailored to the person's tolerance for exercise and should be based on the results of his personal exercise testing.

There are a great number of various exercise programs, from the least strenuous (walking) to the most strenuous (running exercise programs) with the walking-jogging exercise programs in between. There are also exercise programs consisting of a number of basic exercises such as push-ups, sit-ups, toe touching, arm circling, leg lifting, and bending, in addition to running in place.

Most people can achieve maximum benefits from their physical exercise simply by learning to put up with a certain amount of shortness of breath, and by learning to tolerate a certain amount of discomfort while doing their exercise.

This is very similar to the fact that a predominant majority of people can reduce to a desirable weight and maintain this weight simply by learning to give up the feeling of satiety after meals. It has been shown that each person can find for himself how much of this feeling he has to give up, without any need for guidance from the detailed tables and charts in the books on nutrition and dieting and without actually preparing a single dish according to the recipes from such books.

Similarly, those who decide to do their regular, daily physical exercise can draw maximal benefit from it simply by learning to achieve a certain amount of shortness of breath. If such persons choose to achieve a relatively small amount of shortness of breath, then the benefits from their endurance exercises will accumulate in a slow way.

Shortness of breath increases with the intensity of endurance exercises. In doing one's exercise, the aim is to learn to achieve the right amount of shortness of breath and then maintain it. Those who choose to achieve more shortness of breath and put up with a little more discomfort while performing the exercise, will reach a higher level of physical fitness than those who choose to do less.

If you have the opportunity to do your physical exercise outdoors you are fortunate. However, a great majority of city dwellers have to do their exercise indoors; except for walking, which anybody can easily arrange to do outdoors.

It is the consensus of the experts on physical exercise that about 12 minutes of exercise daily is the rock-bottom minimum to achieve fairly good results. Be sure that six minutes of that time you are puffing and panting. If it takes you 12 minutes to begin to puff then continue exercising for six more minutes.

BEST TIMES FOR EXERCISE

Possibly the best time for indoor exercise is in the morning, soon after rising and before breakfast. Naturally you need to provide time for your exercise and plan for it. Try going to bed 15 or 30 minutes earlier than you usually do, and getting up in the morning 15 or 30 minutes earlier, with the intention of using this time for exercise. Another good time for indoor exercise is in the evening, a short time before you go to bed, provided you are not excessively tired from the day's activities. Some general advice: avoid physical exercise when you are tired, under stress, ill, or within one or two hours after meals (meals are another form of stress).

These 12 minutes and more of daily indoor exercise can be used most profitably if they consist of a few minutes of warming-up exercises at the beginning, such as push-ups, sit-ups, toe touching, bending and others, followed by at least 6-8 minutes or more of jogging or running in place. The few minutes of warming-up exercises help to achieve a certain shortness of breath, which should then be maintained during the remaining time of exercise. They also help to provide some exercise to the groups of muscles which otherwise would receive very little activity.

While running or vigorously exercising, stop for a moment and measure the rate of your heart beat (pulse rate) for 15 seconds. Multiply this by four. It should be over 100 beats per minute during good, vigorous exercise. It usually is around 120 to 130 beats per minute, but it should not go more than 145 to 150 beats per minute, the exercise limit a middle-aged person should try not to exceed.

In experiments with persons between ages 15 and 30 doing maximal physical work (running on the treadmill), Dr. Robinson observed that the maximal pulse rate reached values around 190 - 200 beats per minute, while the average maximal values for older persons were consistently lower. Thus, 40-year old persons reached 183 beats per minute, 55-year old persons reached 168 and 70-year old persons only 160 as the highest heart beat rate values, while running on the treadmill.

Also, in doing the same, though lighter, standard exercise, older persons show higher increases in pulse rate and in blood pressure and, at the end of the exercise, they require a longer time for recovery than do young adults. Middle-aged and older persons should be increasingly careful not to approach too closely maximal heart rate values while they are doing their physical exercise, and they should not try to push too hard toward maximal efforts. Persons with a weak heart, heart condition, or heart disease, should be very careful in this regard and they should certainly consult with their physician before they start an exercise program.

Here are three basic exercise programs, from the least strenuous, a walking exercise program, through a more strenuous, a walking-jogging exercise program, to the most strenuous, jogging exercise program. These exercise programs are very flexible. If a person is slow to get in shape, he can stay on the same schedule as long as he needs to. Walking and jogging exercise programs always let the person exercise within his own capability or endurance for exercise.

WALKING EXERCISE PROGRAM

This program is probably one of the easiest exercise programs. It is intended for middle-aged and older persons who can walk at a brisk pace no more than 5 or 10 minutes and even less. Persons who have performed the walk test and can walk at a brisk pace without undue difficulty or discomfort on a level surface less than 5 minutes, are advised during the first week of this program to walk at a brisk pace for 5 minutes or for a shorter time, if they become uncomfortably tired. After a 5 minute walk at a brisk pace, they are advised to walk slowly or to rest for 3 minutes and then again walk briskly for 5 minutes or until they become uncomfortably tired.

During the second week, increase the pace as soon as they can walk 5 minutes without fatigue or discomfort. During the third week, walk at a brisk pace for 8 minutes, or for a shorter time if they become uncomfortable, then walk slowly or rest for 3 minutes, and again walk briskly for 8 minutes or until uncomfortable. During the fourth week, increase the pace as soon as they can walk 8 minutes without fatigue or discomfort. Persons who have completed the fourth week of walking exercise program, can begin the first week of the walking-jogging exercise program.

WALKING-JOGGING EXERCISE PROGRAM

This program is a little bit more strenuous than the simple walking exercise program. It is intended for middle-aged and older persons who have performed the walk test and can walk at a brisk pace for 10 minutes or more. During the first week of this program, walk at a brisk pace for 10 minutes, or for a shorter time if you become uncomfortably tired. After a 10-minute walk at a brisk pace, walk slowly or rest for 3 minutes. After a slow 3-minute walk or rest, walk briskly for 10 minutes or until you become uncomfortable.

During the second week of the walking-jogging program, walk at a brisk pace for 15 minutes, or for a shorter time if you become uncomfortable, then walk slowly for 3 minutes or rest. Real jogging is carefully and gradually introduced only on the third week of this program, or when you can walk at a brisk pace for 15 minutes without becoming uncomfortably tired. By combining walking and jogging (that is, slow, comfortable running), nearly anyone can begin to jog safely and comfortably.

At the beginning of the third week of the walking-jogging exercise program, jog for only 10 seconds (which corresponds to about 25 yards) then walk for one minute (which corresponds to about 100 yards), followed by jogging for 10 seconds again and walking for one minute. Then repeat the entire sequence (10 seconds jogging with one minute walking) ten or fifteen times. The fourth week, jog for 20 seconds (which corresponds to about 50 yards), then walk for one minute, and repeat the entire sequence (20 seconds jogging with one minute walking) 10 or 15 times. Persons who have successfully completed the fourth week of the walking-jogging exercise program, can begin the first week of the jogging exercise program.

In any of these exercise programs, whether they are walking, walking-jogging, or jogging programs, the amount of exercise and exertion can be gradually increased to suit each person's individual pace or endurance capability. You do not and should not accidentally overexert yourself. By gradually increasing the pace and the amount of running, any person can eventually train himself to a high level of physical fitness and endurance. Also remember, these exercise programs which take only a few weeks should become part of a long-range health program. If you intend to exercise only for a few weeks or a few months and then stop, the benefits will be only very short-lived.

JOGGING EXERCISE PROGRAM

This program is more strenuous than the walking-jogging exercise program. It is intended for middle-aged and older persons who have successfully performed the walk-jog test for a total of 10 minutes. During the first week of this program, jog for 40 seconds (which corresponds to about 100 yards) and then walk for one minute (which corresponds again to about 100 yards) and repeat the entire sequence (40 seconds jogging with one minute walking) 9 or 10 times.

During the second week of this program, increase the jogging period from 40 seconds to one minute (which corresponds to about 150 yards), then walk for one minute, and then repeat the entire sequence (one minute jogging and one minute walking) 8 times. During the third week of this program, increase the jogging period from one minute to two minutes (which corresponds to about 300 yards), then walk for one minute and repeat the entire sequence (two minutes jogging with one minute walking) 6 times.

During the fourth week of this program, increase the jogging period from two minutes to four minutes (which corresponds to about 600 yards) then again walk for one minute, and repeat the entire sequence 4 times. During the fifth week, jog for 6 minutes (900 yards), then walk for one minute and repeat the entire sequence (6 minutes jogging with one minute walking) 3 times.

During the sixth week, jog for 8 minutes (or about 1200 yards), and increase the walk from one minute to 2 minutes (or 200 yards), Repeat the entire sequence 2 times. During the seventh week, jog for 10 minutes (or 1500 yards), then walk for 2 minutes and repeat the entire sequence 2 times. During the eighth week, jog for 12 minutes (or 1700 yards), then walk for 2 minutes and repeat the entire sequence (12 minutes jogging and 2 minutes walking) 2 times.

The aim of this jogging exercise program is to increase gradually the jogging periods from less than one minute to over 10 minutes. However, these jogging (or walking) exercise programs should not be considered as something rigid which must be followed exactly at any price. These exercise programs should be understood only as approximate guidelines which provide each person with some idea of how to start his exercise program and how to continue it.

Any physical exercise program can be modified and adjusted to each person's individual needs and endurance. For instance, if the transition from a one-minute jogging period (during the second week of the above exercise program) to a two-minute jogging period (during the third week of this program) is too abrupt, modify and adjust the jogging periods to your individual endurance capacity.

This advice applies to any part of the exercise programs: whenever a schedule seems to be particularly difficult, do *not* advance to the next one. Rather, drop back a week and stay there until you are ready to move up again, or stay with the present schedule until you can complete it comfortably. The theme of jogging exercises is moderation. Joggers never run at maximum effort. Jogging is never competitive.

Jogging is a gradual, moderate exercise that permits you to tone up heart, lungs, and blood vessels while exercising within your own endurance capability. Moderation in jogging underlines the principle of gradually increasing stress. The principle of gradually increasing stress prevents overexertion and the danger of an unaccustomed burden on the heart, lungs, and other parts of the body.

The advice to avoid overexertion or unaccustomed burdens

applies to all exercise programs for middle-aged persons, not just to jogging exercise programs. This advice, however, does not mean that middle-aged and older persons should avoid putting a certain amount of effort into the physical exercises they are performing. On the contrary, each person would be well advised to put as much effort into the exercise as he can with comfort.

In this connection, it is worthwhile to mention that some exercise experts advise regular physical exercise each day for at least 12 to 15 minutes or more, but others advise an alternating program of harder exercise one day (such as a 30 minute workout) and taking it easy the next day. This advice of alternating exercise is based on the observation that those persons who alternate the program of hard exercise one day and rest the next day, progress toward an improved state of physical fitness more rapidly and painlessly, than those persons who exercise daily for 15 minutes, even though both perform about an equal amount of exercise. It appears also that chronic fatigue states are avoided more easily by such alternating exercise programs. Into the alternating exercise programs also would fall the advice to jog for about 30 minutes three days a week, instead of jogging each day for 15 minutes.

When you jog outdoors, try to jog on soft surfaces; the natural cushion of grass, leaves, or pine needles absorbs shock and lessens discomfort. When you can not find a soft surface for jogging, wear properly cushioned shoes. When you develop a cold or any minor illness, do not jog or exercise. When the condition clears, begin jogging or exercise at a lesser level of fitness.

Besides the walking exercise programs, walking-jogging, and jogging exercise programs, there also are the running exercise programs which have their importance mainly for younger persons, and which for middle-aged and older persons very often would be too strenuous. The main difference between jogging and running is that jogging is done at a leisurely pace and is more suited for older people.

Walking and jogging exercise programs usually do without the so-called warming-up exercises. Most exercise programs which do not include warming-up exercises usually start at a very low level of physical fitness (as found in sedentary, middle-aged persons) and aim to increase this level substantially; whereas exercise programs which include warming-up exercises usually start at a relatively higher level of physical fitness and aim more at improving and maintaining this level.

Warming-up exercises consist of a group of exercises each of which has a certain starting position, such as:

(1) standing erect, with feet together (knee-raising, neck swivel, shoulder roll);
(2) standing erect, with feet about 12 - 16 inches apart (such as toe touching, arm circling, lateral bending, arm flinging);
(3) lying on back (such as, sit-ups, chest raising, or leg raising);
(4) lying face down (knee push-ups, another type of chest and leg raising).

Besides these most frequently used warming-up exercises, there are many other variations with less common names, such as big swim, boxer or kickette, kickback and others, and each person should feel free to use his own imagination in selecting his preferred set of warming-up exercises with which he would start his daily exercise program.

For most people it is relatively easy to make it a habit to do their daily physical exercise and to keep this habit for years, hopefully for the rest of their lives. Many people find walking exercise programs not very difficult and continue them even into very old age. Naturally, regular daily physical exercise gives best results if also accompanied by regular eating habits, well-balanced nutrition, and the avoidance of various, health-endangering, disease-inducing and life-shortening errors of everyday life.

PART IV:
Relaxation

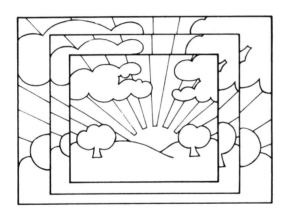

23 | Man-Made Stresses and Chronic Diseases

MANY PHYSICIANS AND HEART SPECIALISTS HAVE REPEATEDLY observed that man-made stresses and emotional pressures are an important factor or cause in the development of chronic diseases, particularly of atherosclerosis, coronary heart disease, and hypertension, which in turn predispose or lead to heart attacks and cerebrovascular accidents (more commonly known as strokes), just to mention the most important ones. In this regard, such man-made stresses present difficulties when one tries to describe "exactly" what to avoid in order to prevent development of chronic diseases.

Not only are there different types of stresses and emotional pressures which vary from situation to situation, but there are also lower and higher levels of such stresses or pressures and, of course, differences among individuals in their resistance to these stresses and pressures (or in their susceptibility to develop one or another chronic disease). Further low-level stress or emotion usually doesn't do any harm, but is often helpful. Consequently, in the avoidance of man-made stresses and emotional pressures, each person will have to use his own judgment based on the general information in the following chapters.

Stress and anxiety have always been an integral part of life but many urban, industrialized societies are now laden with special, man-made, socioeconomic and situational stresses and anxieties which are unique; they have not been previously witnessed in any age of history.

Not every stress or anxiety, however, is a villain to be avoided at any price in an effort to prevent development of chronic diseases. It has been well recognized that there is a great difference between a low-level stress or anxiety, which can induce improved performance and a high-level stress or anxiety, which can sometimes have the most devasting effects and lead to unimaginable consequences. A low-level stress of anxiety tells us that danger is present, that something is wrong and the healthy person, who is not overwhelmed by such stress or anxiety, becomes more alert and more vigilant toward the menacing elements. He responds by searching for what is wrong and by attempting to rectify it, or by an increased ability to cope with the imminent danger.

A high-level stress or anxiety is something quite different. With increasing stress and anxiety, the apprehension turns to a loss of intellectual control, to terror and panic; the individual is paralyzed and unable to cope with the upsetting situation, or to resolve it, and he may literally disintegrate. Chronic stress or anxiety at any level weighs heavily on the individual and what's more, is an important factor contributing to the development of chronic diseases.

When does a low-level stress cease to be harmless, or even helpful, and when does it begin to be harmful or conducive to the development of chronic disease? The dividing line can be based on various criteria. A simple and reasonably good one is the ability to recover and to feel refreshed after a usual amount of night's sleep and rest. If you feel tired or depressed in the morning after what should have been a good night's sleep, you probably had more stress the previous day than you should have taken. Again, there are great individual differences; some persons are more susceptible and get tired more easily than others, and once they have overstrained themselves, they recover more slowly than others so that what is too stressful for some, is acceptable for others.

It is not always easy to pinpoint the most important factors or causes that contribute to the development of a given chronic disease. In situational stresses, in anxieties and emotions, the suspected factors or causes of disease are difficult to measure, for no blood tests exist comparable, for example, to serum cholesterol determinations. Nevertheless, a number of heart specialist-investigators have pointed out that in many relatively young persons who suffer from coronary heart disease, the predominating environmental factors in their life are—various uncertainties of modern life, or dilemmas between what the individual would like to do and what circumstances compelled him to do, or suppressed feelings resulting from crushing situational stresses. It is generally considered that in such circumstances persons with a vulnerable cardiovascular system may develop coronary heart disease more easily than others, including a heart attack if the situational stresses are not relieved.

In one study, the social, economic, and interpersonal relationships of individuals suffering from coronary heart disease revealed in about 60 percent of cases the presence of life situations and dramas in which they were irretrievably caught in a crossfire of emotional stresses, or in a "nutcracker" squeeze between opposing forces, entrapped without respite—at home and/or at work. Some were trapped between the need of economic security and the inability to assert their position, others suffered from financial or business failures, status degradation, belittlement, estrangement, or had feelings of guilt, pangs of conscience or grief. In another study about half the persons who suffered from heart attack (myocardial infarction), showed gradually mounting tension of emotional or situational origin for months and years prior to the onset of heart attack. Most of them had a high sense of responsibility and considered their status in the community of great importance. The type of emotional and/or situational impact, however, varied from one individual to another.

If you consider that the situation in which you find yourself is comparable with or similar to any of the above, the best advice you can follow is to do the essential of what has to be done (never mind the details, or—delegate authority over details to somebody else) without overstressing yourself and, above all, do not worry about the outcome. If you are religiously inclined, adopt the attitude of "doing your best and leaving your worries to God, and the outcome in His hands." If you prefer a philosophical approach, a sort of stoic attitude would be the answer. Both will help to protect you from heart attack and may even save your life.

Recently a number of studies have shown that relatively young victims of coronary heart disease very frequently exhibit a personality structure characterized by an intense and sustained drive to succeed, including ambition, competitiveness, aggressiveness and a profound sense of urgency. They seem to be deeply apprehensive about their careers and, in order to convince themselves of their continued success, they constantly have to find new achievements in other competitive areas, as if haunted by the feeling that one day their talent, or their luck, may simply run out. Their behavior is characterized by a profound inclination and eagerness to compete, by persistent desire for recognition and advancement, by habitual tendency to accelerate the rate of execution of their functions, and by extraordinary mental and physical alertness.

Such persons seem to have to succeed primarily to satisfy some basic neurotic needs. They appear to be excessively driven to achieve self-selected goals; they willingly commit themselves to get things done, but are always unable to overcome the inflexible factor of time itself and are constantly struggling against the competing and obstructing influences of other persons and things, as if to assure themselves over and over again that their luck has not deserted them. Men and women with this personality pattern, immersed as they habitually appear to be in these stresses, often are seemingly content with their multiple professional and social commitments, despite the tendency of these commitments to produce deadlines and to enhance the sense of urgency.

This personality pattern results from the interplay of certain inborn, inherited (or endogenous) factors, together with certain environmental, acquired (or exogenous) factors. It exists particularly in the milieu that characterizes our urban, industrialized civilization, and it is probably increasingly prevalent in the American population, as an accompaniment of new socioeconomic stresses, unique to our modern, mechanized, fast-moving society.

A large study on the incidence of coronary heart disease among competitive-aggressive persons, was made by a group of investigators in California. Men and women with an excessive competitive drive, aggressiveness, and sense of urgency were compared with men and women similar in age and in habits such as diet, smoking, exercise, etc. The second group was different only because of the relative absence of drive, ambition, sense of urgency, desire to compete, and involvement in deadlines.

It was found in this study that men of sustained drive and competitiveness exhibited a several times greater incidence of coronary heart disease and of heart attacks; they had significantly higher serum cholesterol levels (253 mg per 100 ml, on the average), more rapid blood clotting time, and five times greater incidence of arcus senilis (the white line which appears around the cornea of the eye with advancing years) than men who were less prone to compete on a "high-stress" level. These more relaxed competitors also had lower serum cholesterol levels.

In another study, which involved over 1600 individuals of the excessive personality and over 1600 individuals of more reasoned and pragmatic personality, it was observed that the number of deaths due to coronary heart disease and the number of fatal heart attacks was approximately six times higher among individuals of the first type than it was among individuals of the less driven type. Further, it has been specified that men of the excessive aggressive pattern frequently exhibit various typical mannerisms, gestures, and muscular phenomena, such as forceful rapid speech, often explosively uneven and emphatic, accompanied by sudden gestures such as first clenching, desk pounding, and taut facial grimaces. Their locomotion and gestures are rapid, reflecting their enhanced drive, competitive striving, chronic restlessness, impatience, and sense of urgency. In ordinary conversation they have a consistent tendency to emphasize certain individual words in sentences, to hasten the pace of conversation by attempting to either finish the sentences of the other person, or to hasten his rate of speaking by uttering rapidly such phrases as "Yes, yes," or "I see, I see," even before the other person has finished his sentences.

If you identify with or belong to the personality that is driving hard for achievement and if you have deadlines to meet remember Murphy's law, "If anything can go wrong, it will," and start working for your deadline 20 to 40 percent earlier than you would have usually started. Make allowances for lack of alertness in other people; relax and stop thinking that your whole career depends on whether or not you achieve your most recent goals. Your coronary heart arteries are much less strong than your will power to succeed; if they break, none of your past or present achievements will be worth the damage done.

24 | Emotional Pressures and the Development of High Blood Pressure

ONE OF THE MOST FREQUENT CONSEQUENCES OF SITUATIONAL and emotional tensions and pressures is the heavy contribution to the development of high blood pressure or hypertension. How often have you heard or read various admonitions like, "Keep your blood pressure down"? You may have even been wondering: how can a person keep his blood pressure down? And because you have not found any easy or satisfactory answers to this question, you may have asked: is it really so dangerous to have high blood pressure?

Studies indicate that high blood pressure is as dangerous as high cholesterol level in the risk of developing heart attack. In the United States two-thirds of the new cases of coronary heart disease in middle-aged persons develop among those who have either an elevated serum cholesterol level or an elevated blood pressure or both. People with high blood pressure die twice as frequently of heart attack as do people with normal blood pressure. Even what is called "small" elevations of blood pressure increase the dangers of having a heart attack, especially if accompanied by other diseases like atherosclerosis, diabetes, overweightedness, or coronary heart disease.

How frequently does high blood pressure occur? The answer to this question depends on what is really "normal" blood pressure in middle-aged persons, as compared to what is only "considered" by specialists to be a normal blood pressure for this age. There are tremendous differences in interpretation.

The controversy is based on the fact that about 5 percent of men and less than 5 percent of women in the United States maintain the same low blood pressure throughout life, but in the remaining 95 percent of the population blood pressure gradually rises with age. It is one of the most obvious findings in almost all modern, industrialized societies—not just in the United States—that blood pressure on the average is lowest in young individuals and gradually rises with age. In recent years some investigators have drawn increasing attention to the fact that about 5 percent of the population in the United States (and higher percentages in other populations) maintain low blood pressure throughout life.

For over half a century it has been considered that the age increase in blood pressure is perfectly normal, because the rise in blood pressure with age has been observed with what is considered to be "normal" healthy adults of various ages. But is this age increase in blood pressure really normal? If it is normal, as some want us to believe, why then in some people does it stay low throughout life? There are a number of investigators who consider that no satisfactory explanation for the age rise in blood pressure has yet been given. After all, why does blood pressure rise with age?

Should the blood pressure stay low throughout life as it does in about 5 percent of men in the United States? Is the age increase in blood pressure (95 percent of people in our population) truly normal? The answer to this last question is so important because, if it is considered or decided that blood pressure should stay low throughout life (as it does in about 5 percent of men), it would also mean that 95 percent of the population in the United States develops high blood pressure as they grow older.

It may appear almost absurd to interpret these observations to say that about 95 percent of middle-aged and older persons in the United States have high blood pressure. And yet, there are other very important observations in favor of this interpretation. In various populations at a primitive stage of development, no rise in blood pressure takes place. In other words, low blood pressure throughout life in primitive populations is present in 100 percent or all its members.

Certain populations isolated in Polynesia and South America, living without any contact with the outside world, have unusually low blood pressure throughout life, and in three nomadic pastoral tribes in northern Kenya, Africa, no rise in blood pressure with increasing age has been recorded. Of course, these populations do not live under the tensions of modern industrialized societies, which may explain entirely the low blood pressure throughout life. It is of interest to note also that the males in all three tribal groups in Kenya are fairly lean individuals and show no increase in body weight with age; indeed, after 50 years of age there is a notable decline in the mean body weight in all three tribes.

From these observations it is evident that in a number of the less-developed countries around the world, there are communities, ethnic groups, or populations whose way of life, based on a primitive or peasant economic system, have not yet been affected by the inroads of modern civilization and which, consequently, show no age rise in blood pressure. What indications or conclusions should we draw from these observations? No matter what we decide, one thing is certain: low blood pressure throughout life is truly and perfectly normal.

It is very frightening to say that 95 percent of the population in the United States develop high blood pressure in the later years of life. It appears to many investigators of blood pressure that there is something wrong with this kind of conclusion or interpretation, and they apply various devices to make it less frightening or unbearable. The most frequent device along these lines is to declare arbitrarily that a "moderate" rise with age in blood pressure is perfectly normal and that only blood pressures which fall above this moderate rise with age would be abnormal, that is too high.

There are many difficulties with this approach, the first being that there is disagreement among investigators about how much rise with age in blood pressure is still considered normal, or beyond what level such a rise becomes "abnormal". If you place the level (for "normal" rise with age in blood pressure) too low, then the percentage of people with high blood pressure in the United States becomes frighteningly high, but if you put this level higher (by which decision the percentage of people with high blood pressure becomes immediately lower), you face the difficulty of explaining the disconcerting fact that blood pressure should rise so much with age. Why should it rise at all, in the United States, if it does not rise with age in primitive populations?

As a result of these two opposing forces, it is now considered that a reasonable estimate of the percentage of people with high blood pressure in the United States would be around 20 percent, with some estimates going as high as 35 percent (especially in the older sectors of the population), and other estimates as low as 5 percent (especially in the younger sectors of the population). These estimates seem to be considered much less frightening than the original 95 percent, but still comfortably frightening.

The conclusion is that practically nobody is immune to developing high blood pressure. Practically anybody can (and most probably will) develop high blood pressure in the later years of life—unless he is careful to do something about it. In addition, there are indications that great differences exist among individuals in their susceptibility to high blood pressure. For instance, it has been observed that high blood pressure is more frequent among men of broad body build and also more frequent among people who are overweight, but there is more to it than that because there are differences in susceptibility to high blood pressure even among persons of the same body build or of the same degree of overweight.

Some persons are more susceptible than others to high blood pressure or hypertension in the later years of life, even though they all may have very much the same body build or the same amount of overweight or lack of overweight. These differences in susceptibility to high blood pressure have been studied by many investigators. The conclusion is that susceptibility to high blood pressure is inborn, genetic, or inherited; this means, for instance, that if your parents suffered from high blood pressure, chances are that you may have inherited from them a susceptibility to develop high blood pressure in the later years of life.

What would happen if one parent suffered from high blood pressure and the other had normal blood pressure? In such cases, their offspring may or may not inherit the susceptibility to high blood pressure, or may have inherited a "moderate" susceptibility. But whether or not a person develops high blood pressure in the later years of life depends not only on inherited susceptibility, but also on the presence or absence of various environmental factors, such as the amount of emotional tensions or pressures he encounters in life. Now there is no doubt that high blood pressure is the result of the cumulative effect of both environmental and hereditary factors.

There have been attempts to separate hereditary hypertension (sometimes called essential or primary hypertension) from acquired hypertension (sometimes called secondary hypertension). Investigators agree that hereditary (essential, primary) hypertension is rarely manifest in the first two decades of life and develops only infrequently after the fifth decade.

Practically all persons have normal low blood pressure at least up to the age of about 20. Then, sometime between ages 20 to 50 (in most cases between 35 and 45 years) some persons develop high blood pressure.

From various studies on hypertension we now know that not every hereditary (essential, primary) hypertension becomes manifest. In other words, not every person who inherits the susceptibility to high blood pressure really develops it. The important question is to find out why. It has been observed that the causes which contribute to the development of inborn or hereditary hypertension in susceptible persons are the same causes which contribute to the development of the acquired (secondary) hypertension in persons who are not susceptible to hypertension.

The inborn, or hereditary factors determine a stronger or weaker inclination, predisposition, or susceptibility to the development of high blood pressure in the later years of life. For this reason, even those persons who have inherited a stronger susceptibility to hypertension will not develop high blood pressure, if their life is not tense and stressful and if they make specific efforts to be calm and take it easy. For the same reason, even those persons who have inherited a weak susceptibility to high blood pressure may develop high blood pressure if their life is filled with very strong emotional tensions and no efforts are made to avoid them.

The growing disparity between the rising social or professional expectations of middle-aged persons and their declining capacities produces tensions and pressures which are experienced by at least 95 percent of middle-aged persons in the United States (even if they do not admit or are unaware that such tensions or pressures exist), and this is the most important factor in the development of high blood pressure.

This important conclusion is further supported by observations made on a group of young adults in the following interesting experiments. Their blood pressure was measured when they were relaxed, calm, and unsuspecting of the bad news awaiting them. Then some really bad news affecting each of them personally (like a bad loss on the stock market) was announced to each individually, and then the blood pressure was measured again shortly afterward and at half-hour intervals for several hours. In all of them without exception, the bad news was followed by a large increase in blood pressure and the high blood pressure stayed high for several hours.

There were great differences among the individuals in the above experiment. Some persons showed an excessively high increase of blood pressure, and their blood pressure took a much longer time to drop to lower levels, whereas others took the bad news more calmly. But there was not one single person whose blood pressure did not go high after he received the bad news that affected him personally. How much bad news does an average American receive each month, week, or every day? Is it any wonder that he develops high blood pressure as he grows older?

In the light of this, it is worthwhile to mention the effects of sodium and kitchen salt on the development of high blood pressure. Kitchen salt has been under suspicion for a long time as one of the agents in the development and aggravation of high blood pressure. It is not always easy to provide a clear-cut proof as to whether or not such a substance as kitchen salt is involved in the development of something as elusive as high blood pressure. To provide such proof, researchers sometimes have to collect every indication available, such as the observation that in societies where the average salt intake was found to be high, more people in the adult and older adult population have higher blood pressure than in societies where the average salt intake is low.

Then, there is the so-called rice-fruit diet of Dr. Walter Kempner, who showed conclusively that high blood pressure can be significantly reduced, often to normal levels, with his rice and fruit diet. It consists of rice, sugar, fruit, fruit juices, vitamins, and iron (this diet contains 2000 calories as follows: about 15-25 gm of protein, 4-6 gm of fat, 460-470 gm of carbohydrate, 0.25-0.4 gm of sodium and 0.1-0.15 gm of chloride). The amount of fruit juices given daily is usually 700-1000 ml.

Although Kempner believed that the blood pressure reduction was due to factors in his diet, such as rice protein, it has been convincingly demonstrated by others that the low sodium level in the rice-fruit diet is chiefly responsible for lowering blood pressure. The average American diet contains at least 4 gm of sodium; by omitting salty foods and added salt at the table and in cooking, this amount can be reduced to about 1 gm of sodium per day. There is no doubt that rigid sodium restriction to 0.5 gm of sodium per day (or even better, to 0.2 gm) will reduce the blood pressure in a considerable proportion of persons suffering from high blood pressure.

There is no data, however, to predict how many persons with high blood pressure, chosen from the population at large, would respond to a daily sodium restriction of 1 gm by blood pressure lowering, or how great the lowering would be. Nor can it be predicted how often a low sodium diet would prevent high blood pressure in susceptible persons. Nevertheless, experiments with animals have shown that high blood pressure can be induced by the continued intake with food of large or excessive amounts of kitchen salt.

And when excessive salt is fed to pregnant animals, their descendants will also manifest high blood pressure when they attain adulthood. However, in both human and animal studies it was observed repeatedly that some persons, can for years, take in with their food large amounts of salt without developing high blood pressure, whereas others appear to be singularly sensitive to the addition or restriction of kitchen salt to their food. This again points to individual differences among persons in their susceptibility to high blood pressure.

What can a person do in order to avoid developing high blood pressure in the later years of life? Probably the most logical advice is to concentrate one's efforts on reducing the growing disparity between the rising expectations for and the declining capacities of middle-aged persons. This advice can basically be approached from two angles, and it would be preferable to approach it from both angles simultaneously. One angle concerns social and professional activities, for there are many ways to tone down one's activities without hurting one's social or professional standing. Clearly, advice along these lines would be entirely outside the aim or scope of this book.

The other angle concerns the declining capacities of the middle-aged person. The central idea or theme of this book is the many possible ways to protect one's declining capacities for as long a time as possible, while trying to do as much as possible.

To see the complexity of the above task, compare the human body to an automobile, and compare the above task to the assignment of driving a car very carefully without an accident for as long a time as possible. Suppose that, on your thirty-fifth or fortieth birthday, you receive a shining, brand-new car and are told that this will be your last and only car for the rest of your life. Once the car (your body) is no longer in driving condition, you will have no choice but to die.

At the age of 35 or 40, your body is still in a shining, almost brand-new condition. But this is your last and only body for the rest of your life. Once your body is no longer in driving condition, you will have no other choice but to die. If you really had to drive an old beaten-up Ford for the rest of your life, what would you try to avoid? Overheating the motor? Punching the tires? Breaking the axle? There may be thousands of different things which you might be anxious to avoid, depending on how experienced and careful a driver you are. And this is exactly how it is with your body for the rest of your life. If you overheat the motor, or have a comparable accident, something breaks or gets clogged inside your body or your heart, you get a heart attack and you die.

Does the human body contain some device which indicates that the tensions and pressures of everyday life are approaching a dangerous level? Not exactly, but there nevertheless exists something very close to it.

This something is the rate of your heartbeat or pulse rate. As already mentioned, the rate of your heartbeat in the morning after a good night's rest should be around 62 beats per minute, while you are still in bed and below 70 when you get up. If worries did not allow you to fall asleep, the rate of your heartbeat in the morning may be way above 62 or even above 70 beats per minute, even if you stayed in bed for 8 or 9 hours, because sleepless hours in bed do not count as sleep.

If you start in the morning with a heartbeat around 80 per minute or even more, if the usual daily activities make it rise to 90 beats or above and if then some stressful situation with tension or pressures unexpectedly develops during the day and makes the heart rate reach 100 beats per minute (and in some persons even more) it is a real danger sign which *absolutely should not be neglected.* What can a person do when tensions and pressures develop during the day, when bad news arrives and when the rate of the heartbeat reaches 95 to 100 beats per minute or even more?

Particularly dangerous among the various tensions and pressures is the feeling of repressed aggression; that is, anger at somebody or something without the possibility of doing something about it. Repressed aggression results in high blood pressure comparable to the tension created by the steam from water heated in a closed container. If the steam (or hostility) is not allowed to escape, or if hostility is suppressed and not allowed to express itself, then the pressure inside the container, or the blood pressure of the person, may rise excessively and even produce an explosion, either a brain stroke or a heart attack. However, ways to cope with suppressed aggression fall less within the realm of this book and much more within that of a psychiatrist.

It may appear that one cannot do much more to avoid the development of high blood pressure besides avoiding kitchen salt. But this is only the surface; in the chapters on nutrition it has been pointed out that the avoidance of certain nutritional errors of everyday life can help to prevent the development of high blood pressure. In the chapters on physical exercise the type of physical exercise which is particularly helpful in preventing the development of high blood pressure has been pointed out, and in the present chapters on overstrain and lack of relaxation the need for relaxation is being indicated.

25 | Preventive Maintenance or Don't Let Your Molehills Develop into Mountains

EVERYONE IS UNIQUE WITH SPECIAL TALENTS AND WEAKNESSES. Even identical twins are not truly identical; all they share is the same hereditary pattern. Their differences begin before birth, when their position in the womb and their order of birth begin a lifetime of individuality.

Parents who have had more than one child become aware how early differences in physical and psychological make-up show themselves. While still in the crib some characteristics of the individual begin to emerge. One baby will be active and wakeful, another more placid and drowsy. One baby "never cries," another frets just for the fun of exercising his lungs. One baby seems never to be sick; another catches and keeps every cold around the neighborhood.

We cannot change the characteristics that are part of our hereditary pattern. There are no postconception miracles capable of changing the texture of our skin, the pattern of our retinas, or the "programmed" interaction of our organs and organ systems.

However, much can be done to alter the manner in which these patterns affect our health and lives. Ultimately, the responsibility is ours. It is our life. Only we can perform the necessary actions. Nevertheless outside sources of help are available. The purpose of this book is to show how you can help yourself and how you can make use of medical knowledge to make your body as strong and long lasting as possible.

This book is not intended to turn carefree you into a hypochondriac. It is designed to *keep* you carefree, enjoying vigorous health to an age extending past 100. Preventive maintenance does not require constant worrying about health. A little attention focused on the proper problems at the right time will do the job. Confidence and enthusiasm are more conducive to health than worry; a little preventive maintenance is worth months or years of worry brought on by chronic disease.

Our bodies are built for use. They are even designed to absorb a certain amount of punishment or stress and recover completely from its effects. The amount of stress each individual can tolerate without harm varies from individual to individual. And no matter how much stress an individual can take when he is young, as he grows older he can tolerate less of it without permanent damage to himself. Nor can an individual's tolerance to stress be expressed simply. Some people have strong hearts and arteries but are susceptible to diseases like diabetes or high blood pressure, or perhaps their livers or kidneys are less resistant and likely to break down. It is important to learn from a yearly checkup with your doctor what parts of your body are in good condition and what parts are the most susceptible to injury.

Fortunately for us, most of the time all the metabolic and biosynthetic processes of the body function smoothly and efficiently. However, a variety of factors—called stressful agents—can interfere with the functioning of these processes. Infection is one such stressful agent. If you have a cold, your upper respiratory tract is affected. In addition to the sniffling and sneezing and the generally awful feeling, you are probably having difficulty in breathing. One stress often leads to another. A cold that starts in the nose may cause subsequent reactions in the bronchial tubes or the lungs. During an infection, the heart has to work harder. A normal healthy human body is "designed" to accept such stresses with ease.

However, not all of our organs and organ systems are of the same strength. Under stress, one organ may be thrown into disorder before the others. Some people have a combination of two or more susceptibilities which then determine their "susceptibility profile." Depending on differences in susceptibility profiles, some people may be more susceptible to obesity without developing diabetes, other people may be lean and yet susceptible to diabetes, and still others may be susceptible to both obesity and diabetes. Some people are susceptible to coronary heart disease without being susceptible to obesity or diabetes, other people can be susceptible to both obesity and coronary heart disease without being susceptible to diabetes, and still others can be lean and yet susceptible to both diabetes and coronary heart disease.

Some people may be susceptible to hypertension (high blood pressure) in middle age, without being susceptible to obesity, diabetes, atherosclerosis, or coronary heart disease. Other people may have susceptibility to hypertension, combined with the susceptibility to obesity, diabetes, atherosclerosis, or coronary heart disease, or a combination of several. When two or several susceptibilities are combined in one person, they may aggravate each other. Susceptibility to diabetes is aggravated by the susceptibility to obesity, and vice versa. Susceptibility to coronary heart disease is aggravated by the susceptibility to obesity, diabetes, or hypertension, or their combinations, and vice versa.

It is very encouraging to know that even a person who has been genetically afflicted by susceptibilities to all the major chronic diseases, and there are such cases, may have as good a chance as anybody else to live a healthy life past 100 years of age. He need only know his susceptibilities and the specific errors of everyday life that may aggravate them and put his efforts and self-discipline into avoiding them for the rest of his life.

One of the most important points of this book is that even the less fortunately endowed, those whose bodies are less resistant to stressful agents and more susceptible to a variety of health problems, can live long vigorous lives with the use of proper strategies. These strategies will not take a lot of time and attention. In fact, by preventing sickness and weakness, they will free your time and attention to enrich your life.

Strategy only works when it is followed. The plan is not enough, it is the doing that counts.

MOST IMPORTANT PREVENTIVE MEASURES

The first strategy of preventive maintenance is to learn the limits of your physical endurance. Each of us has a limit to the amount of physical activity he can perform at one time, the amount of mental concentration he can exert in one sitting, the amount of emotional strain he can tolerate without beginning to show signs of fatigue. With careful training these limits can be extended upward.

But regardless of what the limits could be, it is the existing limit that will—or will not—make you sick. The strategy for health is to use yourself close to these limits—we are made for use and we thrive on use—but do not exceed these limits. Don't drive yourself until you break down. Our bodies have an adequate warning system, pulse rate, that switches on when we are beginning to crowd our luck. The pulse rate goes up when your daily activities are straining you too much.

Observe yourself to determine what your warning signal is and then respect its function. An overly strained body is a more vulnerable body. Under chronic physical or emotional stress, the body's defense mechanisms begin to falter.

We all have emergencies during which we may feel that we have to ignore the warning signs. Some have to drink another cup of coffee, swallow an aspirin or an antacid. But if you want a long life, a vigorous and a happy one, you don't develop a life style that is one pill-taking emergency after another. Actually resting when you need to, slowing your pace when it gets frantic, budgeting fun into your day or week allows you to work more efficiently afterwards. And it is the best health insurance that money can buy.

The second strategy for health and long life is treating recurrent health problems before they become chronic.

Being susceptible does *not* mean being ill. Being susceptible means only that you *can* become ill under stress. Knowing where you are susceptible can keep you from becoming ill.

Each of us, even the strongest, has a pattern of susceptibility. This pattern reveals which systems in our body are thrown into disorder most easily and which systems need the least care. The degree of susceptibility or strength in each organ or organ system is called our profile of susceptibilities. Much of this profile can be determined from our own observations of ourselves. We know whether we are likely to get sick in flu season, whether we huff and puff when climbing a flight of stairs. Throughout this book a variety of methods to make your self-observations more helpful are given. However, some of the profile can only be filled in with the help of a qualified expert, your doctor.

Preventive health maintenance is the route to extended youth, health, and vigor.

The next few pages contain illustrations of minor difficulties that, uncontrolled, can become major problems. I have deliberately chosen examples that are interesting or are more likely (and may) to touch your life. But, remember, you are not average, you are unique. What we are chiefly concerned with is *your* health and vigor and those strategies that will enable you to keep them both past the age of 100. Except the sections pertaining to exercise and nutrition, which are applicable to everyone, the forthcoming illustrations do not necessarily pertain to you. They are intended to illustrate a process and point up the value of preventive health maintenance as a method of conserving the prime of life.

HAY FEVER, ASTHMA, BRONCHITIS, EMPHYSEMA

While it is true that most victims of emphysema have case histories that include a hay fever type allergy and asthma, the route from hay fever to emphysema is not inevitable. It is equally true that there are those fortunate individuals whose lung tissue is more resistant to stress so that they can live past 100 with not a trace of emphysema in their lungs. But why gamble with your health? Life-shortening errors are easier to avoid than to rectify.

Hay fever is the body's hostile reaction to alien protein. The mechanism for fighting disease in some people is easily roused. The so-called antigen substances contacting the body produce the same reaction at the point of contact that viral or bacterial invaders would. Hay fever was named in a rural age when large segments of the population lived on farms, and it was noticed that many people began sneezing around haying time or after a day's work in the barn. It was not the hay stalk itself but the pollen from the grain head of the grass or other organic dust that caused the defense reactions of sneezing, watery noses and eyes, and the maddening itch under the eyelids. Since then, allergists have discovered that other pollens and the spores of some fungi produce similar reactions. In fact, because the body reacts in a similar fashion to some viruses, colds have many of the symptoms of hay fever; the same antihistamines and anticongestants can be used to control the discomforts of both. In essence, a cold is a viral attack complicated by an allergic reaction.

No one is happy to have hay fever. But in itself, hay fever is a relatively harmless annoyance . . . providing it is short termed. Hay fever becomes more serious if it plagues its victim year round. Those who sneeze and rub their eyes 365 days a year should really make an effort to discover what pollen or other foreign protein or antigen has put their body's defense mechanism in an uproar.

If the substance producing the allergy turns out to be part of the local environment only, the simplest solution, medically speaking, is to move to a noncontaminated region of the country. Most likely the simplest solution will not be feasible. There remains the possibility that your doctor or an allergist can "reason" with your defense mechanisms through a process called desensitization treatment.

Uncontrolled chronic hay fever puts a stress on the entire respiratory system. Chances are that your respiratory system can take this stress for years or even for life without being thrown into further disorder. But there are those who, under this frequent stress, develop asthma and chronic bronchitis, which appear very much like bronchial colds.

The bronchial tubes are the air-conveying system for the lungs. Their inner surfaces are covered with tiny, whiplike hairs that are in continual motion so that under a microscope they resemble a field of wheat in a spring breeze. These hairs are kept moist by small amounts of mucus secreted by cells embedded in the bronchial lining. The moist hairs catch hold of dust and other impurities we breathe and by their wave-like action carry the matter away from the lung alveoli up toward the part of the larger bronchial tubes where sneezing and coughing gets rid of it.

Asthma is accompanied by contraction of the smooth muscles around the bronchial airways, resulting in constrictions that greatly impede the sufferer from exhaling the air he breathes. A victim of asthma can easily breathe in but he has difficulty in breathing out.

Bronchitis (an inflammation of the bronchial tubes whether because of infection, viral invasion, or allergic response) involves a thickening of the inner lining of the bronchial tubes, especially the larger bronchial tubes. The thicker the inflamed lining becomes, the less room there is for the flow of air. Breathing becomes constricted. In response to the inflammation, the bronchial mucus cells become overactive, matting the bronchial hairs and further obstructing the air flow.

It should be obvious that either of these conditions are serious enough to call for medical help. Either of them puts a stress on the respiratory system. Additionally, they also stress other body systems, especially the heart and are accompanied by an impressive amount of discomfort. Nevertheless, it is remarkable how many people suffer from chronic bronchitis for years without seeking medical help. With medical help, the disease can be controlled and eased. Without it, more often than not, the victim's condition becomes progressively worse and can be further aggravated by air pollution and heavy cigarette smoking.

Even so, emphysema is not inevitably the next state. There may be no next stage at all. Beyond suffering and functioning less efficiently than he would have without the disease, the victim may live till the end of his days with periodic bouts of asthma or bronchitis that grow no worse, or only a little worse, than when he was first afflicted.

Nevertheless, emphysema is a possible next step, and the possibility is so unpleasant that it is worth taking the steps while they are still available, to avoid the disease. A study of those who are afflicted with emphysema reveals that 15 years usually go by from the time the patient first suffers shortness of breath with bronchitis or asthma until the day emphysema finally forces him to consult a doctor. Fifteen times 365 is a lot of wasted opportunities to avoid a crippling disease and an ugly death.

In emphysema, lung tissue, long stressed by inflammation and infection, gives way, literally leaving holes in the lungs themselves. Once the lung tissue is damaged in this way, it cannot heal itself; consequently, at the present time emphysema is irreversible; we cannot heal it. The best we can do is to slow down its progress.

Even so, its victim is left in a permanently vulnerable position. His oxygen intake is noticeably lowered. This means that he cannot be as active physically as he could before the disease and that his body continues to age prematurely. In addition to his lessened ability to function, cold or respiratory infection represents a grave danger. His lungs, already damaged, are not as capable of withstanding further attack or stress. And the chance exists that each new cold or bronchitis will worsen his emphysema. In its last stages, emphysema-stricken lungs resemble moth-eaten wool. Smoking, always a gamble, becomes almost suicidal. Air pollution and smog, a stress in itself, may represent such a threat to the sufferer of emphysema that his doctor will advise him to move out of the city.

Sufferer is no cliché when referring to someone with emphysema. In advanced stages, he can barely suck in enough air to sustain life. Taking a shower and dressing in the morning become panting achievements. Hiking, golf, gardening, or even a stroll around the block are forever beyond his capacity.

To find out whether or not you are in the early stages of emphysema, there is a simple test you can give yourself. Hold a lighted match six inches from your mouth. If you cannot blow out the flame without pursing your lips, make an appointment with your doctor immediately.

To those who find they have emphysema, it would be cruel to say you should have made that appointment sooner. Go now. Your doctor can still help you. He will tell you what to do and how to slow down and possibly arrest emphysema's progress. He can teach you exercises that will make the most of the lung capacity you have left. He will give you advice and medication on how to avoid further destruction of lung tissue and he will give you medication that will help you to breathe more freely.

For those who can easily douse the flame with their open mouths, guard this ability, not anxiously, but competently. If asthma or chronic bronchitis become a part of your life, seek help immediately. Don't cheat yourself from easy breathing.

When a person's body is under too much stress, his resistance to chronic disease is at its lowest ebb, especially if he is no longer as young and strong as he used to be. As the years of middle age advance, the individual should avoid physical stress as much as possible because such stresses prepare the way for various chronic diseases to step in.

A little-known body stress that sometimes occurs at night during sleep is the chill that develops when large parts of the body accidently become uncovered and stay uncovered for hours. Such a chill hardly ever leads to serious consequences in young adults, but in middle-aged or older persons this type of chill is frequently an important contributing factor to the development of arthritic pains.

AGE DECLINE IN BODILY FUNCTIONS

It would be helpful for every older adult if he had some information about the limits to which the functional capacities of his body and its organs may have declined, especially if these capacities are near the basal work-output demands of the body, that is to say if these organs can barely supply the needs of the body when it is at rest. This information is particularly important in order to avoid accidents caused by organ strain that can be fatal.

Many studies have been made with this need in mind; it has been well documented that the organs' abilities to meet the body's needs decline with age, some faster in one person than in another. For instance, the amount of blood flowing through the kidneys (or the kidney blood flow) falls by about 60 percent between the ages of 25 and 85. The total lung capacity decreases with age only insignificantly, whereas lung vital capacity falls on the average by 17.5 ml per square meter of body surface per year.

Some physiological functions do not show any particular age decline when measured under resting or basal conditions, but they do show a significant age decline when measured under exercise or stress conditions. For instance, during exercise, the amount of air which has to go through the lungs (i.e., the pulmonary ventilation volume) in older adults rises much more for a given increase in oxygen uptake than it does in young adults. However, pulmonary ventilation volume under resting conditions does not change significantly with age. Similarly, heart rate and blood pressure during standard exercise increase more in older adults and require a longer time for recovery than in younger adults.

These observations indicate that there is an age decline in reserve capacities of the individual and of his organs, even if some physiological functions do not show age decline in their functional capacities. Observations of this kind, made in various research laboratories, are very similar to those which many lay adults have made themselves without the use of any sophisticated scientific equipment, namely that "one gets tired faster and recovers more slowly as one grows older."

It is particularly important to be aware of this age decline in functional and reserve capacities because when the individual's demands from his body and its organs rise beyond the level of their maximal performance, or reserve capacities, these demands become stressful and the organs first try to resist or to adapt themselves to the given stress—somewhat like the "fight or flight" reaction of an animal in face of a danger. If the demands are much too heavy or stressful, and do not allow for a meaningful adaptation or resistance, the organs may break down and fail. It is for this reason that the functional and reserve capacities of the organs, together with their adaptability and resistance to stress, represent an important health asset.

In the 1950s, Dr. Hans Selye, Professor and Director of the

Institute of Medicine and Experimental Surgery at the University of Montreal, Canada, observed that our body responds in a very similar manner to a variety of different factors, such as infections, toxic agents, heat, cold, trauma, muscular fatigue, or nervous strain. Even though the specific actions of all these agents are quite different, they have one feature in common: they place the body in a state of general stress.

Dr. Selye was particularly struck by the fact that, while all the organs of the body show degenerative changes under action of such stressful agents, adrenal glands actually seem to flourish on stress. Subsequently he presented the concept of a general adaptation syndrome, which he divided into three distinct stages: the alarm reaction, the stage of resistance, and the stage of exhaustion. Since then, much has been written about the effects of stress on the human body, and about the fact that our modern way of living is laden with stress and stressful agents. However, very little has been written about the fact that the resistance of the body to stressful agents declines gradually from early adulthood, as documented by many observations and experimental data from research in the physiology of aging.

The consequences of this decline in resistance to stress is that the same amount of stress or stressful agents (no matter of what kind, category, or origin) which in a young adult is not stressful enough to produce even an "alarm reaction," may easily in the same person when he grows older lead to the "stage of resistance" and even to the "state of exhaustion" with undesirable damage to the health of that person. So many people seem to forget this fact; they seem to believe that a strong person who could resist much stress when young and healthy will not reach limits to resistance with age.

At the present time the only way that the age decline in functional and reserve capacities can be slowed down is by careful avoidance of excessive demands upon your body and its organs. This age decline can be reversed to some extent by judiciously chosen activity and physical exercise. However, remember that you further aggravate the decline by indiscriminate and excessive demands upon your functional and reserve capacities.

In fact, it is very easy and tempting for practically every older adult to err by pushing in one way or another beyond the declining limits of these capacities. Even if such pushing does not result immediately in the acute failure of an overstrained organ or organs, nevertheless your resistance is decreased and you have prepared the ground for the onset of chronic diseases. Such excessive demands present themselves or arise under a great variety of forms: bad nutrition, occupational exposure and hazards, and environmental, mechanical and other stresses.

26 | Survival Strategies of Middle Age

WHEN A MIDDLE-AGED PERSON REACHES THE REALIZATION OF the growing disparity between his declining abilities on one side and the rising social and professional expectations on the other side, he is very often confronted with many pressing problems and questions. Should he continue to push in his efforts for further achievements or should he take more care of his health and declining abilities? Which has a greater priority?

How do you tell, or decide, whether or when a person should consult a physician? I reply to this question by another question: do you know, for sure, which physician you would call if you had a heart attack?

The time will inevitably come, sometimes quite unexpectedly, when you will feel very strongly that you need to consult a physician, and then it may make a great difference if you know whom to consult. Plan ahead of time, especially if you are 45 or older. Why postpone looking for the right physician until *after* you had a heart attack? If you start then, it may be too late.

Make an effort to find one or possibly two conveniently located physicians who can be easily contacted at any time of the day or night if need should suddenly arise. Once you have decided on a physician, make an appointment for a visit to get personally acquainted with him. You do not have to have a medical checkup the first time you see your new physician. This may be decided later, depending on a number of intangibles like, for instance, your feeling of general confidence and rapport with the new physician. It is advisable that each person discuss with his physician the question of a medical checkup, because his physician is in a better position than anybody else to advise him.

You will be much more satisfied if you choose to have the medical checkup done by a physician whom you would like to have as your health adviser or personal physician, and to whom you would like to return for future consultations, because he also keeps records about your health. It has been suggested that it would be advisable to keep a copy of one's health records, possibly in the form of a "personal health book," just in case you have to move or something happens to your physician.

Medical examinations have always been rather expensive and time consuming, and it would be unworkable to provide them at periodic intervals for *all* the adults or even older adults in our population (even if we were to overlook the expense) simply because there are not enough physicians to do all the examinations and also to perform all the other primary medical activities. It is one thing to advise or to advocate regular, periodic, medical examinations for all persons in the later years of life; it is another thing to implement these examinations in a meaningful way without using an overwhelming amount of money and time.

Actually, the usefulness of periodic medical examinations has often been questioned on a purely monetary basis. Namely, it has been pointed out repeatedly that it is difficult to estimate the net gain if you compare the examination cost with the wages saved through not getting diseases. The difficulty is further compounded by the fact that in such comparisons it is almost impossible to take into account the purely human factor (such as suffering, deaths etc.), which is even more difficult to evaluate on a "purely monetary basis." For these various reasons it has been frequently emphasized that the need exists for the replacement of periodic medical examinations with some kind of inexpensive, automated, computerized health checkups. What is even more needed for every middle-aged and older person is to make special efforts in order to avoid or to prevent the development of chronic ills and diseases of old age, as they would require excessive medical attention and contribute to overburden the already strained health care facilities.

The first step in this regard is to admit that one's abilities are declining and to avoid overstraining them. However, it is very difficult to write down "exactly" what to avoid, because a given load, stress, or strain—which may be very harmful for some persons—can be perfectly harmless for others. I can give only a general idea of the possible types of stress to avoid; for the rest, each person will have to use his own judgment.

First, in order to improve one's judgment in these matters, it's good for every person to have a more concrete idea about the age decline in functional and reserve capacities of the body and its organs. For this purpose, I have included Figure 5 a simple graphic representation of age decline in maximal performance and reserve capacities of organs, from one of my publications in the *Journal of the American Geriatrics Society.*

FIGURE 5

AGE DECREASE OF MAXIMAL WORK OUTPUT AND RESERVE CAPACITIES

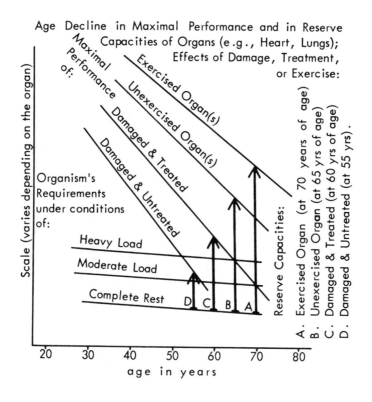

Both the maximal performance and reserve capacities decline with age in all organs whether or not these are exercised, healthy or damaged, treated or untreated. Figure 5 also illustrates graphically that reserve capacities can be very much influenced by environmental factors or causes (see arrows *A, B, C, D*). Thus, reserve capacities of an exercised organ at the age of 70 (arrow *A*) can be higher than the reserve capacities of an unexercised organ at the age of 65 (arrow *B*), which in turn can be higher than the reserve capacities of a damaged and treated organ at the age of 60 (arrow *C*), and still higher than the reserve capacities of a damaged and untreated organ at the age of 55 (arrow *D*).

However, at any age the maximal performance is higher in exercised organs than it is in unexercised, in healthy than in damaged, and in treated than in untreated. It is evident from Figure 1 that, as one grows older, each organ's best effort finally reaches the point where it can barely supply the body's needs even when it is under little or no stress. This point is reached more quickly in the unexercised than in the exercised organs, and in the damaged, untreated than in the damaged and treated, or in the healthy organs.

AGE DECLINE OF MAXIMAL PERFORMANCE BELOW MINIMAL NEEDS

Special situations arise when the best effort of an organ falls below the body's moderate and even minimal needs. When the maximal performance falls below moderate requirements (as when an older person runs too fast), the person has to decrease the load (that is, slow down and take a rest) before he can continue again. When the best effort falls below minimal requirements, which frequently happens during an acute illness, older adults cannot live long without medical help or intervention; in a relatively short time, death through insufficiency of the given organ occurs. In such cases death often can be prevented by medical intervention or treatment, helping to carry the overstrained organ over the stressful period of an acute illness.

At the end of the human life, however, the moment approaches when the decline of reserve capacities below minimal requirement of the body cannot be prevented or remedied by any possible means (at least not at the present time) and the person finally dies of old age. Figure 5 shows that it is possible to attempt to some extent to postpone death from old age (even at the present time) by several means:

1. Keeping reserve capacities as high as possible, which can be done:

(*a*) by avoiding damage of organs through too much stress from various errors of daily living;

(*b*) by treatment of accidentally damaged organs, or

(*c*) by judiciously chosen activity and exercise,

2. Keep the requirements of the body from its organs as low as possible, which can be done in various ways.

For example:

(*a*) the stresses an overweight body places on its organs can be lowered by reducing to normal weight or even to slightly underweight, or

(*b*) the specific requirements of the body from its organs (e.g., kidneys) can be reduced by lowering a specific load (e.g., a diet low on protein and sodium in the case of ailing kidneys) etc.

At the time of life when the individual becomes undeniably aware of the limits and even of the decline in his capacities, abilities, and energies, many individuals are caught in all kinds of stressful situations. Not everyone is able to discover and develop his own strategies or techniques to cope with such situations. At this period of life most people become fully aware that they are growing old and resent it most. What should have become the "indulgence stage of later middle age" often could be called more appropriately the "state of individual strategies," if not the stage of outright defeat. In fact, this period of life can easily turn into a defeat if the individual stresses his body and develops an incapacitating chronic disease or suffers a fatal heart attack. This is precisely what happens each year to hundreds of thousands of Americans in the prime years of life, who die of a heart attack.

There is a simple and easy test which anyone can use at any time of the day to see if he is straining his heart. This test consists of checking the pace of one's heartbeat, and it can be done simply by counting the rate of one's pulse. All that is needed is a stop watch or any watch that has a second-hand sweep. The heartbeat test also gives additional information about the fitness of the heart, how rested the heart is in the morning and how tired it is in the evening.

The usual method of counting one's pulse rate is by placing the index and middle finger of one hand on the little depression on the wrist of the other hand right under the base of the thumb where the beat of the artery can be felt. Another place where the beat can be felt is on the temple in the little depression between the eye and the ear. At first the pulse may be a little difficult to find and to keep track of. Try closing your eyes and concentrating on it until the feel of your pulse becomes familiar. With practice, you will be able to do it easily.

As a basis for comparison, take the rate of your heartbeat or pulse rate in the morning after a good night's rest, while you are still lying down. In men who are in reasonably good physical condition, the pulse rate in the morning in bed is around 62 beats per minute (or a few beats more or less). In athletes, regularly exercising, it usually is a few beats lower, around 58 or 60 beats per minute. After one gets up, the pulse rate usually goes up a few beats. The resting heart rate, while sitting during the midmorning hours, should be below 70 beats per minute in men who are in good physical condition. In women, a resting heart rate below 75 beats is considered a reasonable value.

Often you may start in the midmorning hours with the resting heart rate below 70 beats per minute, and it then climbs in the later afternoon or evening to higher values. If it does, it is always a warning sign which should not be neglected, especially if your heart rate is approaching 90 beats per minute or reaching even higher values. It indicates that your daily activities may be straining your heart; but you must also consider that you may be too tense, that you are smoking too much, taking too much coffee or alcohol (whichever may be the case) or a combination of several. Sometimes an additional reason for the high values in your pulse rate may be that last night you went to bed very late and did not get enough night rest. A too-rapid pulse rate can mean that you are not getting enough exercise on a regular basis so that your heart overreacts to little exertion. If the cause is not obvious to you, you should consult your doctor.

There is a surprisingly large percentage of middle-aged American men whose pulse rates approach 90 or 95 beats per minute and even exceed 100 per minute in the afternoon or evening. There are great differences among individuals in this regard. Some persons can be very active from the early morning until late in the evening and still show a relatively low pulse rate even late in the evening whereas others, the susceptible ones, with much less activity will reach high pulse rates easily. These susceptible persons have to be particularly careful not to strain their hearts.

If you are one of the persons whose pulse rate approaches or exceeds too high values in the afternoon or in the evening, cut down (or out) on smoking, coffee, and alcohol. If this is not enough to lower the rate of your heart beat, lie down for at least ten minutes, and possibly more, without being disturbed by anybody (as if you had an important meeting).

Let me issue a warning: do not go around for days and even weeks with high pulse rates in the late afternoon and evening hours without slowing down and without avoiding various contributing causes like too much coffee, smoking, or alcohol. If do not slow down, you may, at some unexpected moment, have a heart attack.

SIGNS OF HEART STRAIN

Another good way to find out if you are straining your heart is to do some mild physical exercise like ten knee bends in 20 seconds, or walking up one or two flights of stairs, followed by taking one's pulse rate immediately after stopping and then every minute until the mormal pulse rate is restored. The usual good recovery time is under 2 minutes; if the recovery time is between 2 and 3 minutes, it is considered fair, and if it is over 3 minutes, it is considered insufficient. Also, if your pulse rate rises excessively after such mild exercise, if you are breathing heavily and are unable to catch your breath, if it takes you a long time to recover, your heart is not in good condition or you have been straining it lately.

Another extremely important warning sign of heart strain, which a person should be very careful not to neglect, is "skipped heart beats" or extrasystoles. Some describe the feeling "as if their heart turned over in their chest," others merely as a vague feeling that they have missed a heartbeat which often they would not even have noticed, if they had not been taking their pulse or heartbeat at the particular time. Almost everyone experiences an occasional skipped beat of his heart or an extrasystole which, more often than not, passes unnoticed.

Some skipped heartbeats are present in apparently healthy persons, who have no signs of heart disease. For instance, a large number of skipped heartbeats have been documented in active flyers of the United States Air Force. They are more frequent in middle-aged persons than in young adults, and some persons are more susceptible than others. However, many people who experience skipped heartbeats regularly, or even occasionally, have definite signs of heart disease.

Skipped heartbeats often occur in persons with high levels of nervous tension or without adequate rest. Sometimes skipped heartbeats follow heavy meals, or are stimulated by the cumulative effects of heavy meals with excessive use of coffee and tobacco, or both, under high nervous tension without adequate rest, and may disappear after a good rest.

Occurrence of skipped heartbeats should be considered a timely and serious warning that the heart is under undue stress, that the demands which the person is putting on his heart are exceeding the limits of his heart's endurance, either because his heart has already been weakened by atherosclerotic or other changes, or simply because of the age decline in the heart's functional capacity. Skipped heartbeats usually are not present in young adults and develop in susceptible persons some time during middle age.

At an early stage, skipped heartbeats usually disappear after the person has had a good rest, cut out coffee (or at least excesses in coffee drinking), cut down (or out) on smoking and alcohol, and avoided heavy meals. Then the well-rested person usually notices that he can have one or two cups of coffee without provoking skipped heartbeats, but if he is tired, overstrained, or has a third cup of coffee (or a heavy meal), the skipped heartbeats may set in and do not disappear unless he takes a rest in a horizontal position or until the effect of the excess coffee (or the effect of the heavy meal) disappears.

Among major chronic diseases, coronary heart disease is now of epidemic proportions in the United States, 54 percent of all deaths is due to cardiovascular diseases. The heart attacks suffered by President Eisenhower and by other prominent persons, some of which occurred under dramatic circumstances, have brought greater attention to the toll extracted from our population by coronary heart disease. In 1963 there were 547,000 deaths from coronary heart disease, 201,000 deaths from strokes, 75,000 deaths from hypertension—and these numbers keep increasing each year.

As one might expect, coronary heart disease is found to be more common in older people. However, this disease is not just a killer of our senior citizens. At the early ages of 25–29, coronary heart disease ranges among the ten leading causes of death and, by the ages 40–44, it is the leading cause of death and continues as such throughout the remaining years of life. The U.S. National Center for Health Statistics estimates that 3.1 million persons aged 18–79 years have definite coronary heart disease and another 2.4 million have suspected coronary heart disease.

The Korean War created an opportunity to determine how many apparently healthy young men had atherosclerotic damages of coronary heart arteries. Post-mortem examinations were performed on a number of young soldiers killed in combat at an average age of 22. When the coronary arteries of the heart were opened, evidence of atherosclerosis was apparent in many instances.

The accumulation of fatty deposits in the wall of the heart arteries, that untimately leads to their occlusion, was present in over 77 percent of these young men. In 10 percent the process had already occluded over 70 percent of the openings of one or more of the major heart arteries. The diseased heart arteries were not those of sedentary middle-aged men, but those of young active, apparently healthy individuals, representing a group of Americans presumably in better than average health. Despite all external evidence of good health in these young soldiers, heart disease had already begun its deadly process.

The most effective prevention of the heart attack probably begins in early adulthood, as opposed to efforts made after atherosclerotic disease of heart arteries has achieved extensive proportions. However, a great deal can be done to improve the heart and prevent progression of disease, even after surviving a heart attack. Although the process of the atherosclerotic disease of heart arteries begins early in life, it is not until it suddenly occludes the blood flow to an area of the heart muscle that a heart attack (infarction) occurs. Heart attacks are not rare in young men between 30 and 35 years of age, but beyond age 35 the likelihood of heart attacks increases sharply. The American men most susceptible to heart attacks are those between 50 and 60 years of age. After age 60 there is a sharp decrease in the percentage of individuals who have heart attacks.

27 | Need for Relaxation and Rest

FROM WHAT HAS BEEN SAID IN PREVIOUS CHAPTERS, IT SHOULD be evident that adequate relaxation and rest are very important measures for the avoidance of various chronic diseases, especially of heart disease, high blood pressure, and heart attacks. The importance for rest and relaxation increases as the individual grows older, and his abilities to recuperate decline; the time needed for recuperation increases with age.

Just a short rest of 15 or 20 minutes, or catnap, preferably lying down, can make a tremendous difference. In fact, short rests or catnaps are quite common among knowledgeable, middle-aged and older persons, and they are nothing to be ashamed of. It is known that, in order to be relaxed during a period of stress, Theodore Roosevelt and Thomas Alva Edison, both men of action, took catnaps.

Another simple but important measure: avoid working late at night. This becomes increasingly important as one grows older. If you are in your middle years and have emergency work to do, don't let yourself be tempted to take another cup of coffee and work late at night. Instead, just review briefly the essential parts of the work to be done, go to bed at your usual hour, and leave the work for tomorrow. Next day, fully refreshed after a good night's sleep, start to work on your emergency as soon as you can, and you will see what a difference it makes for your health, your feeling of well-being, and even for the work done.

A third simple measure of almost equal importance concerns

the time you may lose from your night's sleep by occasionally staying out late, which often is difficult to avoid. Staying up late in the evening, evidently, is not as tiresome to a middle-aged and older person as working late in the evening. Nevertheless, when a middle-aged or older person stays up late in the evening, he should make it a point to go to bed earlier the next evening, in order to catch up with the sleep he lost the night before, and he should not pile up staying up late one night after another, which otherwise may contribute to the development of chronic fatigue, irritability and exhaustion.

RESIDUAL TENSIONS AND INABILITY TO RELAX

When a person lies "relaxed," in the popular sense, it can be shown in many instances that he still remains tense in various groups of muscles of his body. A tense person may lie in horizontal position apparently quiet for hours, even the whole night long, and yet remain nervously restless and sleepless. Following such 'restless rest' or 'sleepless sleep', the person does not feel refreshed, and he retains his complaints of nervousness, fatigue and exhaustion.

Another common annoyance resulting from excessive strain and tension is the inability to sleep. Insomnia is often the first sign of strain and tension. In fact, if a person cannot sleep when he seeks to do so, it very often is because he is too tense and worried. Lack of sleep is always accompanied by a feeling of residual tensions, and can be overcome only by relieving these tensions. In fact, the first effects of insomnia are further stimulation of both mental and muscular tensions to a high level. Doing away with residual tensions is an essential part of treating insomnia.

THE NEED TO LEARN HOW TO RELAX

Many people do not know how to relax. But is is necessary to discover what techniques are best suited to relaxation, what adjustments in life will minimize worries, and what balance of work and rest will result in best achievements. To begin: learn the difference between normal fatigue and chronic fatigue.

Normal fatigue is part of normal, healthful living. It consists of a general tiredness of the body which can be dispelled by adequate rest and sleep. Chronic fatigue is abnormal fatigue; it usually is not dispelled by a normal amount of rest and sleep. Chronic fatigue often results from disregard of normal fatigue and the need for an adequate amount of rest and sleep to offset it.

There are persons who will always fatigue more easily than others. They will have to accept the fact that they cannot live as vigorous a life as they desire, and they will have to adopt every possible technique to conserve their energy.

Relaxation and doing away with fatigue, exhaustion, and residual tensions usually does not come about very quickly, not even in a person who has experience in relaxation and knows how to relax. Usually, residual tensions and fatigue disappear only gradually. In the beginning, it may take 10 to 20 minutes or even longer to relax completely, and various methods or approaches have been suggested or devised to speed up the process of relaxation.

METHOD OF PROGRESSIVE RELAXATION

Some forty years ago, Dr. E. Jacobson, a clinical physiologist from Chicago, introduced the method of progressive relaxation which consists of relaxing various groups of muscles, one group after another, until the entire body is relaxed. An inexperienced person usually cannot judge accurately whether he is tense or not, because he does not realize which muscles or muscle-groups are tense.

Dr. Jacobson reports a personal inability to fall asleep at night which persisted for hours, while his mental activities continued, regardless of the need for rest. Seeking to discover what it was that seemed to keep him awake, he was always able to identify processes of muscular tension somewhere in the body, and when these were eliminated by relaxation, sleep came. As he studied the muscle tensions further, he noted that subjectively he seemed responsible for them and therefore apparently could undo them, and he concluded that this evidently depended upon his carrying the relaxation sufficiently far.

The ability to relax must be acquired, learned, and cultivated. Whatever the natural inclinations of an individual toward relaxation, there is always considerably more that he can improve, just as a person with a good voice can improve his voice on additional training. Neurotic persons have partly lost the natural habit to relax. Usually they do not know what muscles are tense, cannot judge whether they are relaxed, do not clearly realize that they should relax and do not know how to relax.

In some cases of chronic nervous exhaustion or neurasthenia, relaxation will have to become a matter of habit formation that may require months. For the purpose of progressive relaxation, it is important to remove as much as possible both physical and mental sources of excitement. Since this often cannot be realized entirely, the method of relaxation seeks to lower the nervous reaction even in situations where sources of excitement remain unavoidably active.

The method of progressive relaxation consists of voluntary continued reduction of activity, contraction, or tonus of all muscle groups of the body and of the nervous system. When relaxation is limited to a particular group of muscles or to a part of the body, it is called local relaxation. When relaxation includes practically the entire body, in horizontal position, it is called general relaxation.

In the method of progressive relaxation, general relaxation is progressive in three respects:

1) The person relaxes a group of muscles, for instance, of one arm or one leg, further and further each minute, until complete relaxation is attained.

2) He learns to relax all the principal muscle-groups of his body, one after another.

3) As he practices relaxation from day to day, he progresses toward a habit of repose, tends toward state in which quiet and relaxation is automatically maintained.

The term relaxation is usually applied to nervous as well as to muscular tension because of the difficulty of separating the two types. It is customary to apply the terms tense and tenseness not only to the muscles but also to the individual as a whole. By a tense individual we mean a person who acts as if his muscles were unduly tense; he is overalert, or high-strung in popular terms.

In the technique of progressive relaxation one learns to localize tensions when they occur during nervous irritability and excitement, and then to relax them away. It is a matter of nervous re-education. The approach to progressive relaxation can take many forms, depending upon the condition to be met, whether this condition is acute or chronic, and its previous duration.

Nevertheless, the person must not continue to watch his muscles intently, or else he may fail to relax. In the course of months, when relaxation has been made habitual, moments of attention to muscles while trying to relax become increasingly unnecessary.

Here it is, like in any other learning process, requiring less attention as time proceeds.

Sensations of tenseness or contraction constitute some of the very essence of the processes of attention and thinking, but this does not mean that we are aware of these sensations while thinking. In the method of progressive relaxation, the person is made aware of sensations of tensness, and later he may even observe these sensations taking place while he thinks or is excited. He may note how tense he becomes; and his attention, thus drawn to the point, shows him what parts of his body to relax. Or again, when he becomes tense, the habits of progressive relaxation, which he has newly acquired, may lead him automatically to repose.

HOBBIES AND PLAY FOR RELAXATION

For a great many people the easiest way to avoid chronic fatigue and prepare for relaxation is through satisfactions from creative or challenging activities. Unfortunately, and for various reasons, not all people are able to draw creative or challenging satisfactions from their jobs or professions, but very often they can draw such satisfactions from well-selected hobbies.

The daily activities of many adults can easily become monotonous, dull, and uninspiring, lacking in creative or challenging aspects, and often there is little or nothing they can do about it. Such activities easily make them irritable, tense, or wind them up. After they come home, they need hobbies and play to 'unwind.'

Unfortunately, tense persons very often do not know how to play. They set their minds upon material or self-selected goals and bring themselves to believe that only purposeful activity is justifiable. They seem to find no room in their lives for hobbies and play, which in their opinion serve no useful purpose; they do not seem to realize that relaxation has an important purpose.

Children draw satisfaction from play which challenges their inborn skills, and yet are not too difficult for them to perform. If children cannot play, they too become irritable, tense and wound up and for various reasons similar situations may develop with many adults and older adults. In such situations, the most natural way for adults and older adults to unwind and get rid of accumlated tensions is by engaging in well-selected, enjoyable hobbies and play.

The most important problem is what kind of hobby to select, because the success or failure of a person's efforts to relax through hobbies and play may depend on the right or wrong kinds of hobbies he choses to practice. Very often the kind of hobby which can be most enjoyable to one person may be exceedingly dull and boring to another.

Some people enjoy and relax best going to theater or concert, whereas other people more enjoy various outdoor hobbies. Still others like to collect enjoyable or unusual objects, or to create with their hands. Sometimes the availability of suitable material plays an important role. A great many people unwind and relax best by listening to selected pieces of music, or even by watching their favorite programs on television. There are all kinds of hobbies, activities and play which can be applied toward the general aim of relaxation. And there is no rule nor law to say that a person should have no more than one hobby. Each person can have as many hobbies as he enjoys, but there is one, very special triple hobby which I would advise any person to adopt, in addition to all the others he may enjoy.

1)selecting daily well-balanced foods in the right proportions for you;
2)doing daily a well-balanced physical exercise tailored to your abilities, and
3)practicing daily progressive relaxation, especially when you feel that the tensions of everyday life are mounting too high.

If you will find time to enjoy and practice this 'triple hobby' I have just outlined, as it is also amply discussed in this book, you can be sure that you too will live a healthy, active and very long life, possibly past one hundred.

The Appendix:
How to Survive a
Heart Attack

MUCH OF THIS BOOK CONTAINS ADVICE ABOUT HOW TO AVOID the errors of everyday life that may produce heart attacks. If middle-aged and older persons in the United States would follow this advice, the number of people who die each year from heart attack in this country (over 700,000 each year) would be reduced by as much as 90 percent and possibly more. Unfortunately, in the years to come, people will continue to die of heart attacks in just about the same numbers as they did previously.

This indicates two things: a great majority of people do not make enough effort to avoid various errors of everyday life which lead to heart attacks, and each person should prepare himself very carefully for the possibility that unexpectedly, while he feels perfectly healthy, he may suddenly have a heart attack. Depending on how carefully each person prepares himself for the possibility of having a heart attack, he may, or may not, survive it.

There are quite a number of relatively simple things you can do in order to prepare yourself.

Select a physician ahead of time, whom you would call if you suffer heart attack. Inquire ahead of time about the nearest hospital with a "Coronary Care Unit" to take care specifically of heart attack patients. Try to select a physician who can also be your health adviser in the future. Such a physician should be conveniently located so that he can easily come at any time of the day or night should you suddenly need him. Once you have selected such a physician, make an appointment for a visit to get personally acquainted with him.

Finally, if you have a heart attack, don't postpone having someone call your physician or you may die before he arrives. I stress this because postponing a call to the physician is one of the first mistakes many people make. In one study it was shown that an average of 8 hours passed between the onset of symptoms of the heart attack and the asking for medical help. It has been suggested that one reason for delaying the telephone call to the doctor is an emotional reluctance to admit or to consider the possibility that a specific pain can be so serious as to involve the heart.

Once a person has a heart attack, or even suspects that he may be having one, he should immediately stop doing everything he has been doing and rest comfortably in a horizontal position. Keep warm and quiet, and wait for the physician to come. In order to avoid any unnecessary strain or load to the heart, the victim should not call for the doctor; someone else should call for him, while the victim continues resting in a horizontal position, tries to keep quiet and to calm down, relax, and stop worrying.

The expression "heart attack" generally refers to a pattern of clinical events, experienced by a person when the blood flow in a heart artery is suddenly obstructed for a long enough time to cause the death of a significant segment or portion of the heart muscle and the damage of another portion of the heart muscle, both of which are due to the lack of oxygen. Most frequently the obstruction of the blood flow in the heart artery is due to a blood clot (called an "infarct"). When this happens, suddenly the surviving and undamaged portion of the heart muscle has to take over and perform the pumping work of the whole heart, putting a very heavy stress on this portion of the heart.

If the surviving, undamaged portion of the heart becomes unable to carry the heavy load of pumping the blood, the situation may lead to the failure of the surviving portion of the heart and the death of victim. Possibly the most important, general advice, if you have a heart attack, is: *keep the load on the heart as low as possible!*

STOP ALL ACTIVITY AT FIRST SIGN OF HEART ATTACK

Many persons, the moment they were having a heart attack, were just in the process of doing some very important work; after it, they are unable to resist the desire or the urge to finish "just a few" things they considered to be so very important for the work they were doing. These "few important things" which they decide to finish first result in too heavy a load on the remaining, undamaged part of the heart, lead to the failure of the heart, and kill the person before the arrival of the physician. Such things happen very often. Hospital statistics tell us that, out of each 100 persons who have a heart attack, 20-25 persons will be dead in the first 15 minutes after it because of such unnecessary mistakes or errors. An additional 4-6 persons (out of each 100 who have a heart attack) will die within the first 2-3 hours and about 8-11 more persons will die within the first 24 hours after the heart attack. This makes a total of 32-42 persons (out of each 100 who suffered a heart attack) who die within the first 24 hours after the heart attack.

If you are having a heart attack, the first most important consideration is to survive the first 15 minutes. All other considerations should be ignored. Keep warm, or at least prevent your body from cooling off; cooling off may put an additional load on your heart and keeping warm may be as important as lying in the horizontal position and relaxing. It may not always be an easy task to keep warm, quiet and relaxed, especially if there is pain. Complete and total relaxation is an excellent aid to enduring severe pain.

The second most important consideration for a person who is just having a heart attack is to survive the first 2-3 hours after the heart attack, the time it may take to get him to the hospital. This the physician, who has by now arrived on the scene, will arrange for the patient.

When the physician comes, he will examine you and look for other signs of a heart attack, and will administer medicine to provide psychic sedation and to relieve pain spasm, or discomfort (Demerol, morphine, or other) before the ambulance comes to take you to the hospital. During all this time, you should keep warm, quiet, calm, relaxed, and continue to minimize your physical activity and mental anxiety as much as you can.

The third most important consideration for a person who is just having a heart attack is to survive the first 24 hours after the attack. Don't become one of the 9-11 or more persons (out of each 100 who had a heart attack) who die within the first 24 hours after the heart attack. In this regard, the "coronary care unit" in hospitals, specially devised to take care of persons having a heart attack, is the best place to be.

For a number of reasons each person should learn ahead of time and in all details how it feels to have a heart attack. One reason is to be able to recognize the heart attack once it occurs, or at least have a suspicion that you may be having a heart attack. Sometimes the heart attack is accompanied by nausea, vomiting, hiccups, or abdominal distention, so that the person may mistake it for an episode of harmless indigestion.

The most characteristic hallmark of an acute heart attack is a severe pain or oppression deep in the center of the chest, or along the left or right side of the chest, often radiating from its point of origin toward either shoulder, down either or both arms, or to the neck, jaws, cheeks, or ears. Typically, the pain is described as a compressing, constricting, squeezing, pressing, boring, or burning sensation of such unrelenting magnitude as to be associated with a sense of impending doom. Often the victim of a heart attack feels that the crushing pressure on his chest prevents him from breathing properly.

Particularly dangerous are the so-called silent heart attacks which are accompanied by no pain at all and do not give any warning or impression of imminent danger to life. Fortunately, even the silent heart attacks are accompanied by certain, though less conspicuous, signs indicating that something may be wrong with the heart. First of all, the victim of a silent heart attack has a persistent breathing difficulty which starts more or less suddenly and for no apparent reason, and is often accompanied by weakness and sweating. Breathing may be rapid and shallow. The skin becomes pale, cold, and moist. For no apparent reason, the pulse becomes rapid and weak, though during the first few hours after the silent heart attack, the pulse rate may stay slow and appear normal.

If a middle-aged or older person for no apparent reason suddenly gets a persistent breathing difficulty, and if at the same time his pulse rate becomes rapid; if the breathing difficulty with the rapid pulse rate do not disappear after a good rest in horizontal position, the person should suspect that he may be having a silent heart attack, especially if he also feels weak, is sweating and his skin is pale, cold, and moist. With a silent heart attack sometimes even an experienced physician may have difficulty in making the correct diagnosis and in deciding for sure whether or not a person is having a heart attack. Therefore, often it is advisable to have an electrocardiogram which answers such a question easily and without any doubt. Often the question whether a person is having or has recently had a heart attack can be decided for sure only by taking his electrocardiogram which (if he recently suffered a heart attack) shows certain specific changes, characteristic only of the heart attack.

Recently, there has been considerable evidence to indicate that the silent heart attacks, which are completely painless, occur in at least 1 and possibly 2 out of every 10 persons stricken with a heart attack. These silent heart attacks are among the most dangerous because, when there is no pain, the person may proceed with his usual daily activities as if nothing had happened. These usual activities may put an unsurmountable load on the undamaged, surviving part of the heart and lead to the failure of the heart and to death. Death could have been avoided had he rested immediately in horizontal position and, possibly, had an electrocardiogram made.

IMMEDIATE CAUSES OF HEART ATTACK

It is well known that heart attacks may result from vigorous physical effort, especially when the exertion is static and sustained and when the person is untrained for that particular physical activity. However, previous physical activity, or the lack of it, doesn't necessarily help to decide the nature of the discomforting attack or feelings, because heart attacks may also occur at rest or during sleep (particularly after heavy meals, such as during early morning hours after a heavy supper). In general, heart attacks have so many known and unknown contributing causes that it is very difficult and almost impossible to pinpoint in each particular case the final, last cause which made it occur. Very often, however, the heart-attack-provoking cause is of the kind which puts a very heavy strain or stress on the heart, whether of physical, nutritional (heavy meal), emotional, or other nature.

Immediate hospitalization is important because it greatly increases the chances of survival. Various studies show that half of the people who have died of a heart attack, die outside the hospital. Many of those who died outside the hospital could have been saved had they been transferred to the hospital as fast as possible.

Before hospitals started to have the so-called coronary care units, up to 50 percent of patients in the hospitals died. With coronary care units, the percentage of deaths has been reduced to about 20 percent.

CAUSES OF DEATH IN HEART ATTACK

There are two most frequent causes of death in persons with a heart attack, whether in the hospital or outside. One consists of sudden, very rapid and irregular heartbeats, called arrhythmia(s) which prevent the heart from functioning properly, that is, from pumping the blood. The other consists of cessation of heartbeats or heart arrest.

There are all kinds of arrhythmias in acute heart attack (or myocardial infarction). The important ones are the so-called life-threatening arrhythmias, the most dangerous being the so-called ventricular fibrillation. If arrhythmias are discovered in time—that is, as soon as they start—they can be treated and removed, and the pumping heart function can be restored. However, if the arrhythmias last without medical intervention for only a few minutes, the lack of oxygen (caused by the lack of blood circulation) causes irreparable damage to the brain and the person must die.

The other most frequent cause of death in persons suffering from a heart attack is the cessation of heartbeats or heart arrest, which again can be treated successfully and the person can be resuscitated if the heart arrest is treated immediately after it occurs. Otherwise, even a few minutes of heart arrest lead to irreparable damage of the brain, because of the lack of blood circulation and the resulting lack of oxygen.

The fact that resuscitation efforts are most successful when promptly initiated clearly indicates that all patients with a heart attack should be kept in one area of the hospital where they can be constantly monitored. This is how the idea of "coronary care units" started. Now these units, which are being installed in the hospitals all over the United States, contain special monitoring equipment, in order to allow constant monitoring of the patients to make sure that arrhythmias or heart arrests are not occurring and, if they do, immediate lifesaving action is initiated. Coronary care units further contain defibrillators, external pacemakers and other lifesaving equipment, and are staffed by expertly trained personnel possessing the ability to react almost instantaneously to the critical needs of the patient.

Within the coronary care unit, the nurse has an ideal opportunity to observe the patients for any of the adverse signs or symptoms such as: arrhythmias observed on the monitor; pain in the chest, back, arms, jaw, or any heart burn or indigestion; change in respiration; increased restlessness and confusion; sudden or gradual fall in blood pressure and other changes, which may indicate an emergency or need for intervention. In an emergency, if the physician is not at the bedside within 1 minute, the specially trained nurse is ready herself to institute the lifesaving measures. The most important function of coronary care units is to monitor the patients in early stages of a heart attack, on a 24-hour basis, in order to detect arrhythmias or heart arrests as soon as they occur.

If the victim does not calm down, if he is unable to relax, if he keeps worrying, all his mental stress continues putting an additional load on the heart, which keeps increasing the rate of its beats up to the highest limits to which each particular heart is able to go. But the load continues until the heart is unable to increase the rate of its beats any more—and this is where and when various arrhythmias start. One study of patients in a coronary care unit showed that, when every effort was made to provide patients with a "supportive atmosphere" that relieved anxiety to the fullest extent possible, life-threatening arrhythmias did not occur in over 150 acute heart attacks, whereas without this "supportive atmosphere" they used to be quite frequent. It is tremendously important, then, for each person, who has just had a heart attack, to put special effort into keeping quiet, calming down, relaxing, in order to reduce any possible load on the heart from this direction.

Experience has shown that over 85 percent of the preventable or reversible causes of death will occur during the first 10 days after a heart attack, and the vast majority of these again fall within the 5-7 day period. Patients in the coronary care units have two types of conditions. These conditions are: the acute phase of this illness and the rehabilitation phase. Even though the acute phase may appear to be more dangerous to life, both are about equally important. The rehabilitation phase also has its important signposts, of which possibly the most important is the first bowel movement after the heart attack.

Many common aspects of the everyday life of the person who is recovering from a heart attack must be viewed and evaluated in terms of decreasing the load on the greatly weakened heart. Such an additional load on the weakened heart may come from many unsuspected or unexpected directions. Among these the care of the bowel movement in persons suffering from a heart attack is particularly important. A previously active person who is suddenly hospitalized can easily become constipated. This situation is further aggravated in the presence of a heart attack because certain commonly used medicines have a constipating effect.

Unless attention is given to avoiding constipation, three or four days after the heart attack, an accumulated hard bowel movement has to be passed. This comes at the exact critical time when the newly demaged heart muscle is weakest and most apt to rupture. And rupture of the heart muscle means death. Straining, associated with a difficult bowel movement, is a frequent cause for the giving in of the heart muscle, that is, its rupture leading to instantaneous death. These problems are usually prevented by proper bowel management. It was for this reason, and because he knew that all the individuals in the medical profession would understand its importance, that Dr. Paul Dudley White announced to the world on television when President Eisenhower had his first bowel movement after his heart attack.

For the person who has survived the first 24 hours after his heart attack and also his first bowel movement, the next most important consideration is to survive the first one or two weeks. Unfortunately, there are some important psychological factors, inherent in human nature, which often work against survival and may lead to death—if the victim is too impatient and not careful enough. In almost all victims of a heart attack, the realization that the heart attack has actually taken place and has not resulted in death, evokes a sense of relief. But sometimes it is more than a sense of relief. In some persons the initial feeling of dejection caused by the heart attack is followed by a false bravado, which seems to spring from an unconscious denial that a serious illness has taken place. These persons, in their denial that a serious illness has taken place and that they are still seriously ill, mold the circumstances to provoke another, new heart attack which now becomes fatal.

This interpretation or explanation is supported by the surprising and very important fact that, in about half of those persons who do not survive their heart attack, there is clinical evidence of additional heart attacks. This clinical evidence is supported by histologic evidence indicating that there were in fact two distinct episodes in which heart attacks with obliterations of heart arteries occurred, the second one leading to death. If the second heart attack could have been avoided, the person would have had a good chance to survive.

In such cases, careful microscopic examinations revealed an earlier, still unhealed heart attack with blocking of the heart artery, followed by another fresh episode of blocking or thrombosis, which was distinct histologically from the earlier thrombosis, and which appeared to correspond to clinical events surrounding the rapid death in shock, shortly after the second episode of the heart attack.

The occurrence of a new episode of coronary occlusion by thrombosis (or a new heart attack) while the patient has not yet recovered from the effects of the first occlusion or heart attack, is surprisingly frequent. There are reports that in those persons who died of a heart attack due to thrombosis of a heart artery, over half of the victims showed repetition of the thrombosis. In other words, *over half* of the persons who died of a heart attack were already successfully recovering from a first heart attack, and then provoked another heart attack that killed them.

This tendency, to repetition of the thrombosis, may be due in part to an increased blood clotting, which results in an increased tendency for additional occlusion of heart arteries. But it is also due to "false bravado" and refusal to believe that a serious illness has taken place. Physicians can combat the increased blood clotting with the anticoagulant therapy, but the patient himself also can help by staying in bed, keeping quiet, calm, and relaxed, until his physician gives him the green light to get up. This advice is based on the many unnecessary deaths which could have been so very easily avoided.

If all has gone well during the critical phase of the heart attack, the time comes when the victim must be prepared to return to more normal living. This is done by gradually increasing the amount of time the person may sit up, then gradually increasing the amount of walking he can do around his hospital room and in the hospital corridors. The purpose is to improve gradually the person's ability to take care of all his normal functions.

Most heart specialists do not make an effort to significantly increase the patient's activity until at least three weeks after the initial heart attack has occurred. Dr. Paul Dudley White considers three weeks of bed rest, except for mild bed exercise, necessary for a firm heart muscle scar to begin replacing the damaged heart muscle. If too much activity is permitted too soon, a good scar is not formed and poor healing results.

Also, it takes time to develop new blood vessels and to increase the capacity of previously existing connections among the terminal branches of the major heart arteries. A period of at least 3 to 5 weeks is needed to permit adequate development of new routes to supply blood to the working heart muscle. In most instances, the process will not be complete by then, and will continue for several months thereafter.

A number of specialists have proposed various activity programs for safe return to self-care after a heart attack. They all stress the need to individualize the conditions of the persons treated: no two persons are just alike in severity of the heart attack, age, physical fitness before the attack, and many other characteristics. To start the activity program, there should be an absence of alarming heart signs and symptoms, and a minimum of 15 days must elapse since the onset of heart attack.

One program of graded activity after a heart attack consists of ten levels of activity. It starts with a very low activity level: self-care in bed, like washing face, brushing teeth, eating breakfast.

Activity levels 2 and 3 consist of active exercises in bed such as breathing deeply, moving shoulders through all ranges of motion, flexing and extending the arm, abducting and adducting the arm, raising straightened leg, extending thigh with leg straight.

Activity levels 4, 5, and 6 consist of self-care such as sitting on the side of the bed for a sponge bath, putting on robe or trousers and slippers, and level walking about 35 feet forward and return (just about the distance to the bathroom), increasing gradually up to 100 feet and return.

Activity levels 7, 8, and 9 include walking on incline (up and down hospital ramp 10% grade, 48 feet long). Activity level 10 consists of self-care (grooming, taking tub bath) and stair climbing. Not more than one level of activity is performed by a patient on any one day. Several times during the program an electrocardiogram is made. Testing is not done when the pulse rate at rest is more than 100 per minute.

The tremendous toll of heart disease and heart attacks, amounting to more than 700,000 deaths each year in the United States, has many causes, among which lack of care and ignorance of the average middle-aged and older persons and just plain carelessness, play an important part. However, astonishing results can be obtained where utmost care and timely medical treatment are applied. In this regard, probably no other person in medical history received more intensive treatment and survived so long after so many heart attacks as Dwight David Eisenhower.

To some extent his endurance could be attributed to the quality that laymen call "constitution," but equal credit must go to the cardiology staff and facilities at Walter Reed Army Medical Center. It has been reported that after Eisenhower's first heart attack in 1955, the question arose whether he should have surgery, but the answer was no, and the management of his difficulties with heart arteries was entirely medical.

Following his first heart attack, Eisenhower regularly took anti-clotting drugs. These did not give him complete protection; he had a stroke in 1957. But he made a good recovery, and the only long-term effect he noted was a tendency to reverse syllables occasionally in a long word. He was advised to get all the physical exercise he could. He did not overeat, and he cut down on saturated fats and sweets. This regimen kept Eisenhower's arteries working well for eight full years. Then came his second and third heart attacks in 1965. He recovered astonishingly well for a man then 75 years old. But more episodes were predictable. The 1968 series of heart attacks began in April when Eisenhower was in California. Two weeks later he was well enough to be moved to Walter Reed Hospital, where he soon suffered three more attacks.

In 26 hours after his seventh occlusion of a heart artery, Ike suffered four periods of ventricular fibrillation, in which the heart muscle twitches rapidly and uselessly and produces no beat or blood pumping. But the cardiologists were ready with a defibrillator, a device for giving an instantaneous shock to the heart through electrodes placed against the chest wall, and the heartbeat was restored. Episodes of ventricular irregularity recurred, some of only a few seconds' duration. Throughout this prolonged treatment Ike was cheerful, was not in pain, and rested comfortably. In fact, physicians said, Ike felt well enough to joke with them about all the equipment to which he was hooked up. Since then medical treatment of patients with heart attacks has made further advancements, and what then was available to only a few, is now available to any patient with a heart attack who reaches alive any hospital with a coronary care unit.

References

References Part I:
Keeping Young and
Living Longer

1. Andrew, Warren: *The Anatomy of Aging in Man and Animals.* Grune & Stratton, New York, 1971, 259 p.
2. Bakerman, Seymour: *Aging Life Processes.* Charles C. Thomas, Springfield, Ill., 1969, 189 p.
3. Birren, James, E.: *Handbook of Aging and the Individual; Psychological and Biological Aspects.* University of Chicago Press, Chicago, 1959, 939 p.
4. Bourlière, Francois: *The Assessment of Biological Age in Man.* Geneva, World Health Organization, 1970, 67 p.
5. Bourne, Geoffrey, H. (Ed.): *Structural Aspects of Aging.* Hafner Publishing Company, Inc., New York, 1961, 419 p.
6. Boyd, Rosamonde, R. (Ed.): *Foundations of Practical Gerontology.* University of South Carolina Press, Columbia, S.C., 1969, 270 p.
7. Brues, Austin, M., and George A. Sacher: *Aging and Levels of Biological Organization.* University of Chicago Press, Chicago, 1965, 353 p.
8. Burch, P. R.: *Growth, Disease and Aging.* University of Toronto Press, New York, 1969, 213 p.
9. Comfort, Alex: *Aging: The Biology of Senescence.* Routledge & Kegan Paul, London, 2nd ed., 1964, 365 p.
10. Cowdry, E. V. (Ed.): *The Care of the Geriatric Patient.* The C. V. Mosby Company, St. Louis, Mo., 1968, 3d ed., 430 p.
11. Harman, Denham: "Free Radical Theory of Aging: Effect of Free Radical Reaction Inhibitors on the Mortality Rate of Male LAFI Mice." *Journal of Gerontology, 23:* 476–482, 1968.
12. Harrington, Alan: *The Immortalist.* Random House, New York, 1969, 324 p.
13. Heron, Alastair: *Age and Function.* J. & A. Churchill, Ltd., London, 1967, 182 p.
14. Holečková, Emma, and Vincent J. Cristofalo (Editors): *Aging in Cell and Tissue Culture.* Plenum Press, New York, 1970, 163 p.

15.Hrachovec, Josef, P.: "Translational Control of Protein Synthesis and the Processes of Aging." *Gerontologist, 5* (No. 3, Part II): 27, 1965.

16. ———: "Increase in metabolic Activity in Peritoneal Leukocytes *in vitro* and release of inhibitory substances." *Federation Proceedings, 25* (No. 2, Part I): 538, 1966.

17. ———: "Protein Control of Protein and Nucleic Acid Synthesis in Growth Cessation and Aging." *Proceedings of the 7th International Congress of Gerontology,* vol. I, p. 263–7, Wien.Med.Acad., Vienna, 1966.

18. ———: "Biological Research on Aging." *Science, 159:* 1185, 1968.

19. ———: "Age Changes in Amino Acid Incorporation by Rat Liver Microsomes." *Gerontologia, 15:* 52–63, 1969.

20. ———: "Environmental Health and the Older Adult." *A. M. A. Archives of Environmental Health, 18:* 193–202, 1969.

21. ———: "Health Maintenance in Older Adults." *Journal of the American Geriatrics Society, 17:* 433–450, 1969.

22. ———: "Potentialities for Research on Mechanisms of Aging." *Journal of the American Geriatrics Society, 17:* 1039–1043, 1969.

23. ———: "Aging Research is Coming of Age." *Industrial Research, 11:* 78–80 (Sept) 1969.

24. ———: "What Goals in Biological Research on Aging?" *Geriatrics Digest, 7:* 12–18, (April) 1970.

25. ———: "The Effect of Age on Tissue Protein Synthesis. I. Age Changes in Amino Acid Incorporation by Rat Liver Purified Microsomes. *Gerontologia, 17:,* 1971.

26. ———: "Inhibitory Effect of Gerovital H3 on Rat Brain Monoamine Oxidase. *Federation Proceedings, 31* (No. 2): 604, 1972.

27. ———: "Inhibitory Effect of Gerovital H3 on Rat Brain, Liver, and Heart." *Physiologist, 15* (No. 3): 175, 1972.

28. Marx, Henry: *H3 in the Battle Against Old Age.* Plenum Press, Inc., New York, 1960, 207 p.

29. McGrady, Patrick, M., Jr.: *The Youth Doctors.* Coward-McCann, Inc., New York, 1968, 352 p.

30. Mithoefer, John, C., and Monroe S. Karetzky: "The Cardio-pulmonary System in the Aged," p. 138–164, in: John H. Powers (Ed.): *Surgery of the Aged and Debilitated Patient.* W. B. Saunders Co., Philadelphia, 1968, 611 p.

31. Prehoda, Robert, W.: *Extended Youth. The Promise of Gerontology.* G. P. Putnam's Sons, New York, 1968, 256 p.

32. Ross, Morris, H.: "Aging, Nutrition, and Hepatic Enzyme Activity Patterns in the Rat." *Journal of Nutrition, 97:* 563–602, (Supplement I), 1969.

33. Shock, Nathan, W. (Ed.): *A Classified Bibliography of Gerontology and Geriatrics.* Stanford University Press, Stanford, California, 1951, 599

p. *A Classified Bibliography of Gerontology and Geriatrics. Supplement I.* Stanford University Press, Stanford, California, 1957, 525 p.

34. Shock, Nathan, W.: "Physiological Aspects of Aging in Man." *Annual Review of Physiology, 23:* 97–122, 1961.

35. Shock, Nathan, W.: "The Physiology of Aging," p. 10–43 in: John H. Powers (Ed.): *Surgery of the Aged and Debilitated Patient,* W. B. Saunders Co., Philadelphia, Penn., 1968, 611 p.

36. Strehler, Bernard, L.: *Time, Cells and Aging.* Academic Press, New York, 1962, 270 p.

37. Vedder, Clyde, B. (Ed.): *Gerontology. A Book of Readings.* Charles C. Thomas, Springfield, Illinois, 1963, 403 p.

References Part II:
Dieting and Nutrition

1. Agriculture Handbook No. 8: *Composition of Foods: Raw, Processed, Prepared.* Superintendent of Documents, U.S. Government Printing Office, Washington D.C.
2. Arbeter, A., Echeverri, L., Franco, D., Munson, D., Velez, H., and Vitale, J. J.: "Nutrition and Infection." *Federation Proceedings, 30:* 1421–1428, 1971.
3. Allison, James, B., and William H. Fitzpatrick: *Dietary Proteins in Health and Disease.* Charles C. Thomas, Springfield, Ill., 1960, 86 p.
4. Andres, R.: "Diabetes and Aging." *Hospital Practice, 2:* 63–67 (Oct) 1967.
5. Bajusz, Eors: *Nutritional Aspects of Cardiovascular Diseases.* Crosby Lockwood, London, 1965, 244 p.
6. Barnes, Robert, H.: "Doctors' Dietary Antics." *Nutrition Today,* September 1968, p.21–25.
7. Beaton, George, H., and Earle W. McHenry (Editors): *Nutrition: A Comprehensive Treatise.* Academic Press, New York, 1964.
8. Bennett, Margaret: *The Peripatetic Diabetic.* Hawthorne Books, Inc., New York, 1969, 270 p.
9. Bogert, Lotta, J.: *Nutrition and Physical Fitness.* W. B. Saunders Co., Philadelphia, Pa., 8th ed., 1966, 614 p.
10. Bowes, Anna, D., and Church, Charles, F., and Church, Helen. N.; *Food Values Commonly Used.* J. B. Lippincott Co., Philadelphia, Pa. 10th ed. 1966.
11. Brusis, O. A., and McGandy, R. B.: *Nutrition and Man's Heart and Blood Vessels. Federation Proceedings, 30:* 1417–1420, (July) 1971.
12. Campbell, G. D.: "Diabetes in Asians and Africans in and around Durban." *South African Medical Journal, 37:* 1195–1208 (Nov) 1963.
13. Caso, Elizabeth, K. (Compiled by): "Calculation of Diabetic Diets. Report of the Committee on Diabetic Diet Calculations, American Diatetic Association. Prepared Cooperatively with the Committee on

Education, American Diabetes Association and the Diabetes Branch, U.S. Public Health Service." *Journal of the American Dietetic Association, 26:* 575–583, 1950.

14. Chaney, Margaret, S., and Margaret L. Ross: *Nutrition.* Houghton Mifflin, Boston, 7th ed., 1966, 511 p.

15. Cheraskin, Emanuel, W. M. Ringsdorf, Jr., and J. W. Clark *Diet and Disease.* Rodale Books, Emmaus, Pa., 1968, 369 p.

16. Cohen, A. M.: "Fats and Carbohydrates as Factors in Atherosclerosis and Diabetes in Yemenite Jews. *American Heart Journal, 65:*291–298, 1963.

17. Cooper, T.: "The National Diet-Heart Study Final Report." *Circulation, 37:* Supplement No. 1, 428 p. (March) 1968.

18. Egeli, S. E., and Berkimen, R.: "Action of Hypoglycemia on Coronary Insufficiency and Mechanism of Electrocardiogram Alterations." *American Heart Journal, 59:* 527–540 (April) 1960.

19. Fábry, Pavel, J. Fodor, Z. Hejl, H. Geizerová, O. Balcarová, K. Zvolánková: "Meal Frequency and Ischaemic Heart Disease." The Lancet, ii: 190–191 (July 27) 1968.

20. Fábry, Pavel, and J. Tepperman: "Meal Frequency—A Possible Factor in Human Pathology." *American Journal of Clinical Nutrition, 23:* 1059–1068, 1970.

21. Ford, S., Jr., R. C. Bozian and H. C. Knowles: "Interactions of Obesity, and Glucose and Insulin Levels in Hypertriglyceridemia." *American Journal of Clinical Nutrition, 21:* 904–910 (Sept) 1968.

22. Gofman, John, W., Alex V. Nichols, and E. Virginia Dobbin: *Dietary Prevention and Treatment of Heart Disease.* G. P. Putnam's Sons, New York, 1958, 256 p.

23. Goodman, Joseph, I.: *Diet and Live: A Guide to Corrective Eating.* World Publishing Co., Cleveland, 1966, 300 p.

24. Gordon, Edgar, S., and Marshall Goldberg: "A New Concept in the Treatment of Obesity." *Journal of the American Medical Assoc., 186: 49-60 (Oct) 1963.*

25. Gwinup, Grant, R. C. Byron, W. H. Roush, F. A. Kruger, and G. J. Hamwi: "Effect of Nibbling Versus Gorging on Serum Lipids in Man." *American Journal of Clinical Nutrition, 13:* 209–213, 1963.

26. Gwinup, Grant, R. C. Byron, W. H. Roush, F. A. Kruger, and G. J. Hamwi: "Effect of Nibbling Versus Gorging on Glucose Tolerance." *The Lancet,* ii: 165–167 (July 27) 1963.

27. Gwinup, Grant: *Energetics: Your Key to Weight Control.* Sherbourne Press, Inc., Los Angeles, 1970, 175 p.

28. Hollifield, Guy, Owen, J. A., Lindsay, R. W., and Parson, W.: "Effects of Prolonged Fasting on Subsequent Food Intake in Obese Humans." *Southern Medical Journal, 57:* 1012–1016 (Sept) 1964.

29. Kohn, Clarence: "Feeding Frequency and Body Composition." *Annals of the New York Academy of Sciences, 110:* 395–409, 1963.
30. Kruse, Harry, D.: *Nutrition: Its Meaning, Scope and Significance.* Charles C. Thomas, Springfield, Illinois, 1969, 195 p.
31. Kuo, Peter, T., and David R. Bassett: "Dietary Sugar in the Production of Hyperglyceridemia." *Annals of Internal Medicine, 62:* 1199–1212, 1965.
32. Lusk, Graham: *Nutrition.* Hafner, New York, 1964, 142 p.
33. Martin, Ethel, A.: *Nutrition in Action.* Holt, Rinehart & Winston, New York, 2nd ed., 1965, 298 p.
34. Mayer, Jean: *Overweight: Causes, Cost and Control.* Prentice Hall, Inc., Englewood Cliffs, N.J., 1968, 213 p.
35. Mitchell, H. S., H. J. Rynbergen, L. Anderson, and Dibble, M.: *Cooper's Nutrition in Health and Disease.* Lippincott, Philadelphia, Pa., 1968, 685 p.
36. Munro, H. N.: "Impact of Nutritional Research on Human Health and Survival.: *Federation Proceedings, 30:* 1403–1407, (July) 1971.
37. Ostrander, Leon, D., Francis, Jr., Thos., Hayner, Norman S., Kjelsberg, Marcus O., and Epstein, Frederick, H.: "The Relationship of Cardiovascular Disease to Hyperglyceridemia." *Annals of Internal Medicine, 62:* 1188–1198, 1965.
38. Pike, Ruth, L., and Brown, Myrtle, L.: *Nutrition: An Integrated Approach.* John Wiley & Sons, Inc., New York, 1967, 542 p.
39. Revel, Dorothy, T.: *Dietary Control of Hypercholesteremia.* Charles C. Thomas, Springfield, Ill., 1962, 70 p.
40. Roberts, H. J.: "Afternoon Glucose Tolerance Testing: A Key to the Pathogenesis, Early Diagnosis and Prognosis of Diabetogenic Hyperinsulinism." *Journal of the American Geriatrics Society, 12:*423–472 (May) 1964.
41. Roberts, H. J.: "Spontaneous Leg Cramps and 'Restless Legs' Due to Diabetogenic Hyperinsulinism: Observations on 131 Patients." *Journal of the American Geriatrics Society, 13:* 602-638 (July) 1965.
42. Robinson, Corinne, H.: *Normal and Therapeutic Nutrition.* The MacMillan Company, New York, 13th ed., 1967, 890 p.
43. Ross, M. H.: "Protein, Calories and Life Expectancy." *Federation Proceedings, 18:* 1190–1207 (Dec) 1959.
44. Schachter, Stanley: "Obesity and Eating." *Science, 161:* 751–756, (Aug) 1968.
45. Shock, Nathan, W.: "Metabolism and Age." *Journal of Chronic Diseases, 2:* 687–703, (Dec) 1955.
46. Simonson, E., and Keys, A.: "The Effect of an Ordinary Meal on the Electrocardiogram. Normal Standards in Middle-aged Men and Women." *Circulation, 1:* 1000-1005, (April) 1950.

47. Stare, Frederick, J.: *Eating for Good Health.* Simon & Schuster, Inc., New York, 1969, 190 p.

48. Stillman, Irwin, M., and Baker, Samm, S.: *The Doctor's Quick Weight Loss Diet.* Dell Publishing Co., New York, 1967, 252 p.

49. Stunkard, Albert, J.: "Environment and Obesity: Recent Advances in Our Understanding of Regulation of Food Intake in Man." *Federation Proceedings, 27:* 1367-1373, (Nov) 1968.

50. Vallance-Owen, J.: "Synalbumin Insulin Antagonism." *Diabetes, 13:* 241-246, (May) 1964.

51. Williams, Roger, J.: *Nutrition in a Nutshell.* Doubleday & Co., Inc. Garden City, New York, 1962, 171 p.

52. Williams, Sue, R.: *Nutrition and Diet Therapy.* Mosby, St. Louis, Mo., 1969, 686 p.

53. Wohl, Michael, G., and Robert S. Goodhart (Editors): *Modern Nutrition in Health and Disease.* Lea & Febiger, Philadelphia, Pa., 4th ed., 1968, 1240 p.

54. Wyden, Peter: *The Overweight Society.* William Morrow & Co., New York, 1965, 338 p.

55. Yudkin, John: "Dietary Fat and Dietary Sugar in relation to Ischaemic Heart Disease and Diabetes." *The Lancet, ii.* p.4–5, (July 4) 1964.

56. Yudkin, John: "Evolutionary and Historical Changes in Dietary Carbohydrates." *American Journal of Clinical Nutrition, 20:* 108–115, 1967.

References Part III: Physical Activity and Exercise

1. Ald, Roy: *Jogging, Aerobics and Diet.* The New American Library, Inc., New York, 1968, 191 p.
2. Amery, A., Julius, S., L. S. Whitlock, and J. Conway: Influence of Hypertension on the Hemodynamic Response to Exercise. *Circulation, 36:* 231–237, (Aug) 1967.
3. Astrand, P. O.: "Human Physical Fitness with Special Reference to Sex and Age." *Physiological Reviews, 36:* 307–335, 1956.
4. Bowerman, William, J., and W. E. Harris: *Jogging.* Grosset & Dunlap Publishers, New York, 1967, 127 p.
5. Brunner, D., and E. Jokl: *Physical Activity and Aging; with Special Reference to the Effect of Exercise and Training on the Natural History of Arteriosclerotic Heart Disease.* University Park Press, Baltimore, London, Tokyo, 1970, 315 p.
6. Cooper, Kenneth, H.: *Aerobics.* M. Evans and Co., New York, 1968, 182 p.
7. Cooper, Kenneth, H.: *The New Aerobics.* M. Evans and Co., New York, 1970, 191 p.
8. Covalt, Nila, K.: *Bed Exercises for Convalescent Patients.* Charles C. Thomas, Springfield, Illinois, 1968, 228 p.
9. De Vries, Herbert, A.: "Exercise Intensity Threshold for Improvement of Cardiovascular-Respiratory Function in Older Men." *Geriatrics, 26:* 94–101, (April) 1971.
10. De Vries, Herbert, A.: "Prescription of Exercise for Older Men From Telemetered Exercise Heart Rate Data." *Geriatrics, 26:* 102–111, (April) 1971.
11. Etter, Mildred, F.: *Exercise for the Prone Patient.* Wayne State University Press, Detroit, 1968, 161 p.
12. Falls, Harold, B.: *Exercise Physiology.* Academic Press, New York, 1968, 471 p.

13. Hanson, John, S., Burton S. Tabakin, and Arthur M. Levy: "Compara-tive Exercise. Cardiorespiratory Performance of Normal Men in the Third, Fourth and Fifth Decades of Life." *Circulation, 37:* 345–360, (March) 1968.

14. Hanson, John S., B. S. Tabakin, A. M. Levy and W. Nedde: "Long-Term Physical Training and Cardiovascular Dynamics in Middle-aged Men." *Circulation, 38:* 783–799, (Oct) 1968.

15. Jokl, Ernst: *Heart and Sports.* Charles C. Thomas, Springfield, Illinois, 1964, 117 p.

16. Jokl, Ernst: *Nutrition, Exercise and Body Composition.* Charles C. Thomas, Springfield, Illinois, 1964, 115 p.

17. Jokl, E., and J. T. McClellan (Editors): *Exercise and Cardiac Death.* University Park Press, Baltimore, London, Tokyo, 1971, 185 p.

18. Julius, S., A. Amery, L. S. Whitlock, and J. Conway: "Influence of Age on the Hemodynamic Response to Exercise." *Circulation, 36:* 222–230, (Aug) 1967.

19. Karvonen, Martti, J., and Alan J. Barry (Editors): *Physical Activity and the Heart.* Charles C. Thomas, Springfield, Illinois, 1967, 405 p.

20. Katz, L. N.: "Physical Fitness and Coronary Heart Disease. Some Basic Views." *Circulation, 35:* 405–414, (Feb) 1967.

21. Lake, Lorraine, F.: "Exercise," p. 79–99, in: E. V. Cowdry (Ed.): *The Care of the Geriatric Patient.* The C. V. Mosby Company, Saint Louis, 1968, 3d ed., 430 p.

22. McDonough, John, R., Fusako Kusumi, and R. A. Bruce: *Variations in Maximal Oxygen Intake with Physical Activity in Middle-aged Men. Circulation, 41:* 743–751, (May) 1970.

23. Roskamm, H.: "Optimum Patterns of Exercise for Healthy Adults." *The Canadian Medical Association Journal, 96:* 895–899, (March) 1967.

24. Rudd, Jacob, L., and Reuben J. Margolin: "Physical Fitness in Mainte-nance Therapy for Geriatric Patients." In: Rudd, Jacob, L., and Reuben J. Margolin (Editors): *Maintenance Therapy for the Geriatric Patient.* Charles C. Thomas, Springfield, Illinois, 1968, 293 p.

25. Sidney, Licht (Ed.): *Therapeutic Exercise.* Elizabeth Licht Publisher, New Haven, Connecticut, 2nd ed., 1961, 959 p.

26. Skinner, J. S., H. Benson, J. R. McDonough, and C. G. Hames: "Social Status, Physical Activity, and Coronary Proness." *Journal of Chronic Diseases, 19:* 773–783, 1966.

27. Stoboy, H.: "Physical Fitness Testing Methods and Criteria." *Transactions of the New York Academy of Sciences, 30:* 483–496, (Jan) 1968.

References Part IV: Relaxation

1. Agate, John: *The Practice of Geriatrics.* 2nd ed., William Heineman Medical Books, Ltd., London, 1970, 589 p.
2. Bortz, Edward, L.: *Creative Aging.* The Macmillan Company, New York, 1963, 179 p.
3. Burges, Ernest, W.: *Aging in Western Societies.* University of Chicago Press, Chicago, 1960, 492 p.
4. Busse, Ewald, W., and Pfeiffer, Eric (Editors): *Behavior and Adaptation in Late Life.* Little, Brown and Company, Boston, 1969, 395 p.
5. Clark, Margaret, and Anderson, Barbara G: *Culture and Aging.* Charles C. Thomas, Springfield, Illinois, 1967, 487 p.
6. Cumming, Elaine, and Henry, William E.: *Growing Old.* Basic Books, Inc., New York, 1961, 293 p.
7. Destrem, Hughes: *La Vie Apres 50 Ans.* Editions du Centurion, Paris, France, 1966, 254 p.
8. Field, Minna: *Aging with Honor and Dignity.* Charles C. Thomas, Springfield, Illinois, 1968, 204 p.
9. Filip, Ladislav, Doc., MUDr.: *Jak Zít po Padesátce (How to Live After 50).* Státní Zdravotnické Nakladatelství, Praha, Czechoslovakia, 1969, 221 p.
10. Hoffman, Adeline, M. (Editor): *The Daily Needs and Interests of Older People.* Charles C. Thomas, Springfield, Illinois, 1970, 493 p.
11. Jacobson, Edmund: *Progressive Relaxation.* University of Chicago Press, Chicago, Illinois, 1938, 494 p.
12. Kohler, Mariane: *The Secrets of Relaxation.* Stein and Day, New York, 1969, 125 p.
13. Neugarten, Bernice, L. (Editor): *Middle Age and Aging.* University of Chicago Press, Chicago, 1968, 596 p.
14. Rathbone, Josephine, L.: *Relaxation.* University of Chicago Press, Chicago, 1938, 494 p.

15. Rudd, Jacob L., and Margolin, Reuben, J. (Editors): *Maintenance Therapy for the Geriatric Patient.* Charles C. Thomas, Springfield, Ill., 1968, 293 p.
16. Simon, Alexander, and Epstein, Leon, J. (Editors): *Aging in Modern Society.* American Psychiatric Association, New York, 1968, 248 p.
17. Stotsky, Bernard, A.: *The Elderly Patient.* Grune & Stratton, New York, 1968, 160 p.
18. Vedder, Clyde B. (Editor): *Gerontology: A book of Readings.* Charles C. Thomas, Springfield, Ill. 1963, 403 p.
19. ———: *Problems of the Middle-aged.* Charles C. Thomas, Springfield, Ill. 1965, 202 p.
20. Vedder, Clyde B., and Lefkowitz, Annette, S.: *Problems of the Aged.* Charles C. Thomas, Springfield, Ill., 1965, 259 p.

References
Appendix:
The Heart Attack

1. Baldry, P. E.: *The Battle Against Heart Disease.* Cambridge University Press, Cambridge, 1971, 189 p.
2. Begerowich, Jonas, Fenig, S., Lasser, J., and Allen, D., "Management of Acute Myocardial Infarction Complicated by Advanced Atrioventricular Block." *American Journal of Cardiology, 23:* 54-65, (Jan) 1969.
3. Bellet, S.: "Significance of Arrhythmias in Middle Life." *Postgraduate Medicine, 39:* 186-191, (Feb) 1966.
4. Blakeslee, Alton, and J. Stamler: *Your Heart Has Nine Lives. Nine Steps to Heart Health.* Prentice Hall, Inc., Englewood Cliffs, N.J., 1963, 269 p.
5. Blumenfeld, Arthur: *Heart Attack: Are You a Candidate?* Paul S. Eriksson, Inc., New York, 1964, 372 p.
6. Boylan, Brian, R.: *The New Heart.* Chilton Book Company, Philadelphia, Pa., 1969, 211 p.
7. Day, Hughes, W.: "Acute Coronary Care—A Five Year Report." *American Journal of Cardiology, 21:* 252-257, (Feb) 1968.
8. Flynn, R. L., and Fox, III., Samuel M.: "Coronary Care Programs in the United States." *Israel Journal of Medical Sciences, 3:* 279-286, 1967.
9. Friedberg, C. K. (Ed.): *Acute Myocardial Infarction and Coronary Care Units.* Grune & Stratton, New York, 1969, 288 p.
10. Grace, William, J., and Keyloun, Victor: *The Coronary Care Unit.* Meredith Corporation, New York, 1970, 223 p.
11. Harris, Raymond: *The Management of Geriatric Cardiovascular Disease.* J. B. Lippincott Co., Philadelphia, Pa., 1970, 288 p.
12. Hurwitz, M., and R. S. Eliot: "Arrhythmias in Acute Myocardial Infarction." *Diseases of the Chest, 45:* 617-626, (June) 1964.
13. Kuhn, L. A.: "Shock in Myocardial Infarction—Medical Treatment." *American Journal of Cardiology, 26:* 578-587, (Dec) 1970.

14. Lamb, Lawrence, E.: *Your Heart and How to Live With It.* The Viking Press, New York, 1969, 280 p.
15. Lown, B., and Arthur Selzer: "The Coronary Care Unit." *American Journal of Cardiology, 22:* 597-602, (Oct) 1968.
16. Pickering, George: *High Blood Pressure.* J. & A. Churchill, Ltd., London, 1968, 717 p.
17. Raab, W. (Ed.): *Prevention of Ischemic Heart Disease. Principles and Practice.* Charles C. Thomas, Springfield, Illinois, 1966, 466 p.
18. Scheidt, S., Ascheim, R., Killip III., T.: "Shock After Acute Myocardial Infarction. A Clinical and Hemodynamic Profile." *American Journal of Cardiology 26:* 556-564, (Dec) 1970.
19. Zohman, Lenore, R., and Jerome S. Tobis: *Cardiac Rehabilitation.* Grune & Stratton, New York, 1970, 248 p.

REFERENCES

INDEX

INDEX

B

Balanced diet best, 43
Bennett, Margaret, 109
Biosynthetic processes, 7-8
Björksten, Dr., 9
Blood clotting, 208, 215
Blood flow after fatty meal, 50-51
Blood vessels increased with exercise, 136
Blood washing or plasmapheresis, 10, 26
Body tissues lose from no exercise, 125
Body types, 66-68
Brain cell loss, 8
Brain damage and heart attacks, 212
Bread exchanges, 105-106
Bronchial tubes, 186
Bronchitis, 185, 186-187
Brown-Séquard, Charles Eduard, 15-16
"Burning calories," 48, 90
Butenandt, Adolph, 16

C

California Aging Association, 23
Caloric intact calculated, 90, 91, 92, 97, 119, 127
Calcium loss from bones during inactivity, 131
Campaign against sugar consumption needed, 84
Campbell, Dr. G. D., 82
Canadian Council on Nutrition, 90, 92
Cancer, 38
Carbohydrates, 44, 80, 93, 103, 104, 133
Cardiac output, volume of blood moved by heart, 133, 136
Cessation of heartbeats, 212

Chapman, Dr. Carleton B., 132, 133, 154
Charles University, Prague, 137
Checkups, medical, 193
Chevalier, Maurice, 34
Chilling at night, 188
Cholesterol, 72, 73, 79, 116, 170
Chronic diseases:
    decline with treatment, 37
    and exercise, 127
    interrupts life span, 36, 37
    and medical examinations, 193
    and relaxation, 201
    and stressful conditions, 53, 167, 168
Chronic fatigue vs. normal fatigue, 202-203
Churchill, Sir Winston, 144
A Classified Bibliography of Gerontology and Geriatrics by N. W. Shock (1951), 12
Coffee and heart strain, 197, 198, 199
Cohen, Dr. A. M., 83
Cohn, Dr. Clarence, 73, 117
Columbia University, New York, 98
Cooper, Dr. Kenneth H., 134, 135, 153, 154, 155
Cornell University Medical College, New York, 130
"Coronary Care Unit," 207-209, 211-213
Crawford, Joan, 62
Creighton University School of Medicine, Omaha, 77
Cross-linked molecules and enzymes, 9

D

Dangers in improper exercising, 146-148

Exercises, categorized, 139-140
Exogenous (environmental) factors in
    personalities, 170
*Extended Youth, Promise of Geronto-
    logy* by Robert W. Prehonda, 7

F

Fábry, Dr. Pavel, 72, 74
Falling domino theory, 13-14
Fast, 48 hours to begin weight
    reduction, 112-113
Fat content, 44, 103, 104, 105, 133
Fat exchanges, 104-105
Fatty acids, 44, 47-48
Flu, 38
Food and Agriculture Organization of
    the United Nations, 92
Food and Drug Administration, 20
Food Exchange System, 94-95, 97, 99,
    102-110
Food faddists, 45
Forecasting human life span, 7
"Fountain of Youth" cure of Voronoff,
    16
Fountain of youth search depends on
    research, 11
French, Dr. C. F., 118
"Fresh-cell-therapy," 17-18
Fruit exchanges, 107, 108
Fuel for body building, 44, 48
Functional capacities decline, 3-4
Funding needed for research on aging,
    22
Furnam, Dr. R. H., 116

G

Gardberg, Dr. Manuel, 74
Genetic obesity, 65-66

Gerontology, 11-12
Gerovital H3, 19-20
Glucose tolerance test, 58-61
Goddard, Dr. Robert H., 22
Goldberg, Dr. M., 112, 113
Goldberger, Dr. Emanuel, 84
Gordon, Dr. E. S., 112, 113
Gorging vs. nibbling, 72-73, 74, 77
Gwinup, Dr. Grant, 72

H

Hadassah Medical School, Jerusalem,
    79, 83
Hamburger, Dr. Walter W., 64
Harman, Dr. Denham, 9
Hay fever, 185-186
Heart arrest, 212
Heart attacks:
    after static exertion, 143-144, 211
    prevention of, 200
    survival of, 207-217
Heart diseases, 38
    and blood pressure, 172
    and causes, 136
    and diabetes, 55
    and exercise, 126-127, 145-148,
        158
    and heavy meals, 51-52, 75
    and ischemia, 51
    and maximal oxygen uptake, 134
    and overeating, 47, 74
    and relaxation, 201
    research on, 84
    and signs of strain, 198-200
    and stress, 167, 168-171
    and sugar consumption, 80, 83-84
    and susceptibility, 182-183

Heart strain testing, 196-200
Heartbeat rate, 52, 196-197
Heavy meals dangerous for weak
　　hearts, 51-52
Heparin, 51
Hereditary factors in individuality, 181
Hereditary hypertension, 175
High blood pressure:
　　and age levels, 173, 174
　　causes of, 175
　　and diets for, 177
　　and emotional pressures, 172-176
　　and exercise, 127, 130, 137, 141,
　　　142
　　found in what circumstances, 38,
　　　77
　　and heavy meals, 76
　　and overeating, 47
　　rare in primitive cultures, 173-174
　　and relaxation, 201
　　and use of salt, 177-178
High-level stress, 168
Hobbies for relaxation, 206
Hollifield, Dr. Guy, 73, 112
Hrachovec, Josef, 194
One hundred-year life span, 5-6, 36
Hunger vs. appetite, 98-99, 100-101
Hyperglycemic, 55
Hyperinsulinemia, 61
Hypertension:
　　and age, 175
　　and diabetes, 55, 58, 62
　　and emotional stress, 172
　　and exercise, 137
　　and heavy meals, 76
　　hereditary and acquired, 175, 183
　　and overeating, 77
　　and stress, 167
Hypertriglyceridemia, 61
Hypoglycemia, 75, 76
Hypoglycemic shock, 102

I

Infection as stressful agent, 182
Insomnia, 202
Insulin, 54-55, 66, 70, 80, 102
Insulin antagonist theory, 56-57
Intercellular spaces between cells,
　　clogged in old age, 10-11
Ischemia, 51
Isometric exercise, 139, 140-141,
　　142-143

J

Jacobson, Dr. E., 203
Jogging exercise program, 160-162
Johnson, Dr. B. Connar, 77
Jones, Dr. R. J., 116

K

Kempner, Dr. Walter, 177
The Ketogenic diet, 117-118
Ketone substances, 117
Ketosis, 117
Keys, Dr. Ancel, 74, 77, 130, 131
Knowles, Dr. Harvey C., 61
Korean War, 200
Král, Dr. Jirí, 136

L

Lack of exercise and its effects, 125,
　　130-135
Lamb, Dr. Lawrence E., 147
Life expectancy:
　　defined, 37, 38
　　increased by preventing chronic
　　　diseases, 37

Life span:
  defined, 36-37
  potential available to all, 38
Limits of physical endurance, 183-184
Lind, Dr. A., 142
"Lipogenesis," or increased synthesis
  of fat, 73
Longevity:
  and environmental factors, 39
  runs in families, 38-39
Low-level stress, 168

M

McCussick, Dr. Victor, 62
Malnutrition, 45
Market Research Corporation of
  America, 70
Maturity-onset diabetes, 53-54, 60
Maugham, Somerset, experimented
  with cell therapy, 18
Maximal oxygen uptake, 131-136, 154
Mayer, Dr. Jean, 68
Mayo diet, 113-114
Meat exchanges, 104
Medicaid, 22, 26
Medical examinations, 193
Medicare, 22, 26
Mesomorphs, 66, 68
Meyer, Jean, 88
Michael Reese Hospital, Chicago, 73,
  117
Middle age:
  adjustment to, 33-34
  awareness of, 30
  and blood pressure, 173, 174-175,
    178-180
  and decline in body's ability to
    burn fuel, 48-49
  and diabetes, 60

and exercise, 126-128, 129, 140,
  147, 149-155, 156-163
and heart disease, 199-200
and overeating, 86-95
and preventive measures, 183-191,
  192-200
and sugar intake, 84
and survival of a heart attack,
  207-217
and when it starts, 29
Milk exchanges, 106-107
Molecular gerontology, 11
Molecules of human body replaced, 8
Monoamine oxidase, 20
Muscle fibers and exercise, 125
Myths:
  on longevity, 38
  on remedies for long life, 5

N

National Aeronautics Space Adminis-
  tration (NASA), 79
National Research Council, 90, 92
Neurotic drives behind goals, 33, 34
The New Aerobics by Dr. Kenneth H.
  Cooper, 134
New York University, 10
Nibbling:
  decreases levels of fat, 72
  natural in man, 71
  vs. gorging, 72-73, 74, 77
Niehans, Paul, 17-19, 31
"Night-eating syndrome," 69-70
Normal fatigue vs. chronic fatigue,
  202-203
Northwestern University Medical
  School, Chicago, 146

Nutrition:
    bad eating habits and their effect on, 4
    and balanced diet, 43, 45, 94-95
    and digestion, 43
    as fuel for the body, 44
    and overeating, 47
Nutrition Books: Recommended and not Recommended, published by the Chicago Nutrition Foundation, 116

O

Obesity, 47, 80
    causes of, 63-64, 96, 111-113, 182-183
    definition of, 49
    and diabetes, 55, 56-57, 61, 62, 66
    and emotion, 64-65, 70, 96
    genetic, 65-66
    more in endomorphic types, 66, 68
Olson, Dr. N. A., 79
Olson, Dr. R. E., 116
1.5 mile test, 155
Orentreich, Dr., 10
Ostrander, Dr. Leon D., 84
Outside influences slowing down aging process, 8
Overeating:
    causes triglycerides to be stored, 48
    effects of, 56
    greatest nutritional problem, 47
Overstrain, 4
Overweight:
    and blood pressure, 172
    and body builds, 88
    definition of, 49
    more in endomorphic types, 66, 68

and the importance to reduce, 63
    in West Germany, 64-65
Oxidation of fats and aging process, 9
Oxygen, as combustion agent, 133

P

Pain and heart attacks, 209
Pancreas, 54, 60
Parson, Dr. William, 73, 112
Passive exercise, 139
Pennsylvania State College, Department of Nutrition, 118
The Peripatetic Diabetic by Margaret Bennett, 109
Physical activity and dieting, 121-122, 127
Physical activity best for rejuvenation, 126, 128, 136, 138
Physician, choice of, 192, 207
Physiological functions and age decline, 189-191
Placebo effect of revitalization experiments, 18
Plasmapheresis or blood washing, 10, 26
Pneumonia, 38
Potential of one hundred years life span, 5-6, 36
Prediabetic state, 53, 75, 76
Prehoda, Robert W., 7
Preventive measures for long life, 4, 5
    and physical endurance, 183
    with treatment of health problems, 184-188
Procaine hydrochloride, 19
Procaine injections, 19
Program for exercising, 150-155, 156-163

Progressive relaxation, 203-204
Protein, 103, 104
Protein synthesis, need for in cell
    divisions, 13
Psychological effects:
    with heart attack, 214
    on nutrition, 45, 48, 98
    in overeating, 63-65, 70, 96, 111

R

Rand Corporation, Santa Monica,
    California, 7
Recognition of heart attack, 210
Recovery from heart attack, 216-217
Regularity in exercise, 146, 157
Rejuvenationists, 5
    Dr. Björksten, 9-10
    Dr. Harmon, 9
    Dr. Orentreich, 10
Rejuvenators or "youth doctors," 21
Remineralization of bones from
    exercise, 126
Repressed aggression, harmful to
    body, 179-180
Research:
    on age decline, 194-200
    on diabetes, 56-57, 82
    on diets, 111-113, 116-117, 118
    on eating habits, 71-77
    on the effect of sweets, 78-84
    on exercise, 129-131, 142
    to extend life, 4-5, 8, 39
    on heart attacks, 213
    and high blood pressure, 176-180
    and its history, 15-21
    on maximal oxygen uptake, 132-135
    needs financial support, 9, 22
    neglected, 15
    on nutrition, 49, 69

on overeating, 64, 65-66, 69
on physiological decline, 189-191
and the Rand Corporation, 7
stages of, 11-12
on weight fluctuation, 93
Respiratory diseases, 38
Restless legs, 76
Retirement funding, 27
Revitalization experiments:
    Aslan, 19, 20
    Brown-Séquard, 15-16
    Butenandt, 16
    Niehans, 17
    Steinach, 16
    Voronoff, 16
Rhythmic exercise vs. static exertion,
    143-144
Rhythmic exercises, 139, 141, 142
Rice-fruit diet for reducing blood
    pressure, 177
Roberts, Dr. H. J., 75, 76
Robinson, Dr. S., 134, 135, 158

S

Salt and its effect on high blood
    pressure, 177-178
Satiety, 98, 99, 100
Schachter, Dr. Stanley, 64, 98
Self-discipline in healthy life, 5, 129
Selye, Dr. Hans, 189-190
Senility, 24
    and antioxidants, 24
    fear of, 31
Sheldon, 66
Shock, N. W., 12
Shortness of breath and effectiveness
    of exercise, 150, 157
Silent heart attacks, 210-211

Six minutes of endurance exercise beneficial, 150
"Skipped heart beats," 198-199
Sludging of blood cells, 50-51
Smith, Kline and French Laboratories, 7
Smoking:
    and emphysema, 187
    and heart strain, 197, 198, 199
Snacks that are beneficial, 81
Stamler, Dr. Jeremiah, 146
"Starvation diabetes," 60
State University of Iowa, 79
Static exertion vs. rhythmic exercise, 143-144
Statistical Bulletin, (1959), 87
Stein, Dr. Y., 79
Steinach, Eugen, 16
Stillman, Dr. I. M., 114, 115-116
Stravinsky, Igor, 31
Stressful conditions:
    changed in recent years, 167-168
    and effect on blood pressure, 172-177, 179-180
    effect on dynamic processes of life, 53, 182
    and effect on heart diseases, 167, 168-171
    and exercise, 157
    shorten life, 4
The Struggle for Survival (1940-65) by Lord Moran, 144
Strunkard, Dr. Albert J., 69-70
Stroke volume in blood moved by heart, 132-133, 136
Sugar glucose:
    in blood, 47-48, 70, 73, 75, 79-80
    and diabetes, 53-54, 56-60, 66, 102
    and exercise, 127
    and oxygen uptake, 132
    supplied by carbohydrate foods, 44

Susceptibility to disease, 39, 62
"Susceptibility profile," 182-183, 184
    advertised overly for consumption, 80
    consumption increased in last century, 78-79
    overuse dangerous for body, 55-56

T

Tennis for exercise, 141-142
Tenseness, 204-205
Tests to measure exercise tolerance, 152-155
Therapeutic exercises, 140
Thrombosis, 215
Tissues (body) weakened with stored fat, 50
Tolerance for glucose varies, 58, 61
Toxic substances in cells contributing to aging, 10, 13
Triflycerides, 44, 47-48, 61, 72, 73, 79, 80, 132
Tulane University, Department of Medicine, 74
12-minute test, 153

U

U. S. National Center for Health Statistics, 200
University of California at Los Angeles, School of Public Health, 12
University of Chicago, 116
University of Cincinnati College of Medicine, 61
University of Illinois, Urbana, 77

University of Istanbul, Turkey, 75
University of London, England, 78
University of Michigan, 84
University of Minnesota, 130
University of Montreal, Canada, 190
University of Natal, Africa, 82
University of Oklahoma Medical
    Center, 116
University of Southern California
    (USC) Gerontology Research
    Center, 12-13, 129
University of Texas, Department of
    Medicine, 73
University of Virginia School of
    Medicine, 73
University of Wisconsin Medical
    School, 112, 113
Upjohn Company, 9

V

Vallance-Owen, Dr. J., 56
Vasoligature, 16
Vegetable A exchanges, 107
Virginia University School of Medicine,
    112
Voronoff, Serge, 16

W

Walk-Jog Test, 152-153
Walk Test, 152
Walking exercise program, 158-159

Walking-jogging exercise program,
    159-160
Wall Street Journal, 70
Walter Reed Army Medical Center, 217
Warming-up exercises, 162-163
Water intake and weight, 93
Water retention in weight problems,
    111-112
Weight averages:
    and body builds, 88
    and interpretation, 86-87, 90
    tables, 85, 88, 89
    in various parts of the world, 87
Weight loss and gain fluctuation, 92-93
White, Dr. Paul Dudley, 141, 146, 214,
    215
White, Dr. Philip L., 116
Wilhelm, Dr. C. W., 77
Winitz, Dr. Milton, 79

Y

Your Heart and How To Live With It
    by Dr. Lawrence E. Lamb, 146
Your Heart Has Nine Lives by Dr.
    Jeremiah Stamler, 146
Youth:
    and blood pressure, 176-177
    and energy, 3
    and exercise, 129
    and heart disease, 200
    and stress, 182, 190
Yudkin, Dr. John, 78, 83